D1366657

How Things Really Work

HOW THINGS REALLY WORK

LESSONS FROM A LIFE IN POLITICS

By Bill Hobby

With Saralee Tiede

DOLPH BRISCOE CENTER FOR AMERICAN HISTORY
The University of Texas at Austin
Austin, Texas

Frontispiece: Hobby with typewriter at the *Houston Post*, 1952. *Courtesy of the Hobby family.*

*When it comes to government and how to get things done, Bill Hobby was
as adroit and as clever as anyone I've ever known. There have been very few
people in my life that have had more impact on me than Bill Hobby.*

—former Texas Governor Ann Richards

About *How Things Really Work*:

Past and Present Public Officials

My friend Bill Hobby has written a book that should be read by every student of Texas government. It is a classic text—by a man who has been there—on how state government is run.

—former Texas Governor Mark White

Bill Hobby innately understands Texas and its priorities and challenges. He has always been eager to be out in front of difficult issues if he thought they paved the way for a better Texas.

—former Texas Lieutenant Governor Ben Barnes

Lieutenant Governor Hobby and I were of different parties and, at times, of different philosophies. Nevertheless, I regard him as one of a very limited class known as great Texans.

— former Texas Lieutenant Governor Bill Ratliff

Bill Hobby is one of the best public servants I've ever known. A true statesman, he led the Senate with integrity and respected the legislative process. Reading *How Things Really Work* is a great reminder that we do our best work when we put the interests of the people of Texas first and don't care who gets the credit.

—former Texas Speaker of the House Pete Laney

Bill Hobby isn't just a politician—he is a true statesman. As lieutenant governor, he went out of his way to work with members based on their ability, as opposed to whether somebody had an R or a D behind their name. And he demonstrated the type of leadership that is sorely needed across our country today.

—Texas Senator Rodney Ellis

Bill Hobby was my first intellectual lieutenant governor. He read books and could actually write one. I'm glad he was and he did.

—former Texas Senator Babe Schwartz

A "must" text for any course on civics, Texas government, Texas history, or public policy. Bill Hobby not only tells us how it worked in the "kinder, gentler days," he lays out a road map for a return to sanity in a world where "politics" has gone mad with "get the other guy."

—former Texas Senator Max Sherman

Texas historians, journalists, educators

Bill Hobby tells good stories in *How Things Really Work* and gives us an insider's view to a challenging, interesting, and productive period in Texas political history.

—Ted Fehrenbach, historian and author of *Lone Star*

No one knows more about Texas politics than Bill Hobby, and few people tell better stories. In *How Things Really Work*, this Texas legend is at his perceptive, funny, and provocative best.

—H. W. Brands, historian and author of *Lone Star Nation*

The Texas lieutenant governor, who presides over the Texas Senate, is the most powerful in the country. Much of that reputation flourished in the eighteen years that Bill Hobby quietly but effectively held the office, through some trying economic and social times. Like the good racquetball player he is, Hobby stood in the middle of the court, without much visible motion, but causing others to move a lot.

—Dave McNeely, columnist and author of *Bob Bullock: God Bless Texas*

Bill Hobby and Saralee Tiede have written a superb book. As lieutenant governor, Bill Hobby was enormously successful—he knew how things worked in politics and what did not work. But it is the stories that are the most fun. Anecdotes about Bill Clements, Ann Richards, Tom DeLay, and many other Texans are plentiful.

—Mark Yudof, president, University of California

In *How Things Really Work: Lessons from a Life in Politics*, Bill Hobby deploys two of the most devastating weapons known to political battle: a sharp wit and a long memory

—John Wilburn, opinion editor, *Houston Chronicle*

CONTENTS

Foreword

I N NOVEMBER 1972 AN OVERWHELMING MAJORITY of my fellow Texans elected Bill Hobby the lieutenant governor of our great state. Bill's election proved to be one of the most positive developments in the political and legislative history of the Lone Star State. Not only did Bill serve in that powerful office for an unprecedented eighteen years, but, in my opinion, he also established an unrivaled record as the best lieutenant governor in our history. The voters of Texas must have shared my opinion, because they continued to return Bill Hobby to office as long as he was willing to serve.

During my time as governor of Texas from 1973 until 1979, it was my privilege to work closely with Bill Hobby in our joint effort to provide the people of Texas the benefits of good government. Under the provisions of the Texas Constitution, the lieutenant governor is elected independent of any other state official, so he and I ran separate election campaigns. Although I certainly was aware of Bill and his outstanding reputation as a Houston businessman and civic leader, I did not know him personally until we were inaugurated in January 1973.

At the inauguration ceremony on the steps of the Texas Capitol, Bill Hobby took his oath of office and then delivered a speech in which he made generous and gracious comments about me, pledging that, in performing the duties of lieutenant governor, he would remain "at the right hand of Dolph Briscoe, whom we principally honor here today." After the inaugural parade down Congress Avenue, Bill and I hosted a public reception in the great rotunda of the Capitol. There were no special or invited guests for this event. Bill and I felt strongly that we should be available to greet and shake the hand of any member of the general public who wanted to attend. The recent Sharpstown scandal had badly eroded the public's trust in its state officials, so we wanted to throw open the doors of the Capitol for an event that symbolized our determination to run a state government that would be open to the scrutiny of the people.

The inaugural events gave Bill and me an opportunity to get better acquainted. A few days after the inauguration, Bill came to my office and told me that he was eager to establish a harmonious and collaborative working relationship. We agreed that Bill would be the one to work directly with the members of the Senate in all legislative matters, but only after he and I conferred and reached an agreement on general legislative direction. I thought that was a good deal, because he and I had very similar goals, and the lieutenant governor has the overwhelming power in the Senate. To put it another way, I understood that as governor I shouldn't try to go around him unless we had a serious disagreement over some very critical issue.

Bill Hobby was true to his word. We quickly developed an excellent working relationship. In the years that we served together, even when we disagreed on specific issues, Bill was always a steadfast friend. We collaborated whenever we could, and, in those few cases when we couldn't, our disagreements never became angry or disrespectful. Because his father had been governor of Texas, Bill had tremendous respect for the office, which was very helpful for our relationship. Bill is a man of absolute integrity, which sadly is not true of every politician. The entire time I was governor, he and I stayed on the same page, and we never had a serious problem. The vast majority of the Senate shared my positive view of their presiding officer. He never had a problem with the members of the Senate. He treated them right, always with respect, and they all respected him. They loved him.

Bill decided to retire from elected office in 1991, but he did not retire from public service. He selflessly continued to take time away from his highly successful communications business to teach, to advise, and to provide generous financial support to charitable and educational causes. Thankfully, Bill also has taken time to write this book. I am delighted that he has, not only because it makes enjoyable and interesting reading, but because this book serves the cause of history. As a member of one of the most historically influential families in Texas history and as one of the state's most important political and business leaders, Bill Hobby has been a history maker as well as a witness to history. I am grateful that he has preserved his memories and that he has now made them available to us all.

DOLPH BRISCOE

Editor's Preface

BILL HOBBY JR. HAS THE HISTORICALLY UNIQUE DISTINCTION of having served as lieutenant governor of Texas for a period of eighteen years, a longer tenure than any other previous occupant. As created by the Texas Constitution of 1876, the lieutenant governor is a popularly elected official who serves as the presiding officer of the Texas Senate and is first in the line of succession in the event of the death, removal, or resignation of the governor. Because senate rules confer on the lieutenant governor decisive authority over senate procedures, committee appointments, and the assignment of bills to specific committees, the position has evolved to become one of the three most powerful offices in Texas state government. Serving from January 1973 until January 1991, Lieutenant Governor Hobby presided over the Texas Senate during a period of rapid and historically unprecedented demographic, cultural, political, and economic change. Because Bill Hobby occupies such a significant position in the political and legislative history of Texas and because he has been such an insightful observer of "how things really work" in state government, the Dolph Briscoe Center for American History decided to publish his fascinating and informative memoir, not only for the historical record but for the civic good.

The Briscoe Center's publication of *How Things Really Work: Lessons from a Life in Politics* also comes from its role as a history center whose mission is to support, facilitate, and disseminate research based largely on its collections. The Center proudly serves as the archival home of Bill Hobby's extensive collection of official papers documenting his service as lieutenant governor. The Center also houses the official papers of former Texas governors Dolph Briscoe (1973–1979) and Mark White (1983–1987), whose terms ran concurrently with ten of Hobby's eighteen years in office; as well as the official papers of former United States senator Lloyd Bentsen (1971–1993) and several individuals who served as Texas's representatives to the U.S. Congress during the years that Bill Hobby was lieutenant governor. This massive collection of historically valuable records provides a critical and comprehensive primary resource for anyone conducting research in the political and legislative history of Texas from the early 1970s through the early 1990s. The publication of Bill Hobby's legislative memoir provides an especially notable addition of information to this already impressive resource.

The publication of *How Things Really Work* has been made possible by support from the Center's Dolph Briscoe Fund for Texas History, established by former governor Dolph Briscoe in 2008.

DON CARLETON, PH.D.
Executive Director
Dolph Briscoe Center for American History
University of Texas at Austin

Author's Preface

I HAVE SPENT MOST OF MY LIFE IN AND AROUND TEXAS GOVERNMENT. A political, or public service, gene lurks in my family's DNA. It has expressed itself now for four generations.

Both my grandfathers and a great-uncle were in the Texas Legislature. Both my parents were public servants. My father was lieutenant governor (1915–1917) and governor (1917–1921). I was lieutenant governor (1973–1991). My mother was parliamentarian of the Texas House from 1925 through 1931. Mother was the first director of the Women's Army Corps in World War II and the first secretary of health, education, and welfare (1953–1955).

In fact, Hobbys have infested the Senate chamber off and on for 137 years. My grandfather Edwin Hobby was a senator (1873–1879). When my father presided (1915–1917), his father-in-law, Bronson Cooper, was a former senator (1880–1884) who had succeeded Edwin Hobby in the same Piney Woods seat. My daughter Laura Beckworth's father-in-law, Lindley Beckworth, was a senator (1970–1971). When Lt. Gov. Ben Ramsey presided (1951–1963) I was his parliamentarian (1959).

After I presided (1973–1991), my son Paul was Lt. Gov. Bob Bullock's chief of staff (1991–1992).

Paul ran unsuccessfully for state comptroller in 1998. He was chairman of the Texas General Services Commission (1995–1997) and assistant U.S. Attorney for the Southern District of Texas (1989–1992).

I grew up in the newspaper business and reported on the Fifty-fifth Session of the Texas Legislature in 1957.

All this is by way of saying that the workings of government were a part of household conversation—and of life—from childhood.

What follows is a reflection on those experiences. Until the mid-1980s, partisanship—called "faction" by the nation's founding fathers—was not a big factor in Texas government. There were no party caucuses in the legislature. Democratic presiding officers appointed Republicans and Democrats as committee chairmen as seniority and experience, not party, dictated. Seniority and experience, for both Democrats and Republicans, was respected when legislative and congressional redistricting time came around. By the time I left office I had presided over thirty-three sessions and seventy-nine senators.

As long as Texas-born leaders of either party—Lyndon Johnson, Sam Rayburn, Dwight Eisenhower—held sway in Washington, partisanship, if not ignored, gave way to the national interest.

But as voters became more partisan, so did Texas government. Elected officials take an oath "to faithfully execute the duties" of their office and "to the best of my ability preserve, protect, and defend the Constitution and laws of the United States and of this State, so help me God." That oath doesn't say "Republican" or "Democrat," but those unsaid words seem to have crept in somehow.

Government is about education, health care, public safety, and transportation—not about abortion, homosexuality, or evolution. Our country was founded—and our Constitution written—by folks who didn't want other folks telling them what to think about religion or anything else.

Memoirs are by definition nostalgic. Nostalgia is not my purpose. But I do hope to convey something of my admiration for the people that I had the honor to work with, the spirit of the times, and a sense of how things actually worked—at least in the legislative process.

BILL HOBBY

Acknowledgments

S
ARALEE AND I WISH TO ACKNOWLEDGE all those who patiently and ably assisted us in recreating this history. Diana Hobby used her considerable editing talents and helped with facts and recollections. Delores Chambers, my longtime executive assistant, was invaluable in locating photographs and sources. I am indebted to Patsy Spaw, now secretary and historian of the Senate, and to her predecessor, Betty King, for adding facts and corrections. My Senate colleagues Max Sherman, Ray Farabee, "Babe" Schwartz, Bill Ratliff, and others helped recall events and anecdotes. Sharon Scarborough of Senate Media Services allowed us to ransack their files for photographs. Political columnist Dave McNeely gave the manuscript a careful read and ferreted out a number of errors.

The staff at the Legislative Reference Library patiently helped retrieve news clips that were invaluable to this account. We used online resources such as the Texas Almanac of Politics and the Senate Rules.

Specific chapters depended heavily on good sources, including: James A. Clark and Weldon Hart's biography of my father, *The Tactful Texan: A Biography of Governor Will Hobby*; Steven Fenberg's *Brother, Can You Spare a Billion: The Story of Jesse H. Jones*; *Barn Burning, Barn Building* by Ben Barnes; *Lines in the Sand: Congressional Redistricting in Texas and the Influence of Tom DeLay* by Steve Bickerstaff; *The Miracle of the Killer Bees* by Robert Heard; *John Hill for the State of Texas: My Years as Attorney General* by John L. Hill Jr. with Ernie Stromberger; *Bob Bullock: God Bless Texas* by Dave McNeely and Jim Henderson; *Dolph Briscoe: My Life in Texas Ranching and Politics* by Dolph Briscoe as told to Don Carleton; and *West Texas Time Machine: Creating the Hobby-Eberly Telescope* by Tom Sebring with Frank Bash, Steven Weinberg, and Joel Barna.

My friends in higher education, Bill Cunningham, Peter Flawn, Jerry Supple, Malcolm Gillis, Ken Ashworth, Art Smith, and David Bell, helped me with facts for the chapters on higher education.

However, there would be no book without the Dolph Briscoe Center for American History at the University of Texas at Austin. Don Carleton, who directs this vital and growing center, agreed to publish it and cast his discerning eye on the contents. We are indebted to Erin Purdy for her excellent ideas on promotion and to Holly Z. Taylor for her skillful, meticulous editing and many ideas for improvement. Hal Richardson scanned the photographs from the Hobby family and tracked down additional images from the Briscoe Center's collections.

BILL HOBBY
SARALEE TIEDE

INTRODUCTION

BETWEEN 1968 AND 1999, two Texas lieutenant governors lit up the sky with their outsized personalities and flamboyant ways. Ben Barnes was a political rock star whose meteoric rise was cut short at an early age by scandal, real or perceived. Bob Bullock was alcoholic, manic-depressive, and a naturally cantankerous soul famous for his flamethrower temper and his Machiavellian manipulations.

Between them, serving eighteen years, still a record for longevity in that Texas post, was Lt. Gov. Bill Hobby. Bill Hobby, as humorist Larry King noted, could take the excitement out of an earthquake. When Hobby left office in 1991, those of us on his staff made him a present of a mock historical marker, which praised him as an "enduring Texas landmark." We cited his innovative legislative techniques—"one publication compared him to a glacier," his dapper way of dressing (not!), and his "colorful expressions such as 'watch the legislative process' and 'if it isn't broke, don't fix it.'"

The good news is that he didn't fire us. The fact is that this very improbable politician was one of Texas's most progressive and dedicated public servants, fulfilling in every respect his campaign promise to "be a good Lieutenant Governor. Honestly."

In many ways, Bill Hobby is the polar opposite of the successful politician. He isn't particularly good at public speaking. He is not a glad-hander, and he doesn't enjoy small talk. We used to joke that the most dangerous place to be was between Gov. Mark White and a TV camera and between Bill Hobby and the door.

He was notably media adverse. Despite a career in newspapers, he gave a terrible interview, preferring a simple "yes" or "no" to any elucidating answer, and he had a disconcerting habit of walking away in the middle of an interview. I remember one time when I was a reporter sitting bewildered in his office for a good ten minutes before I realized he wasn't coming back and that I would have to slink out of his office. Was it something I said?

Hobby's wit is so dry and razor sharp that sometimes the target didn't even know he had been dismembered. Once, when the famously voluble Sen. A. R. "Babe" Schwartz asked on the Senate floor, "May I speak

Executive Assistant Saralee Tiede is emphatic. Hobby is unimpressed, c. 1988.
Photograph courtesy Senate Media Services.

briefly?" Hobby responded from the podium: "You may, but I doubt that you can."

Hobby was an intellectual among good ol' boys and supercharged backslappers—someone who does math for recreation, who later became so enamored with statistics that he began spending part of each summer at the Inter-University Consortium for Political and Social Research at the University of Michigan. He once gave friends T-shirts printed with George Bernard Shaw's quotation, "The mark of a truly educated man is to be moved deeply by statistics."

He is soft-spoken, mild-mannered, patient, and temperamentally well suited for the compromise and give-and-take of a successful legislative session.

While Hobby was in office, Texas was evolving from a one-party Democratic state to a two-party state. After he left office, Democrats would eventually become the minority, unable to win a single statewide office. The state was also going through a painful transition from its big-oil and big-agriculture economic base to one more dependent on technology.

Hobby saw those changes coming. The politics interested him little; he saw his party forsaking moderates like himself and believed there was little he could do to change the situation. He recognized the economic evolution, understood it, and did his best to prepare for the changes by bolstering the state's education system. He understood that prosperity would depend, as he said, not on what came out of the ground but on what came out of people's heads.

Understand that the standard political way of dealing with changing paradigms is more often (a) blaming it on one's predecessor; (b) deciding it is an aberration and not a trend; or (c) opting for some quick and easy action, whether or not it addresses the problem. Dealing with the 2008 energy crisis by suspending the federal gasoline tax for three months qualifies as (c).

Hobby did not opt for the easy solution. Texas's past as a frontier state, a ranching state, and an oil-producing state did not put a premium on education. Texans still admire self-made men who pull themselves up by their bootstraps, usually without the benefit of much schooling. And, like most people, Texans weren't eager to tax themselves to pay for much of anything, including a better education system.

Furthermore, Hobby's education program was going to take a long time to produce results, which is anathema in politics, where you need good numbers before the next election. No matter, he supported it anyway, because it was the right thing to do. He didn't turn Texas into one of the nation's highest achievers in education rankings, but he moved the ball forward.

He took on the life-and-death issues in health and human services. Most office holders consider progress in health and human services fraught with peril because, for the most part, entitlement programs are enormous money pits that defy easy answers. Hobby knew that dollars spent on prevention, whether in health care or social ills, could save money in the long term.

Hobby genuinely liked the appropriations process, and he understood the state budget well enough to describe in it very simple terms. If you want to scrub the budget, he would tell people, you have to answer these questions:

1. How many felons do you want to release so you can close some prisons?
2. How many universities do you want to close, including at least one in your district?
3. How many children do you want to cut off health care?

He also liked redistricting, that decennial exercise in matching politics with the newest census in order to reapportion the population into congressional and state legislative districts. He found redistricting an interesting mathematical challenge complicated by various rules and regulations imposed by the Voting Rights Act.

His father had opposed Prohibition, and Hobby inherited a healthy contempt for the many attempts to modify human behavior by passing laws. "It's foolish to have laws against things people are going to do anyway," he told the *Houston Post* in 1974. The subject was parimutuel betting, which was eventually legalized in Texas, but he felt the same way about laws against serving mixed drinks and escalating penalties on drug crimes.

He was protective of constitutional rights. In 1980, when Gov. Bill Clements was supporting Ross Perot's war on drugs, Hobby stood in lonely opposition to the wiretap bill. "The governor wants to wiretap the dope dealers, but that's OK—he's only going to tap the guilty ones," he said. He assigned the bill to Sen. Oscar Mauzy's Criminal Jurisprudence Committee, where it was unlikely to get even a hearing. But when it became clear that the bill had broad majority support, he pried the bill out of committee and stood back while the Senate passed it.

Hobby respected the Texas Constitution, antiquated or not. "When in doubt, read the directions," he would say sometimes when a legislative dilemma presented itself. He recognized its limitations and was one of the strongest voices supporting the Texas Constitutional Convention of 1974. This effort to adapt the 1876 constitution to twentieth-century needs ended in failure over a minor issue—right to work—but Hobby had to watch the entire process from the sidelines after the attorney general ruled that a statewide elected official could not preside over the convention.

The following year, he worked to salvage the best of the convention's work. The Senate passed the bill revising the constitution in one day's time with Hobby working the floor to get the four-fifths vote necessary to suspend the rules. He doggedly supported the new constitution as it went to the voters in November, even though Gov. Dolph Briscoe, Comptroller Bob Bullock, and a host of special interests opposed it. Once again, it was doomed. There has been no subsequent effort.

Hobby let it lie. His hero was Sam Houston, of whom he said in a San Jacinto Day essay: "Houston was a frontier fighter. He was not one for the romantic, futile and fatal gesture. Houston was not one to die for a cause. He was one to get the other fellow to die for his cause."

When Hobby came to office, the pundits were not much impressed. His lack of style and talent for understatement was too big a change from the norm. "Bill Hobby arrived as an enigma and in two sessions has done little to shed light on his political beliefs or for that matter his abilities," said *Texas Monthly* in its "Ten Best, Ten Worst Legislators" article in June 1975. "For the second consecutive session, he managed to cast himself in the villain's role on major legislative issues. . . . Two years ago he dillydallied on reform bills. This session he played footsie with the lobby on utility regulation." Still there was some faint praise: "On both occasions, Hobby came to life at the 11th hour and forced workable bills through what had been a reluctant Senate. . . . It means that Hobby is either much weaker— or much stronger—than people thought."

Even so, Hobby was building a reputation for being fair and even-handed and letting the Senate work its will. Senators took note that even when he personally felt strongly about legislation, as he did about Governor Clements's wiretap bill, he would not stand in the way of majority rule.

That reputation suffered in 1979 when Hobby tangled with the Killer Bees. *Austin American-Statesman* columnist Dave McNeely wrote: "Hobby has always rhymed with lobby, but only this session has that taken on any major significance. . . . For whatever reasons, Hobby has funneled controversial lobby-backed business-oriented legislation through the Economic Development Committee which is completely stacked in favor of business interests, with the result that legislation slid through like it was greased."

At that time, a group of liberal-to-moderate senators had begun calling themselves the Killer Bees, and they absented themselves from the chamber rather than vote on a presidential primary bill favoring home state candidate John Connally. The Senate lost a quorum, and no business could be transacted.

Hobby came out the villain in the piece, since he had changed the order of business to put the primary bill at the top of the calendar, short-circuiting a two-thirds vote to bring it to the floor. The Killer Bees came back when they wanted to. The primary bill died. Hobby joked with the runaways when they came back and did not retaliate against any of them. He said afterward that messing with the Senate calendar was the biggest mistake he made as lieutenant governor.

It is standard in Texas when a long-serving public official leaves office that all faults are forgotten and all transgressions forgiven. Even by that standard, the praise for Hobby was extraordinary and heartfelt.

Texas Monthly, once so critical, noted that Hobby "usually gets what he wants—not because he demands it but because he is so far ahead of other leaders that he sets the agenda for the entire state."

"Bill Hobby has been the most important person in state government perhaps since Sam Houston," said Texas historian T. R. Fehrenbach. "He did a very important thing—he held the vital center and saved the sum of things."

"Hobby's record in office displays a consistency—for leadership, consensus building and the ability and willingness to compromise—that must be unsurpassed in the history of that office," said a *San Angelo Standard-Time*s editorial.

Gov. Ann Richards said, "Of all the people I've known that have brought about change in Texas, Bill Hobby has been the most effective."

And George Christian, press secretary to President Lyndon Johnson and advisor to countless political figures, said, "For eighteen years, he's been the conscience of the state."

Hobby, of course, did not leave public service. He served on the Texas Parks and Wildlife Commission. He taught public affairs and statistics at the Lyndon B. Johnson School of Public Affairs at the University of Texas at Austin. He was chancellor of the University of Houston System. He headed the Commission on a Representative Student Body on behalf of all state universities, public and private, and accomplished other things too numerous to mention.

I have been privileged to know Bill Hobby as a reporter, a staffer, and a friend since the mid-1960s. I have not seen any other Texas leader with such a commitment to doing the right thing without regard for personal advancement. His contributions to the state are extraordinary. In 1975, when he had only been in office two years, Hobby told columnist Winston Bode, "If at the end of whatever period of time I am privileged to serve the state of Texas, it is recorded that I cared about, that I preserved, that I protected, that I defended, and that I extended the fundamental liberties of every citizen, I shall leave a happy man." He has achieved that goal.

SARALEE TIEDE

How Things Really Work

Ancestors

THE BATTLE OF CORPUS CHRISTI was a Civil War engagement that was little noted nor long remembered because neither the Union nor the Confederacy was very proud of it. As in many other acts of war, politics, or government, however, the Hobby family was involved. As far as we know, the Hobbys had been in Texas for only about two years when the battle was joined, and not one but two Hobbys were present at this footnote in Texas military history.

Luckily for the Confederates, the Union commander at first had a ship, the USS *Arthur*, which had too deep a draft to navigate the shallow passes through the coastal barrier islands, so the small, fleet Confederate blockade runners were able to move some cotton down the coast. But the commander, acting Lt. J. W. Kittredge, wasn't easily daunted. He got some shallow-draft vessels from New Orleans, captured a few more, and sailed into Corpus Christi Bay in August 1862. That's where my ancestors enter the story.

Corpus Christi was defended by the Eighth Texas Confederate Infantry Regiment, seven hundred local volunteers organized and commanded by my great-uncle, Maj. Alfred Marmaduke Hobby. My grandfather, Capt. Edwin E. Hobby, who came to Texas from Florida in 1860, was captain of Company D. When Kittredge landed and demanded to inspect government buildings, Uncle Marmaduke said no. Kittredge agreed to a forty-eight-hour truce, and when nothing happened after forty-eight hours, Uncle Marmaduke moved his forces, which included three old cannon and three lighter-weight guns, to earthworks that had been erected by Gen. Zachary Taylor in 1845.

With the *Arthur* in range, Uncle Marmaduke opened fire on August 16, and the ships withdrew. The next day, Union soldiers landed a howitzer south of my great-uncle's battery and commenced firing. They were repulsed with a cavalry charge and again withdrew, this time for good. The battle was hailed as "the Vicksburg of Texas," since the only Confederate casualty was Uncle Marmaduke, who was wounded slightly.

I much prefer the family account of the battle: In August 1862, Union gunboats bombarded Corpus Christi for three days. The bombardment didn't do much damage because the cannonballs didn't explode.

The cannonballs didn't explode, the story goes, because the gunboat crews had replaced the gunpowder with booze. When the cannonballs landed, the bungs popped open, and the booze dribbled out. Needless to say, the defenders soon caught on, had their hot toddies, and discipline deteriorated. The defense was relatively successful even though Uncle Marmaduke's and Grandpa's troops got pretty disorganized. What reluctant gunners those Union sailors must have been!

Whatever the situation, both sides withdrew, the coast remained under Union blockade, and in 1863 the starving citizens of Corpus Christi offered allegiance to the Union in return for food and protection.

Both Uncle Marmaduke and Grandfather Edwin were authors and legislators: Edwin represented the Piney Woods District of East Texas from 1873 to 1879 in the Texas Senate. He then became a district judge in Polk and Livingston counties and a Supreme Court commissioner from 1879 to 1888 and wrote a textbook on land law.

In those days, the Supreme Court appointed district judges as commissioners to write opinions and help handle the case load. The Texas Supreme Court was then a circuit court sitting in Houston, Galveston, Dallas, Austin, and other cities. Their Austin dormitory was in the Capitol space where the lieutenant governor's office is now, a space that was later occupied by my father and then by me.

Grandpa must have been a pretty colorful judge. He was described by an acquaintance as "a little man physically, yet he wore a Prince Albert coat, a big black slouch hat and high-heeled boots. He also wore red flannel underwear, a prevailing custom in his days. Judge Hobby, while District Judge, frequently walked from one courthouse to another." Those high-heeled boots must have made the walk from Livingston to Moscow pretty rough. He was not re-elected in 1888 and moved the family to Houston.

Marmaduke represented Galveston in the Texas House from 1859 to 1863. He wrote *The Life of David G. Burnet* (1871) and numerous poems.

WILL HOBBY

WHEN I WAS BORN IN 1932, my father, Will Hobby, was fifty-four years old. Eleven years earlier, he had left public service to return to the newspaper business after serving as lieutenant governor and governor. His life and times are ably chronicled in a book, *The Tactful Texan* by James A. Clark with help from Weldon Hart.

My father was born in Moscow, which in 1878 was the largest town in Polk County, Texas, having a sawmill, cotton gins, and even a railroad. My grandfather, Edwin P. Hobby, was district judge until he lost an election and moved his family to Houston. Once there, young Will became enamored with newspapers, which were to be his life's work. My father quit school at sixteen to work in the circulation department of the *Houston Post*, keeping the out-of-town circulation lists in order.

In short order, he became a reporter, city editor, and managing editor, and began taking an interest in politics. It would have been hard in that atmosphere for him to ignore politics even if politics weren't in his genes. The *Post's* editor, a colorful ex-Confederate officer named Col. Rienzi Johnston, was a member of the Democratic National Committee (he was later a U.S. senator and a Texas state senator). By 1904, Will Hobby was organizing the Young Men's Democratic Party and recruiting young men to the cause. He was rewarded by being made secretary of the State Democratic Executive Committee.

When he put together the investors to buy the *Beaumont Enterprise* in 1907—becoming editor and general manager—he required political help to meet his objectives for Beaumont, including a deep-water ship channel. The legislature needed to create a navigation district to make that possible. Congress had to permit someone other than the Corps of Engineers to build the channel. Fighting for industry and river traffic for Beaumont, my father got what he wanted—a contract was let for the Sabine-Neches project in 1912.

So, by the time he was thirty-six, my father was a crusading newspaper editor, a civic leader, and a successful businessman, well known and well liked. Still, he was recruited to run for lieutenant governor in 1914 mainly

Will Hobby with Bill Hobby, 1937. *Courtesy of the Hobby family.*

because of his views on Prohibition. James E. Ferguson, then a political newcomer who would later be known as "Pa" Ferguson, was running against Prohibition. Tom Ball, a politically popular Houstonian, was running as a "dry." The only candidate for lieutenant governor when my father was recruited was also a "dry." My father believed that Prohibition was taking up legislative time that should have been spent on more important issues.

In some ways, my father didn't measure up to the political stars of the early twentieth century—stirring orators with imposing features and grand statures. He was quiet, modest, unpretentious, and rather short. As he was a last-minute entry into the lieutenant governor's race, it took him some time after announcing his candidacy to put together a platform. When he did, it had a decidedly progressive look. He wanted state aid to broaden home ownership, improvements in schools and state institutions, minimum rental fees for tenant farmers, flood control and land reclamation, simplified civil and criminal law codes, and an end to corporate campaign contributions.

My father took office as lieutenant governor in 1915 just short of three months after his surprise announcement that he would run. The margin was less than eight thousand votes. Soon afterward, he married Willie Chapman Cooper, the blond and beautiful daughter of former East Texas congressman and state senator Bronson Cooper, who worked with my father on the Beaumont waterway. Amazingly enough, during his two-year term many of Will Hobby's campaign promises were enacted into law, including providing aid to tenant farmers and rural schoolchildren as well as authorizing local governments to levy taxes for public schools.

I cannot say whether I learned my political philosophy from my father or whether it was just in my DNA, but, in fact, his mindset was much like my own. He believed in cooperation in government between the three branches created by the Texas Constitution—the executive, the legislative, and the judiciary. In his 1915 inaugural address he said, "So I indulge the hope that cordial relations and a common aim and a common purpose will prevail with the legislative and executive departments of the government, and that aim and that purpose will be to advance the material welfare of Texas."

He also believed that real progress meant progress for everyone, rich and poor alike. "If we let the poison of filthy disease percolate through the hovels of the poor, death knocks at the palace gates. If we fail to provide education and leave to ignorance any portion of our race, the consequences of ignorance strike us all and there is no escape. We must all move together and we must all keep together," he said at a memorial service for Southeast Texas pioneer Henry Rosenberg in Galveston.

Make no mistake—my father was no liberal. As editor of the *Houston Post*, he opposed a third term for Franklin Roosevelt and castigated the Supreme Court Roosevelt appointed to carry out his New Deal policies. But in a segregated Texas, he was a distinct moderate.

Gov. Jim Ferguson was impeached in 1917 after being indicted by a Travis County grand jury on charges of misapplication of public funds, embezzlement, and diversion of a special fund. But the real reason was his high-handed treatment of the University of Texas.

Ferguson vetoed the University of Texas appropriation because the university regents wouldn't fire the president, who wouldn't fire professors the governor didn't like. (Accidentally or intentionally, Ferguson didn't veto a particular assistant math professor. That's micromanaging.) Ferguson summoned Regent George Washington Littlefield and told him he would not veto the appropriation if President Robert E. Vinson resigned. President Vinson asked Littlefield how he should respond. Littlefield said "I would tell him to go to hell!" Vinson said that the expression was "somewhat out of line with my own customary forms of expression" but asked Littlefield "to convey the substance of his statement to the Governor as my reply, leaving the exact verbiage to [Littlefield's] own discretion."

President Vinson also got divine guidance. Texas Episcopal Bishop George Herbert Kinsolving was closely associated with the University of Texas. As Vinson later told the story: "Just at that moment the ringing of the telephone interrupted the proceedings and the voice of Bishop Kinsolving came to my ears. 'No matter how I know it, but I know what is going on,' he said, 'but don't you resign.' That message had much to do with the decision then made."

Ferguson vetoed the appropriation that same afternoon, and the University of Texas was in the ditch. But then a remarkable thing happened, probably unique in the history of public education. Two of the regents pledged their fortunes by personally guaranteeing the university's budget of $1,627,404. Littlefield and George Washington Brackenridge were longtime regents who disliked each other intensely. They had served on opposite sides in the Civil War, Littlefield as a Confederate officer, Brackenridge as a U.S. Treasury agent. They disagreed, often bitterly and personally, about almost everything except the welfare of the university. Both had given enormous amounts of money to the university, and various structures on the UT campus are named for them. Brackenridge also gave the city of San Antonio the park that bears his name.

The House then impeached Ferguson, and the Senate removed him from office. Technically, Ferguson wasn't impeached because of the veto, but the veto was the proximate cause. There were plenty of other grounds—among them misusing public funds. He was also selling pardons. But it was the University of Texas veto that really got him in trouble. The legislature reappropriated the money. My father, who had succeeded Ferguson as governor, signed the bill, and all was well. My father beat Ferguson in the next election by a large majority.

Left to right: Dan Moody, James Allred, Ross Sterling, Coke Stevenson, Pat Neff, Miriam Ferguson, and William P. Hobby Sr. *William P. Hobby Sr. Family Papers, Dolph Briscoe Center for American History, di_04915.*

Ninety years later, Gov. Rick Perry was pretty confused about the powers of the governor and the powers of the legislature. He didn't like the way higher education is funded, specifically special items, which he wanted to veto. Special items are usually research and public service projects undertaken by universities that reflect the special needs of the communities the universities serve. These items are "special" because they are not funded by the formulas that generate the money for teaching and apply only to a specific university. Perry didn't care that higher education is poorly funded—at that time Texas ranked fiftieth in percentage of high school graduates and twenty-seventh in college graduates.

At the University of Houston, for example, space exploration in conjunction with NASA and superconductivity to increase the efficiency of power transmission are special items. So is the Center for Public Policy, which does research on government issues, frequently with the support of the National Science Foundation or the city of Houston.

Special items are covered by a provision in the education code that appropriates money for higher education in a lump sum. In other words, the governor would have to veto an entire university, not just a particular item. Just as in "Pa" Ferguson's time, the issue remains the power of the governor vs. the power of the legislature.

As impeachment proceedings got underway in 1917, my father became acting governor, although Ferguson continued to occupy the governor's office in the Capitol and the Governor's Mansion. On September 25, after the Senate had sustained ten articles of impeachment, Ferguson was removed from office and Will Hobby became governor.

The times were not auspicious. World War I was underway, Texas was in the midst of a terrible drought, and pink bollworms were tearing up what survived of the cotton crop. A horrendous influenza epidemic waited in the wings. Ferguson's allies—and there were many of them—bitterly resented his impeachment.

My father went to work, securing an impressive amount of legislation in the fourth called session, including a law giving women the right to vote in Democratic primaries, ratification of the constitutional amendment prohibiting the sale or consumption of alcohol, and a number of other new laws. He accomplished his aims mainly by working quietly and effectively with the legislators, staying off the floor of the House and the Senate, and letting the credit go to others.

In those days governors had two-year terms. Will Hobby was no sooner inaugurated than he was campaigning against the former governor, Jim Ferguson. The Senate had barred Ferguson from public office, but my father never raised the issue. It was up to the people to decide.

It wasn't a pleasant campaign. Ferguson called my father a "political accident" and a "weakling" and then got personal, saying that Hobby was "a misfit whom God has failed to endow with the physical attributes which make up a man." My father responded: "I will admit that the Supreme Being failed to favor me with physical attributes pleasing to Governor Ferguson, but at least he gave me the intelligence to know the difference between my own money and that which belongs to the state."

My father won election overwhelmingly in 1918 and focused on:

- Health care—too many young Texans had been rejected for military service for health reasons
- Education—free textbooks
- Prison reform—ending the practice of allowing farmers who leased prison land to work convicts under contract.

Gov. Will Hobby signing the resolution memorializing Congress to ratify the Nineteenth (Women's Suffrage) Amendment, 1919. *William P. Hobby Sr. Family Papers, Dolph Briscoe Center for American History, di_04213.*

One of my father's major accomplishments was his support of the Women's Suffrage Amendment. He had succeeded in getting the Texas Legislature to pass a bill giving women the right to vote in Democratic primaries, which were then tantamount to general elections, but Texas voters rejected a state constitutional amendment to give women the right to vote in general elections. My father spoke strongly in support of the Nineteenth Amendment to the U.S. Constitution. Despite the rather recent defeat of the Texas law, the legislature agreed and ratified the federal suffrage amendment on June 28, making Texas the first Southern state to do so. Hobby also spoke in support of the amendment in Oklahoma and Tennessee.

The legislature also passed my father's proposal to provide free textbooks to schoolchildren. There were other major bills—one of the stiffest prohibition acts in the nation; oil and gas law that included the "Relinquishment Act," which gave former owners of state land one-half the mineral rights; some water conservation measures; and the creation of the

Texas Library and Historical Commission. He sent Texas Rangers to the Oklahoma border when Oklahoma claimed oil from the Burkburnett field in the bed of the Red River.

But in 1920, Will Hobby decided not to run for re-election, saying he would not "complicate the political situation" when there were such well-qualified candidates as former U.S. senator Joe Bailey, two former Speakers of the Texas House, and a state attorney general. He did, however, successfully run for delegate-at-large to the Democratic National Convention, pointing out that "under my administration the doors of the university, which I have found closed, have been opened, and the doors of the saloons, which I found open, have been closed."

Before he left office, my father had to deal with the pink bollworms, which were such a severe problem that the federal government was considering a quarantine of Texas cotton. He talked the feds out of quarantining cotton shipments long enough to pass legislation to pay farmers to destroy infested crops and to begin a state control program. Over half a century later, Gov. Dolph Briscoe would perform a similar service to cattlemen by calling a special session to fund brucellosis (screwworm) control. Will Hobby also found a little money left in the state treasury and was able to push through a long overdue teacher pay raise.

My father made frequent pardons. In 1917 he asked a committee to tour the prisons and look for deserving prisoners who had no friends or relatives to intercede for them. At Christmas he pardoned thirty-five "forgotten men." At the end of his term as governor he pardoned a convicted murderer, who helped raise me. At that time, the Governor's Mansion was staffed by prison trusties. George was a trusty. He was part black, part Indian. After George was pardoned, he worked for our family for fifty years, mainly driving my father and working at the office. George kept greyhounds to hunt rabbits, and I used to hunt with him and his dogs near our house, usually on a field near Main and Bellaire where Glenn McCarthy's Shamrock Hotel used to be and where the Texas Medical Center is now.

Pardons then and now generate a lot of controversy. In 2000, President Clinton's end-of-term pardons were criticized. But executive clemency, as presidential or gubernatorial pardons are called, are neither all bad or all good.

Gov. Sam Houston pardoned murderess Mary Monroe because the Texas Supreme Court opinion upholding her conviction had been written by Oran Roberts, then heading the convention that would lead Texas into secession. "I'll pardon her," Houston said. "No citizen should be deprived of liberty by such a fellow." The pardon itself simply reads "It being shown to me by petitions and facts presented that there is reason for the exercise of executive clemency. . . ." Seems reasonable to me.

Houston well knew that there are injustices in the "justice" system that can lead to locking up people for no good reason. Look at the recent spate of convictions overturned by DNA evidence. As governor, Houston pardoned more people (including several imprisoned slaves) than any of his predecessors.

The ability of the sovereign to correct injustice is well founded in history and much needed in fact. It's one small weight in the balance against a prosecutor (Kenneth Starr, for example) gone mad in a system that needs more such weights. Take President Clinton's pardon of Susan McDougal. McDougal was one of the few people to do prison time as a result of Starr's Whitewater investigation. She served eighteen months, including eight months in solitary confinement, for civil contempt because she refused to answer three questions before a grand jury on whether President Clinton lied. She is now an advocate for prison reform.

Because Congress can make nutty laws, pardons can at least help correct legislative abuses and restore some sanity to the system. President Clinton's pardon of a woman who was in the federal pen for having an eagle feather is but one example.

Before and after my father served as governor, attention was focused on pardons during the administrations of governors James E. and Miriam A. Ferguson. "Ma" and "Pa" Ferguson pardoned hundreds of prisoners, many of whom were in prison because they had violated Prohibition laws. Prohibition of alcohol was the religious right's war on drugs three generations ago. Prohibition laws filled the prisons and ruined lives then just as marijuana laws do now. The Fergusons rightly concluded that the state was better served by these men being home supporting their families. The Fergusons, like President Clinton, were accused of selling pardons. There was no credible evidence that they did so.

Just as Sam Houston did, the Fergusons used the power of the pardon to remedy racial injustice. When Ma Ferguson took office in 1925 she pardoned many black convicts, including John Ed Patten. Patten was a Fourth Ward businessman in Houston who in 1918 had committed the crime of defending himself when attacked by a policeman who was likely doing a bit of racial profiling. Patten was also Barbara Jordan's grandfather. The incident took place on San Felipe Street, just a few blocks from where my office is located.

After finishing his term as governor in 1921, my father went back to Beaumont to run the *Enterprise*. Within two years he had bought up his competition, the *Beaumont Journal*, and moved back to Houston, where

Family portrait: From left, Bill Hobby, Jessica Hobby, Oveta Culp Hobby, William P. Hobby, c. 1941. *Courtesy of the Hobby family.*

he was recruited by Ross Sterling, a founder and president of Humble Oil and Refining Company, to run his newly combined *Houston Dispatch* and *Houston Post*. In 1929 Willie Cooper Hobby, his wife of fourteen years, died quite suddenly of a cerebral hemorrhage. Two years later, in 1931, he married my mother, Oveta Culp.

I grew up listening to my father's stories, enjoying my trips with him to Austin, swimming in Barton Springs, and visiting his friends. One was Edgar "Commodore" Perry, who built the Austin hotel that bore his name. Another was T. C. "Buck" Steiner, who ran the Capitol Saddlery on Guadalupe Street. Buck was a colorful guy, a rodeo bull rider who has his own wing in the Rodeo Hall of Fame. He opened Capitol Saddlery in 1930 and owned a lot of land around Austin, including Steiner Ranch, which is now a subdivision. When I was lieutenant governor, I frequented Buck's establishment, which was close to the Capitol, visiting with Buck as he sat in a big armchair by the old-fashioned counter. As long as he lived he called me "Young Hobby."

One of my parents' close, longtime friends was Jesse Jones, a Houston entrepreneur who started out in the lumber business and became a banker, developer, and publisher of the *Houston Chronicle*. In 1945, President Roosevelt was sworn in for the fourth and last time. My parents came to Washington for the inauguration. I was in Form II (eighth grade) at St. Albans School in Washington.

The ceremony took place on the South Portico of the White House because President Roosevelt was too sick to go to the Capitol. He had a reception at the White House for a small group of Cabinet members, congressional leadership, Supreme Court justices, and the like. My father went as the guest of Jones, who was then secretary of commerce, having been appointed by Roosevelt in 1940.

Mother and I watched the inauguration from the roof of the Washington Hotel. The weather was cold and rainy. My father had intended to join us for lunch after the ceremony, but after a while he called and said he was going to lunch with Mr. Jones. When my father came back to the hotel that afternoon he told us how extraordinarily cordial the president had been to Mr. Jones, how he and Mr. Jones had gone back to the Wardman Park Hotel for lunch, and how Mr. Jones had received a letter at the hotel from the president dismissing him from the Cabinet. FDR ousted Jones to appoint his outgoing vice president, Henry A. Wallace, to that post.

Oveta Culp Hobby

MY MOTHER, OVETA CULP HOBBY, also carried the public service gene. She was born in 1905 in Killeen, a small town in Central Texas. She died ninety years later, having lived a life of exceptional public service and professional achievement.

She was introduced to state government by her father, Isaac W. Culp, a lawyer, minister, and legislator. "Ike" Culp was elected to the Texas House of Representatives in 1919 and took his fourteen-year-old daughter to Austin during the sessions. She became a committee clerk and parliamentarian of the House of Representatives before she turned twenty-one, while also attending classes at the University of Texas and auditing lectures at the law school. She was recalled to that job three times, in 1927, 1929, and 1931, once replacing the parliamentarian of the time who had a heart attack just before the session.

Around 1929, during the Great Depression, Mother was a clerk at the Texas Banking Commission. There were not enough bank examiners to cope with all the failing banks. The banking commissioner said "Miss Culp, I want you to examine a bank in Temple." "But commissioner, I'm not a bank examiner," Mother replied. "You are now," said the commissioner.

When she first went to Houston, Mother went to work for a Houston law firm, then for the *Houston Post-Dispatch* as assistant to the cartoonist. That's where she met my father. They were married in 1931. Entrepreneurs together, they built the *Post* into a communications company that published three newspapers and operated six television stations and two radio stations in five states.

One of the stories my father liked to tell about my mother involved Huey Long, who was governor of Louisiana from 1928 to 1932. In 1932, the Louisiana State University football team came to Houston to play Rice. Long came with the team. "The Kingfish" was famous for his populist policies and his fiery rhetoric. At the time of his visit to Houston he had been elected handily to the U.S. Senate but stayed on as governor to push through his road-building program and other unfinished business.

That year, Texas Gov. Ross Sterling, oilman and publisher of the *Houston Post*, had been defeated for re-election in the Democratic primary

Bill Hobby and Oveta Culp Hobby, 1949. *Courtesy of the Hobby family.*

by Ma Ferguson and was suing her for election fraud. At that time, my father was president of the *Houston Post* and a friend of Walter Monteith, the mayor of Houston.

The mayor asked my father to go with him early that Saturday morning to meet the train and welcome Governor Long. The train got in, the band got off and set up their music stands on the platform beside the train. The band played while the fans got off, then the team. Now it was time for Governor Long to get off. The band played on and on. Finally the governor got off, somewhat the worse for the long train ride.

The mayor presented the governor with the key to the city. Then, since the mayor was having a brunch for Governor Long, my father got in the mayor's car with Long and Monteith to go to the mayor's house. In the car, Governor Long clapped my father on the knee and, blowing his whiskey breath in my father's face, asked: "Hobby, are you a friend of Sterling's?"

"I hope so, Governor. I work for him." my father replied.

"Tell Sterling to keep his ass out of the courthouse. Being counted out is the same as being voted out. I know. I've done it both ways," said Long.

He was right. "Ma" Ferguson served that term as governor. She had previously been governor from 1925 to 1927.

At the brunch, a stag affair, a woman dressed as a waitress came up and offered them coffee. Much to my father's surprise, the waitress was my mother. Mother explained that she had always wanted to meet Huey Long, and she found a way to do it.

"Where did you find that cute young thing?" asked Long.

"I found her in an orphanage" said my father.

"Imagine that" said Long. "A cute young thing like that, and no kinfolks."

Mother was "the first woman who . . ." did any number of things, but she never thought of herself as a feminist or pioneer. As she put it, she just did the next thing that came along.

The "next thing" in public service was the Women's Army Corps. She was its first director; they called her "the little colonel." She was next called to serve in President Dwight D. Eisenhower's administration, first as Federal Security Administrator, then as the first secretary of the Department of Health, Education, and Welfare (HEW).

The hardest time of her life came at HEW during the polio epidemic of the early 1950s. Polio, which paralyzed its victims for life, was a huge public health problem. Many parents kept their children out of schools, swimming pools, or any public place they could catch the disease.

Bill Hobby with his mother, WAC Commander Oveta Culp Hobby, at Fort Hood, Texas, c. 1942. *Courtesy of the Hobby family.*

William P. Hobby Sr. and Oveta Culp Hobby with President Eisenhower when Mrs. Hobby was appointed secretary of health, education, and welfare on April 11, 1953. *Courtesy of the Hobby family.*

Dr. Jonas Salk, financed by the Red Cross, had started working in 1947 to develop a vaccine. In 1954, massive tests of the vaccine started in the United States and Canada. The number of polio cases decreased dramatically among the test groups.

My mother appointed a commission of epidemiologists, headed by the dean of the University of Michigan Medical School, to evaluate the vaccine. The commission approved the vaccine, and my mother authorized its distribution. When I was in Ann Arbor almost fifty years later, I met the doctor who had arranged the news conference at which the approval was announced. Small world.

But some of the vaccine was bad and caused cases of polio as well as several deaths. Mother became ill with grief. But the Salk, and later the Sabin, vaccines ultimately wiped out polio.

In May 2007, I got an e-mail from Roderick Welsh, the sergeant-at-arms of the Texas House, who told me that he was in possession of a portrait of my mother that had recently hung in the House parliamentarian's office. Walsh explained that when the House parliamentarian had vacated her position rather abruptly, he had been asked to return the portrait to me.

Denise Davis was that House parliamentarian. After she finished her undergraduate work at the University of Texas at Austin and before she entered UT Law School Davis worked in the correspondence department of my office. She worked under my highly competent office manager Stella Bryant and got a healthy dose of mentoring in the process.

Once she earned her law degree, Davis worked for the Legislative Council, then for Sen. Rodney Ellis (who also worked for me when he was a student at the Lyndon B. Johnson School of Public Affairs), then for Supreme Court Chief Justice Tom Phillips before becoming general counsel to Lt. Gov. Bill Ratliff in 2001.

In that job, Davis occupied an office right off the Ben Ramsey Room in the Capitol. There was a portrait on the wall of some no doubt distinguished fellow who had died some time ago. Denise wanted something better. On the list of available art she found only two female subjects: Sen. Barbara Jordan, whose portrait hangs in a place of honor in the Senate chamber and may not be moved, and a portrait of my mother, Oveta Culp Hobby.

Davis thought that a portrait of the head of the Women's Army Corps and the secretary of health, education, and welfare would be more inspirational than one of an unknown man. When she became House parliamentarian, she asked and received my permission to move the portrait across the aisle to her House office.

Davis resigned her job, writing out her resignation letter on a laptop while sitting at the podium during the late night hours of May 25, 2007. The 80th Legislature was in its final days, and House Speaker Tom Craddick was under attack by a sizeable number of House members who wanted to replace him as Speaker. Members were asking procedural questions, the gist of which was whether Craddick would recognize a motion to vacate the chair.

Another House member, Rep. Harold Dutton, was sitting on the podium with Craddick at the time, and the Speaker apparently liked Dutton's answer better than the legal advice from his parliamentarian. After he consulted with Dutton and announced his answer—that the Speaker's power to recognize or not recognize was absolute and could not be appealed—Davis resigned.

I picked up my mother's portrait at the Capitol and took it to Killeen, where I was dedicating a historical marker about my mother. The mayor plans to hang the portrait in city hall. Davis later became chief of staff for Joe Straus, the House Speaker who succeeded Craddick.

4

School Days

I was born in Houston in 1932. I share my January 19 birthday with my mother and my sister, Jessica. I went to elementary school at Kinkaid. When my mother joined the army I followed her to Washington and entered St. Albans School in 1943.

I lived at school. The dormitory master was John Davis, a historian and kind and patient man, my oldest friend. I took Spanish, American history, European history, and sacred studies from him. I was one of his protégés, as were many others.

One of my schoolmates at St. Albans was Mike Collins, the astronaut, who, as he put it, "drove the getaway car" during Apollo 11, the 1969 moon landing mission. Mike piloted the command module that circled the moon while Edwin Aldrin and Neil Armstrong walked on it.

Mike always got the job done.

Mike played left guard and I played center on the football team. Single-wing centers used to take a lot of punishment. During one game, I was slow getting up from a scrimmage, mainly because I had been hurt. Mike pulled me up and asked "Which one?" "64," I said. After the next play they carried 64 off, and he didn't come back.

Years later, I visited Mike in Washington, D.C. He had been named director of the Smithsonian National Aerospace Museum, and I wanted to show him a *Houston Post* editorial I had written commending him. He told me some of his experiences in running the new museum. When he took the job, the museum was still under construction, so the contractor tried out the "new boy."

"General, construction costs have gone up 1 percent a month since we bid this job, and we are losing our ass. We can only put in three elevators instead of the four in the contract."

"We paid for four elevators. We'll get four elevators," Mike replied.

When the staff wanted to change the plans he told them they had excellent ideas. "If you had had them six months ago, we might have used them, but you didn't and we won't."

The *Washington Post* applauded him for bringing in the museum on time and on budget.

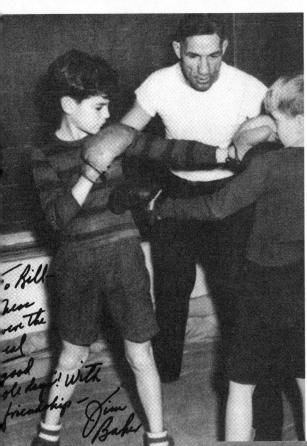

Bill Hobby and Jim Baker (later to be secretary of state) duke it out in 1939. *Courtesy of the Hobby family.*

Bill Hobby playing football, c. 1943. *Courtesy of the Hobby family.*

5

IN THE NAVY

AFTER GRADUATING FROM ST. ALBANS IN 1949, I entered Rice University in Houston. Almost immediately, I tried to enlist in the Naval Reserve Officers Training Corps, but they turned me down because I am colorblind. The commander of the Naval ROTC at that time was Leonard Sparks Mewhinney, brother of Hubert Mewhinney, my mentor on the *Houston Post*. Captain Mewhinney told me to apply to Officer Candidate School, where they could get a waiver for color blindness.

So, when I was a senior at Rice, I tried again. The recruiting officer was a crusty old seadog who told me that even if I were accepted, I could only be a "limited duty officer"—not eligible for command at sea, fit only for such stuff as communications and intelligence. Certainly no red-blooded American boy would want to do that! I allowed as how I was willing to try. That's how I got into Naval Intelligence.

I spent three of the most interesting years of my life in Naval Intelligence. After Officer Candidate School in Newport, Rhode Island, I went to the Naval Intelligence School in Washington, D.C. One of my shipmates was Donald Morris. We were closing up one night in 1954 when he invited me home for dinner. He told me that his sister-in-law was in town and his wife had told him to "bring home a tall one."

Diana Stallings was visiting her sister, Sylvia Morris, from Virginia, where she taught at Chatham Hall. She was the daughter of Laurence Tucker Stallings, a Southern journalist, author, playwright, and critic who won fame and fortune writing powerful, unvarnished accounts of battle. Stallings was horribly wounded and won the Silver Star and the Croix de Guerre for his bravery at Belleau Wood during World War I. While attacking an enemy machine gun, Stallings's kneecap was blown off, but he pressed on and threw a grenade that destroyed the enemy position. Stallings eventually lost that leg to amputation after a bad fall on the ice some years later. That battle became a critical part of his novel *Plumes*, which was made into the popular silent movie *The Big Parade*.

Wedding photo, 1954. From left, Gordon Marshall, Oveta Culp Hobby, Diana Hobby, Bill Hobby, Helen Poteat Marshall, William P. Hobby Sr. *Courtesy of the Hobby family.*

Stallings met Diana's mother, Helen Purefoy Poteat, at Wake Forest University, where her father, Dr. William Louis Poteat, was the revered president of the university. Poteat, who came from a slaveholding Baptist family, was a professor of natural science and biology before being named president of Wake Forest, and he strongly believed in the teachings of Charles Darwin on evolution. Such views were controversial at a Baptist institution, but Poteat survived as president from 1905 to 1927, and in 1925 he helped defeat a legislative attempt to ban the teaching of evolution.

Laurence Stallings and Helen Poteat lived in New York, where he was a reporter and later a critic for the *New York World*. During that time, he teamed up with playwright and journalist Maxwell Anderson to write the play *What Price Glory?* That play ran for 433 performances on Broadway and was so successful that Stallings was able to retire to Forest Home, the

Bill Hobby and Diana Poteat Stallings cut their wedding cake, 1954. *Courtesy of the Hobby family.*

Poteat plantation in Yanceyville, Caswell County, North Carolina. Later he moved to Hollywood and wrote a series of screenplays, including the John Ford movies *She Wore a Yellow Ribbon* and *3 Godfathers*.

Diana and her older sister Sylvia had been raised in New York and Yanceyville. As a girl, Diana had attended Chatham Hall in Chatham, Virginia. She was an English major with a degree from Radcliffe College.

Diana and I were married later that year—1954—in a ceremony at Forest Home, with me in my navy dress whites. After we married, Diana got her master's degree in English at Georgetown University. Much later, when I was lieutenant governor, she earned her doctorate in English from Rice University.

While we lived in Washington, she worked for the Central Intelligence Agency and translated the stuff economists wrote into English. Her office was in "Temporary M," a frame building left over from World War II—the same building where Mother had worked fifteen years earlier.

Diana's colleagues were former newspaper editors and English professors. The father of one of them was Robert Selph Henry, a Civil War historian. When Mr. Henry was a reporter on the *Atlanta Constitution*, one of his colleagues was writing a Civil War novel, and, at her request, Mr. Henry advised her on historical matters. He also reassured the young writer. "Peggy, if this doesn't get published," he would say, "just remember what a good time you had writing it." His concern was misplaced. "Peggy" was Margaret Mitchell, and the book was *Gone with the Wind.*

6

REMEMBERING LBJ

THE LEGACY OF LYNDON BAINES JOHNSON, our thirty-seventh president, has become tragically tangled in the memory of the Vietnam War, a war he inherited from President John F. Kennedy. It was a war LBJ didn't want and couldn't end. Vietnam cannot be ignored; we would have been far better off if President George W. Bush had had any memory or understanding of the pain of such a divisive war. History will be kinder to Lyndon Johnson and recognize his incredible contributions to social justice, education, and space exploration. And surely, there was no majority leader of the U.S. Senate who was more adept at having his way or more colorful in getting things done.

When I was a young lieutenant j.g. in Naval Intelligence in Washington in the mid-1950s, Johnson was majority leader. He had been elected to the Senate in 1948, became minority whip in 1951, minority leader in 1953, then majority leader in 1955.

The main reason that I knew Lyndon Johnson was because of my relative Posh Oltorf, a longtime friend and campaign manager for LBJ. While I was in Washington, Posh was a lobbyist for Brown and Root.

There is no end of stories about Posh. Frank Calvert (Posh) Oltorf was born January 20, 1923, in Marlin. He graduated from Marlin High School in 1940 and attended Rice Institute in Houston. He was a distant Pettus cousin and close friend. We knew one another for fifty years.

Posh served in the army in India during World War II. After the war he came home to Marlin, started law school at the University of Texas, and was elected to the legislature. Born to be in politics, Posh was one of the youngest members of the legislature when he represented Falls County for two terms. He then became Brown and Root's Austin (and later Washington) lobbyist. Brown and Root was a large Houston construction company, founded by brothers George and Herman Brown, with some big government contracts. It is now KBR, Inc., a subsidiary of Halliburton.

When Posh came back to Texas, he became a legislator and rancher. He was a wonderful storyteller with a great knowledge of history and a keen sense of humor. He could entertain an audience of one or hundreds.

Hobby greets former Lt. Gov. Ben Ramsey and Hobby's cousin Posh Oltorf at the Senate podium. *William P. Hobby Sr. Family Papers, Dolph Briscoe Center for American History, di_05743.*

The University of Texas Press published his book *The Marlin Compound* in 1967. Diana Hobby helped edit the book.

In 1955 Posh was entertaining Sen. Lyndon Johnson at Huntland, George and Herman Brown's farm near Middleburg, Virginia, when Johnson had his first heart attack. Posh called the doctor and rode in the ambulance with Johnson to the Bethesda Naval Hospital in Maryland.

At that time Diana and I were living in Washington in a garage apartment in McLean, not far from where Lynda Johnson and Chuck Robb live today.

Posh, Diana, and I had many good times in Washington. Posh, Les Carpenter, who with his wife, Liz Carpenter, ran a Washington news service for southwestern newspapers, and I had nearly the same birthdays (January 18, 19, 20) so we had joint birthday parties. (Liz Carpenter, of course, became a highly placed aide to Senator Johnson and press secretary to Mrs. Johnson when LBJ was president.) The guests were mainly members of the Texas congressional delegation, including Senator Johnson, and the Texas press corps.

On one of those occasions and not long after Johnson's heart attack, I called Walter Jenkins, Johnson's longtime administrative assistant, to invite the senator to the party. Walter, of course, told me that the Johnsons were not going out in the evening because of his health. I told Walter that I realized that, but asked him to let the Johnsons know we were thinking of them and would miss them.

About eight the night of the party Walter called to say that Johnsons had just left the office and were on the way to my house.

Panic! Diana had just put dinner in the oven, but she took it out quickly. I looked up the number for the Bethesda hospital and wrote it in big letters inside the telephone book cover. I had visions of the majority leader dying in a lieutenant j.g.'s apartment. But he didn't. All went well!

Johnson's Persuasiveness

Senator Johnson did not like to be left alone. When Mrs. Johnson and their daughters, Lynda and Luci, went back to the LBJ ranch in Stonewall, Texas, in the summer, Johnson moved into the Mayflower Hotel and asked Posh to stay with him.

Posh woke up one such morning to find that Johnson, the Senate majority leader, had already been through the Sunday papers and was impatiently waiting for seven a.m. to begin calling senators.

The first phone conversation went like this:

LBJ: "Good morning, [Senator] Dick [Russell], this is Lyndon. Dick, I just want to know who you want to fill the vacancy on the [Senate] Foreign Relations Committee. Then we can all get behind him."

RUSSELL: [*Inaudible*]

LBJ: "Dick, that's the very man I was thinking of. But, Dick, we have a problem. I've been calling around, and a lot of them want Estes [Kefauver]."

RUSSELL: [*Objects*]

LBJ: "Dick, Hubert [Humphrey] has a lot of support. I'm afraid Hubert is the only one we can beat Estes with."

[*Russell reluctantly agrees.*]

A few more such calls and Hubert Humphrey was on the Foreign Relations Committee.

Diana's Birthday Present

Lyndon Johnson had not been president long when Ben Haynes, the CIA man in Houston, said he had to see me immediately on a grave matter of national security. His CIA boss also had flown from Washington just for this meeting.

The national security matter he referred to was a story in that morning's *Washington Post* that said, quite accurately, that President Johnson had called his director of Central Intelligence, Adm. William Rayborn, to the White House. The meeting, from Rayborn's point of view, did not go well, so he went back to his office in Langley and asked the CIA librarian to get him books about the Texas Hill Country so that the admiral could learn more about President Johnson's background and understand him better. The librarian called two bookstores: The Bookman in Houston run by Grace David and her son Dorman; and the Brick Row Bookshop run by Franklin Gilliam in Austin. They, of course, cleared their shelves of books by Walter Prescott Webb, Bill Porterfield, Frank Dobie, and Roy Bedichek and shipped the books off to Langley. (I doubt that the admiral had a chance to read the books before Johnson fired him.)

The "grave matter of national security" was "Had the story come from a leak within the agency?" Could I find out?

"Probably," I said. So I called Grace David and told her I would like to come out to the store to buy a birthday present for Diana. I suggested that Larry McMurtry, whom Diana and I knew well and who worked in the store, would do a better job than I of picking a book.

I told the CIA folks that I would have to buy a book. "Buy the whole bookstore," said the man from Washington.

Ben and his boss followed me to the store and parked around the corner. Grace had several books laid out and served coffee. I asked her if she knew that she had made page one of the *Washington Post* that morning. Of course she didn't, so I told her about the story.

Grace laughed and said she had told the story to the *Post* correspondent in Houston a few days before. I bought Diana's present, an early Yeats edition, and left.

I went around the corner and reported the highly predictable news to the CIA and showed the sales slip for $14.97. Ben showed up the next day with a check for $14.97.

Diana was delighted with her present, and national security was preserved.

LBJ's Gavel

When I began running for lieutenant governor in 1971, I went to see President Johnson at his ranch office. He told me that he would support me against anybody except George Christian. Christian was LBJ's former press secretary, a prince of a man. George lent his astute advice, boundless wisdom, and political good sense to me as long as he lived.

In the bookcases on the office walls were many gavels LBJ had used in presiding over the U.S. Senate as majority leader and vice president. He presented me one that had belonged to President Andrew Jackson, made from wood that had come from Old Hickory's office. Of course, I used that gavel the first day I presided over the Texas Senate.

Years later I showed the gavel to Harry Middleton, director of the LBJ Library in Austin, and told Harry how I had acquired it. I was not sure whether LBJ had given me the gavel or lent it. "Well, Bill," said Harry, "there were only two of you in the room, and you're the only one still alive." Foolishly, I gave the gavel back to the LBJ Library.

LBJ's Last Inauguration

In January 1973, the day before Dolph Briscoe and I were sworn in, I called President Johnson to invite him to the inauguration.

"Mr. President," I said, "I know you have received an invitation, but I didn't want the day to pass without telling you how much it would mean to me and Diana and my mother if you would come to the inauguration."

"Well, when is it?"

"Tomorrow, Mr. President,"

"I know it's tomorrow, but what time."

"Noon, Mr. President."

"Noon! That's when I take my nap. You're just trying to kill a sick old man!" He slammed the phone down. Later in the day Mary Rather, LBJ's secretary, called Bill Jenkins to say that President and Mrs. Johnson were coming. Bill Jenkins, a cousin of LBJ's loyal staff person Walter Jenkins, was on my staff handling inaugural arrangements.

Bill asked me where I wanted President and Mrs. Johnson to sit. "Next to Diana and me on the platform. Where else?" I said.

"There isn't room for them on the platform," said Bill.

"Well, Bill, I expect there are seats on the platform for Diana and me. The Johnsons can sit there. I'll stand out in the crowd and raise my right hand and swear to "preserve, protect and defend the Constitution of the United States and this state."

"I knew that's what you would say, but I figured it was better to leave the meeting, talk to you, and go back to the meeting with your decision," Bill said.

It turned out there was room for the Johnsons on the platform after all. After the ceremony, LBJ was mobbed by well-wishers. It was a great last hurrah.

He died a week later.

Hobby with LBJ at the inauguration in 1973, a week before the former president died. *William P. Hobby Sr. Family Papers, Dolph Briscoe Center for American History, di_05746.*

Posh and Robert Caro

Ann Fears Crawford, an historian in Austin, invited me one day in the late 1970s to a dinner she was having the next week for somebody she had never met. "Somebody" was Robert Caro, the Pulitzer Prize-winning biographer of Robert Moses, the visionary and very controversial "master builder" of New York City. Ann told me she was having the gathering because Caro "is just beginning a biography of Lyndon."

I went and brought my cousin Posh because he had been a good friend of LBJ. Posh and Caro became friends, a relationship that lasted the rest of Posh's life.

Posh was valuable to Caro in many ways. He was a frequently cited source, and he had entrée into Johnson circles that Caro rarely had. Caro interviewed Mrs. Johnson once, and only once, early in his research. Mrs. Johnson immediately sensed that Caro would do a hatchet job on LBJ and cut him off.

Thereafter George Christian and Jack Valenti, former White House staff and close associates of LBJ's, would not talk to Caro either. But Ed Clark did. Ed was a principal source for Caro's second volume, *Means of Ascent*. Caro told Posh, as he had told Ed, that he regretted that he had never been able to interview John Connally. Connally would never answer Caro's letters or calls. Ed replied that interviewing Connally was not important, that Connally had "just been LBJ's errand boy." Clark and Connally had never liked each other.

Posh relayed that remark to Connally, who then had Caro down to his Floresville ranch for a few days and answered his questions profusely. Connally said he wanted to be sure that LBJ's side and his own side of the story were told. Caro sent other messages to former LBJ staffers through Posh.

New York Sen. Pat Moynihan had worked for Robert Moses as a young man. Harry Middleton was a close LBJ associate and founding director of the LBJ Library. After Caro's first LBJ book came out, Moynihan told Harry that he wished Harry or Mrs. Johnson had told him that Caro was working on LBJ. "I would have told you Caro is a snake in the grass," said Moynihan.

Posh died in 2004.

Lady Bird Johnson

The Hobbys and the Johnsons have been friends for three generations now, bound together by broadcasting and government. Mrs. Johnson was the broadcaster in the family. Luci Baines Johnson grew up in both businesses, as did I.

Sam Ealy Johnson, President Johnson's father, and I. W. Culp, my grandfather, served together in the Texas House of Representatives.

Mrs. Johnson began her broadcasting career as the owner of a radio station in Austin and then bought a television station. Of course the call letters of both stations were KLBJ (the radio station remains KLBJ but the television station is now KTBC). Mrs. Johnson later bought stations in other Texas cities.

Lady Bird Johnson and Bill Hobby, 1989. *Courtesy of the Hobby family.*

Being married to a public official is no easy task for a woman. Mrs. Johnson was the only such wife and mother I ever knew who enjoyed it. Lynda Johnson Robb and Luci Baines Johnson reflect what a great job she did.

Wildflowers were, of course, Mrs. Johnson's passion. She started a program to beautify Texas highways by sponsoring a contest among Highway Department district engineers to see who could most beautify their highways. She later founded the Lady Bird Johnson Wildflower Center in Austin.

The Lady Bird Johnson Wildflower Center is working on several projects that use native plants to combat climate change. Global warming is caused by carbon dioxide. Plants inhale carbon dioxide and exhale oxygen. In urban areas, well-planned landscapes can not only pull CO_2 from the air, but store it in the soil for decades.

One Wildflower Center product, done in cooperation with the Seattle-based environmental company Mithun, is an open-user, web-based carbon calculator that can aid developers in calculating the total carbon footprint of their projects. This project goes hand-in-hand with the Wildflower Center's work to set standards for sustainable landscapes and on green roofs, which reduce energy demand in the buildings beneath them.

The center also preserves seeds of species of flowers that would otherwise become extinct. That environmental research will continue because, a year before Mrs. Johnson died, the center became a part of the College of Natural Sciences at the University of Texas at Austin.

President Johnson is memorialized by the Lyndon Baines Johnson Library and Museum and the LBJ School of Public Affairs in Austin, where I used to teach. I am honored to be a trustee of the Lyndon B. Johnson Foundation, which benefits the school and the library.

LBJ left his letters and tapes to the LBJ Library with a stipulation that they not be released until fifty years after his death, in 2023. Mrs. Johnson concurred with Harry Middleton's decision to start releasing the material as soon as possible. Harry didn't "break the seal" without Mrs. Johnson's approval, and the first tapes were released on November 20, 1993. That was a wise decision that has served LBJ's memory well.

The archiving process is long and tedious. Under federal law archivists must have security clearances. There is also concern about releasing information that may have been acquired by breaking the security codes used by other nations, thus compromising our country's ability to get certain kinds of intelligence. Perhaps 20 percent of the information has now been published electronically or in print, beginning with the material relating to the Kennedy assassination.

We are farther down that road than we would have been but for Mrs. Johnson's concern about the openness and availability of public documents, tapes, and videos. In contrast, former president George W. Bush loves secrecy and made information in more recent presidential libraries harder to get.

Mrs. Johnson finished the course and kept the faith. Well done, thou good and faithful servant. We shall not see her like again.

7

Newspaper Days

MY FATHER WAS A NEWSPAPERMAN. He started working as a clerk on the *Houston Post* before he finished high school. When he was drafted to run for lieutenant governor in 1914, he was editor and half-owner of the *Beaumont Enterprise*. He and his brother Edwin had also briefly owned the *Waco Morning News*, which they bought in 1913 and sold soon thereafter.

My father returned to Beaumont after he left office as governor, where he bought the *Beaumont Journal* and merged it with the *Enterprise*. By 1924, however, he had expanded his Beaumont interests about as far as he could, and he accepted Ross Sterling's offer to become general manager of the *Houston Post-Dispatch*, created by combining the *Post* and the *Dispatch*, Sterling's other daily, into one morning newspaper.

Sterling became governor of Texas in 1931, just as the Great Depression was deepening. He was in financial trouble and sold a major interest in the *Post-Dispatch* to J. E. Josey, a former citizen of Beaumont who very soon announced that Will Hobby would be president and publisher. In 1939, my father bought what was then named the *Houston Post*.

My parents borrowed the money to buy the newspaper from Jesse Jones, a Houston pioneer in lumber, real estate, and banking. My father had a warm, long-lasting friendship with Mr. Jones, probably starting at the time of the 1928 Democratic National Convention in Houston. Mr. Jones, the party's national finance chairman, had engineered the decision to make Houston the convention site, and my father, as publisher of one of Houston's two newspapers, became an enthusiastic ally.

Mr. Jones had acquired the *Houston Chronicle* in 1926. The afternoon paper was founded by *Houston Post* reporter Marcellus E. Foster in 1901. It grew to be the largest newspaper in Texas and a persistent and powerful competitor to the *Houston Post*. Even though Mr. Jones and my family were business competitors as long as they lived, they were friends and members of the "8F Crowd" of prominent Houstonians who met in Room 8F of the Lamar Hotel to work out city and state problems. That room was dubbed the "unofficial capital of Texas" because these power brokers decided the fate of politicians and programs alike.

Mr. Jones may have been willing to loan my father money to purchase the *Post* in 1939 because, at that time, he had interests in both papers. The *Post's* bank, owned by Ross Sterling, had failed, and Mr. Jones's bank, the National Bank of Commerce, paid the depositors and foreclosed on the *Houston Post*. Both papers owned radio stations, and the FCC then prohibited multiple ownership in a market.

The reason that Mr. Jones was able to be involved was that before he went to Washington in 1932 to serve on the Reconstruction Finance Corporation (RFC) board, he had saved Houston's banks. In effect he created a Houston Deposit Insurance Corporation before Congress created the federal version, the Federal Deposit Insurance Corporation (FDIC).

In the 1930s the nation was sinking into the Great Depression and Texas with it. Cotton prices plummeted, and millions were unemployed. By 1933, just as Franklin Delano Roosevelt was being sworn in, the U.S. banking system was in full collapse.

In 1931, the Public National Bank, owned by W. L. Moody of Galveston, and the Houston National Bank, owned by Governor Sterling, were in deep trouble. Public National was sure to close, to be followed by Houston National. Hundreds of smaller banks were also at risk.

According to Steven Fenberg, author of the oral history on Jesse Jones that led to a documentary titled *Brother, Can You Spare a Billion, the Story of Jesse H. Jones*, "Jones saved the banks not by passing a law but by calling together Houston's bankers to hammer out a bailout plan." They met in his office atop the Gulf Building on Sunday afternoon, October 25, 1931. The meeting was long and rancorous. At two a.m. Monday morning, Mr. Jones called another Houston icon, Capt. James A. Baker, for support. Captain Baker, vacationing in Massachusetts, helped persuade the holdouts. The group finally agreed to supply $1.25 million ($14 million in today's dollars) to guarantee the deposits in the troubled banks. I don't know if the banks stayed open, but the depositors were protected. The 1931 bailout money came from twelve local banks; the electric, gas, and telephone companies; and Anderson Clayton & Co. Captain Baker had earlier kept a murderer and a forger from stealing the money William Marsh Rice had left to found Rice Institute. He was the grandfather of James A. Baker III, President George H. W. Bush's secretary of state.

By Tuesday morning, Mr. Jones's National Bank of Commerce owned Public National Bank. Joseph Meyer owned Houston National. The pool formed by the local leaders was sufficient to pay depositors, to support the transition, and to guarantee Houston's banks.

A couple of days after the emergency meeting, Jones wrote Captain Baker, "My telephone talk with you the other night gave us real courage after several days and nights of a very harrowing experience. I felt that none of us had a right not to stop the tragedy that would have followed our failing to do that which we did."

According to Fenberg, Jones's actions helped save Houston's banks. "As a result of Jesse Jones's initiative, and because local leadership put community well-being first, Houston banks did not fail during the Great Depression," he said.

Other cities were not so fortunate in their leadership. Jones wrote a letter of thanks to one of the bailout opponents who came around at the last minute, "I believe that all we have done, are doing and must continue doing, is necessary for the general welfare. We cannot escape being our brother's keeper."

Fenberg said, "After Jones went to Washington as a board member of the RFC, he urged Henry Ford to form a pool to save Detroit's banks, similar to what had successfully been done before in Houston. Only this time, instead of only local and private action, the federal government, through the RFC, was a willing participant."

Jones agreed to lend $65 million ($833 million today) to the Union Guardian Trust Company if Ford agreed to contribute to the rescue fund and allow smaller depositors and investors to have first claim on the bank's resources before he collected his $20 million ($244 million today) in deposits. According to Jones, "Mr. Ford refused to put his chips into the kitty and said, 'Let the crash come. There isn't any reason why I, the largest individual taxpayer in the country, should bail the government out of its loans to banks.'"

The result was predictable. Jones recalled, "The closing of all banks in the motor capital was the principal prelude to the collapse, during the next three weeks, of the nation's entire financial system." Jones asked the J. P. Morgan Bank to form a pool to save the New York banks. Morgan refused, and the New York banks also failed. The Great Depression was on.

Another Houston banking story from that era also illustrates the value of putting community well-being before self-interest. Jake Friedman ran a gambling house called "Domain Privee" in a colonial mansion off South Main, and many prominent Houstonians were his clients. He did his banking at Judge Jim Elkins's City National Bank in Houston. There was a run on City National, and depositors were lined up around the block to take their money out. Friedman sat down at Judge Elkins's desk on the bank floor and asked the judge if he should take his money out.

Judge Elkins said, "Mr. Friedman, if you tell me now that you are withdrawing your money, I will lock the doors and close the bank. If you leave your money in, we may make it." Friedman left his money in, and the bank did not close. He never had any banking problems in Houston and eventually moved to Las Vegas and built The Sands in the early 1950s.

Judge Elkins and his friend William Ashton Vinson founded the law firm of Vinson & Elkins, which now has offices around the world and employs more than seven hundred attorneys. Elkins got his title serving as county judge in Huntsville before moving to Houston in 1917.

Jones knowingly explained to a colleague after finalizing Houston's 1931 bailout, "Other communities are having plenty of bank troubles, and all of them will pay dearly for not stopping the fire before it starts."

Back to 1939. My parents' loan agreement with Mr. Jones was onerous, preventing them from drawing a salary. They sought relief by trying to borrow the money from Fred Florence at the Republic National Bank in Dallas to pay off their loan from Mr. Jones.

"Will," said Mr. Florence, "you're publishing a newspaper in Houston. You ought to do your banking in Houston." "But if you have any problems with those country bankers down there, show them this." Mr. Florence then wrote the terms under which he would lend the money on his personal notepaper and signed it. On the strength of that note my parents borrowed the money from Judge Elkins's First City National Bank and paid off Mr. Jones.

I once told that story to Ted Strauss, brother of former ambassador and National Democratic Committee chairman Bob Strauss and husband of former Dallas mayor Annette Strauss. As a young man, Ted worked for Mr. Florence. Ted said that Mr. Florence frequently wrote such notes that you could "take to the bank" anywhere in Texas.

When my father went to work at the *Houston Post* (in the mailroom), it already had a reputation as a writer's newspaper. Rienzi Johnston, who had joined the Confederate army as a drummer boy and ended up as a lieutenant and was briefly a U.S. senator, was editor-in-chief. He was considered one of the South's leading editors. Marcellus E. Foster, who founded the *Houston Chronicle*, started on the *Houston Post* and covered the Spindletop oil boom for the *Post*. William Sydney Porter, described as a "columnist with a deft, original touch," was at the *Post*. My father was particularly attracted to Porter, who was, like him, a high school dropout. One day a man came into the *Post* business office looking for Sydney Porter. My father was happy to direct him to the right man. Unfortunately, the visitor had come with a summons charging Porter with embezzlement, something that had apparently occurred during his brief career as a bank teller. As my father told it, Porter told people he was leaving for Austin,

Hobby in the pressroom at the *Houston Post*, c. 1972. *Courtesy of the Hobby family.*

but he actually ended up on a banana boat headed for Honduras. It was only when his wife became ill that he returned to Austin, was arrested, and served a term in the federal penitentiary. William Sydney Porter, of course, was the famous writer O. Henry.

My father became chairman of the *Houston Post* board in 1955, and my mother became president and editor. He died in 1964. I started working at the *Houston Post* during the summer while I was in high school, throwing a paper route. My first editorial job was doing obits—it's a good first job because you have to get it right. If you don't, people tend to complain.

At Rice University, I was editor of the student newspaper, the *Thresher*. I was officially editor of the *Thresher* my junior year, but basically I had put the paper out ever since I was a freshman. The previous two editors recognized the talents of a kid who could write the heads and make up the paper so they didn't have to.

I was the police reporter on the *Houston Post* during my senior year at Rice. In those days the dean of police reporters was Jack Weeks of the *Houston Chronicle*. One of the other reporters, a guy who worked for a radio station, was the butt of all jokes. One day, Weeks came into the police station pressroom and said, "Did you hear what just happened? The police chief just went over to the courthouse and shot the county judge." The radio guys had microphones on their desks so they could broadcast directly from the police station, so this poor fellow goes running for his microphone to broadcast the big news, but he couldn't find it. The other reporters had taped his microphone to the ceiling.

The guy's name was Marvin Zindler. Later on he would become a reporter for KTRK-TV in Houston and gain some degree of notoriety for "exposing" the Chicken Ranch, a LaGrange establishment that became famous in Larry King's play *The Best Little Whorehouse in Texas*.

Sheriff Jim Flournoy of Fayette County was big buddies with the Chicken Ranch madam, which you know if you saw the play or movie. One time after his stellar work of investigative reporting, Zindler went to LaGrange to ride in a parade. Flournoy beat the hell out of him, and no one lifted a finger to help Zindler. I think Zindler filed charges, but they never came to trial.

The Day before Kennedy Died

NOVEMBER 21, THURSDAY, 1963—HOUSTON—The Kennedys and Johnsons came to Houston for a dinner for Congressman Albert Thomas at the dedication of the Albert Thomas Convention Hall. My secretary Logan Adams and I went to what is now Hobby Airport to greet Vice President Johnson. Logan was not interested in Kennedy or Johnson. She just wanted to see Jackie Kennedy.

On the way to the airport, Logan noticed a big sign advertising the Carousel Motel. Logan said there was a new nightclub by that name in Dallas that was popular with the college students. The nightclub was mysterious and romantic because it was run by a gangster! Three days later the Carousel nightclub would become famous because the gangster was Jack Ruby, who murdered Lee Harvey Oswald in the Dallas police station on Sunday morning, November 24, 1963.

Jack Valenti and I met at the airport. Jack was then a *Houston Post* columnist and owner of the Weekley and Valenti advertising agency. As the *New York Times* noted, it was in his *Houston Post* column in 1956 that Valenti lionized Lyndon Johnson as "unbending as a mountain crag, tough as a jungle fighter." Maybe because of that, Jack had become an advisor to LBJ. After the Houston dinner Jack went on to Fort Worth with Vice President Johnson and rode in the Dallas motorcade. Kennedy and Johnson went on to the dinner. I went back to the office.

The Day Kennedy Died

"BUREAUS DOWNHOLD. DALLAS ITS YOURS"

NOVEMBER 22, 1963—HOUSTON—I was managing editor of the *Houston Post*. At about 12:45 p.m. I was handed this Associated Press wire copy:

A206'DN

BULLETIN

DALLAS, NOV.22 (AP)-PRESIDENT KENNEDY WAS SHOT TODAY JUST AS HIS MOTORCADE LEFT DOWNTOWN DALLAS. MRS. KENNEDY JUMPED UP

AND GRABBED MR. KENNEDY. SHE CRIED, OH., NO!" THE MOTORCADE SPED ON.

MM1239PCS A NM

A07'DN

K

BULLETIN MATTER

DALLAS-FIRST ADD KENNEDY SHOT X X X SPED ON.

AP PHOTOGRAPHER JAMES W. ALTGENS SAID HE SAW BLOOD ON THE PRESIDENT'S HEAD.

ALTGENS SAID HE HEARD TWO SHOTS BUT THOUGHT SOMEONE WAS SHOOTING FIREWORKS UNTIL HE SAW THE BLOOD ON THE PRESIDENT.

ALTGENS SAID HE SAW NO ONE WITH A GUN.

MM1241PCS

208DN'

BULLETIN MATTER

DALLAS-SECOND ADD PRESIDENT SHOT X X X

APEREPORTER JACK BELL ASKED KENNETH O';$9,,3)), PRESIDENTIAL 7$ 8! (9

DALLAS-SECOND ADD PRESIDENT SHOT X X X

AP REPORTER JACK BELL ASKED KENNETH O'DONNELL, PRESIDENTIAL ASSISTANT, IF KENNEDY WAS DEAD. O'DONNELL GAVE NO ANSWER.

KENNEDY WAS REPORTED TAKEN TO PARKLAND HOSPITAL, NEAR THE DALLAS TRADE MART, WHERE HE WAS TO HAVE MADE A SPEECH.

BELL SAID KENNEDY WAS TRANSFERRED TO AN AMBULANCE. HE LAAAAAAAAAAA

I went to the "wire room" to read the news service printers. The room was already beginning to fill up as the word spread around the building. The AP Atlanta Bureau had been filing a story when Dallas broke in:

BULLETIN

DALLAS—PRESIDENT SHOT

The wire was silent for a minute or so. Atlanta started babbling again.

New York broke in:

BUREAUS DOWNHOLD. DALLAS ITS YOURS.

The story began to unfold. Gov. John Connally was severely wounded. (When Connally died in 1993, doctors attributed his death in part to that wound.) Priests were called to Parkland Hospital. Last rites were administered. Kennedy died.

Vice President Johnson was already aboard Air Force One at Love Field, where the Secret Service had taken him for security. He sent for Judge Sarah T. Hughes to administer the oath. Mrs. Kennedy, in her blood-spattered dress, boarded the plane with President Kennedy's coffin. Johnson took the oath, flanked by Mrs. Johnson and Mrs. Kennedy.

Here I was, hanging over the printer, aware that this was the biggest story I would ever handle, aware that my reputation as a newspaperman would depend on what I did in the next few minutes. But I didn't know what to do. Managing editors are supposed to know what to do.

J. D. Hancock, the city circulation manager, was standing beside me at the printer. I had known J. D. most of my life. He had been selling the *Houston Post* for fifty years. "Bill, you're going extra, aren't you?" said J. D. Suddenly I knew what to do—put out an extra edition.

But how?

Television news had pretty well killed off extra editions. The last extra

✝✝ EXTRA ✝✝

Written and Edited
To Merit Your Confidence

THE HOUSTON POST 10¢

HOUSTON 1, TEXAS, FRIDAY, NOVEMBER 22, 1963

TELEPHONE PA 3-5321, WANT ADS CA 3-1342

JFK Assassinated in Dallas;
Gov Connally Is Wounded

Suspect, 24, Is Held in Death

By FELTON WEST, Post Staff Correspondent

DALLAS — President John F. Kennedy was shot fatally about 12:30 PM Friday while riding in a motorcade here. An assassin's bullet hit him in the right temple.

The President died about 1 PM in Parkland Hospital in Dallas, where his Secret Service driver rushed him without stopping after the shooting.

Slightly more than two hours later, Lyndon B. Johnson took the oath of office as President of the United States.

TEXAS GOV John B. Connally, who was riding in the President's car at the head of the motorcade, also was shot and seriously wounded. He also was taken to Parkland Hospital and operated on for a chest wound.

A shot evidently went through his body, either entering or coming out the right chest. He also suffered other wounds.

The Dallas Police Department later arrested a 24-year-old man, identified as Lee H. Oswald, in connection with the slaying of a Dallas policeman shortly after President Kennedy was assassinated.

Oswald was pulled screaming and yelling from the Texas Theatre in the Oak Cliff section of Dallas. A policeman, M. N. McDonald, cut across the face in a scuffle with Oswald, who brandished a pistol, quoted Oswald as saying after he was subdued:

"Well, it's all over now."

A LARGE CROWD had gathered to see the arrest. Police held the crowd back, because some persons apparently thought the arrested man was involved in the murder of Mr. Kennedy.

The officers who was shot, J. D. Tippet, had been killed by a man answering Oswald's description to the neighborhood. Oswald was described as about 5 feet 6, weighing approximately 150 pounds, with skimpy blond hair and dressed in ragged trousers and a sports shirt.

The President's death was confirmed to a reporter about 1:36 PM by a Catholic priest who said he had given the President the last rites of the Catholic church.

The priest refused to identify himself but he was believed to be Father Oscar Huber, pastor of the Holy Trinity Parish in Dallas, a Vincentian father who was taken to the hospital earlier by police.

OFFICIAL ANNOUNCEMENT of the President's death was not made until 1:33 PM.

At that time Malcolm Kilduff, an assistant White House press secretary, who was in charge of press arrangements for the two-day trip to Texas, announced with tears streaming down his face that the President had died at 1 PM of a gunshot wound in the brain.

"I have no details regarding the assassination," Kilduff said. He said Mrs. Kennedy was not hurt but declined to discuss her condition.

Vice President and Mrs. Lyndon B. Johnson, whose car had been following the President's car in the motorcade with only a carload of Secret Service agents between them, raced along behind the President's car to the Parkland Hospital.

THERE, SECRET Service agents, perhaps as many as half a dozen, quickly surrounded them and took them somewhere inside the hospital. Their whereabouts could not be determined at the time of the announcement of the President's death.

Kilduff said that the vice president left the hospital about 30 minutes after President Kennedy died. He said that Mrs. Kennedy would return to Washington immediately.

He said the President never regained consciousness after he was shot.

It was not learned immediately where Mrs. Kennedy was in the hospital when her husband died. Kilduff said only doctors were with Mr. Kennedy at the end. He died in an emergency admittance room on the first floor of the hospital.

THE ASSASSINATION occurred near the intersection of Commerce, Main and Elm Streets, near downtown Dallas, as the President's open-topped car was near a railroad underpass.

Mr. Kennedy was riding in the right rear seat of the car with Mrs. Kennedy beside him at the left. Gov Connally was in a seat just in front of the President, with Mrs. Connally beside him on the left. In the front seat was a driver, with a secret service agent.

It could not be learned immediately what happened but apparently one or more persons with one or more rifles opened fire.

Sen Ralph W. Yarborough, Texas Democrat, was riding with Mr and Mrs Johnson in the third car in the procession, with only a carload of Secret Service agents in an open car between the President's car and the vice president's.

Afterward, at Parkland Hospital, Sen Yarborough, trembling, described as best he could what happened. He said he heard two shots either close together and then another. It did not sound like firecrackers or pistol shots but rather like shots from a deer rifle.

YARBOROUGH THOUGHT the President's car was moving about 25 miles an hour at the time.

A few instants after the shots, Yarborough said, the

See JFK on Page 3

PRESIDENT JOHN F. KENNEDY, 36TH EXECUTIVE OF THE UNITED STATES
As He Paid Tribute to Congressman Albert Thomas in Houston Thursday Night

Pictures of President Kennedy and Vice President Johnson in Texas before . . . and moments after the shooting are on Pages 4 and 5 of this section.

Connally Operated On; Pulse 'Good'

By NEIL ADDINGTON
Post Austin Bureau

AUSTIN—Gov John Connally's condition, as reported by his doctors at 2:40 PM, was:

"He is in the operating room, will be more probably two more hours; condition indeterminable surgery."

Charles Tarr opened his chest. Probably four bullets entered through the lung; the bullet did not hit any heart; he was severely injured. Long was still full. His heart intensified to assure artery through the wound.

He pulse, blood pressure and other vital signs were good and his color normal.

ADMINISTRATIVE at the Capitol said that the governor was the thick of a finest, Dr. N. A. Yearwood of the Department. Dr. A. Public Safety's emergency wound what the governor's belief passed the governor's belief and apparently went all the way through the governor.

The nurse suffered a Yarborough said the governor's aides told Texas State officials told, Connally tried to speak...

See CONNALLY on Page 3

Rocking Chair JFK Trademark

The old-fashioned rocking chair came into its own today when President Kennedy installed one in his office at front of the fireplace. It had been used by the President then an emotionally gesture said to do much.

In James Trump he gave speak when President Kennedy finally installed one in his office, at the request of his physician, believing that cause of a good light-backed chair was a fine way to relax, and soon became that the President liked on so much.

He said she had not permitted the rocker, however, in his New York office when he first came to use it to the New York area to become the vice president of a back injury in 1961. He found it exceedingly comfortable and at his request carried one into the White House.

Nation Is Shocked At News

FROM POST NEWS SERVICES

The nation reeled in shocked disbelief Friday at the news of President Kennedy had been shot and killed by an assassin. Business came to a near standstill and front court is dead.

"Is it true?" a New York said.

"How did it happen?" said another person.

But the big question in cities across the nation was who would want to commit murder for the President.

In downtown Manhattan's garment district a newspaper headline extra sold out in from a crowd near business.

The short shaken crowd was silent. This question, unceasing silence was asked in the Bowery, among skid row derelicts and among the elected officials.

See NATION on Page 3

See JFK on Page 3 *See CONNALLY on Page 3* *See NATION on Page 3* *See JOHNSON on Page 3*

LYNDON B. JOHNSON NOW PRESIDENT
Vice President Was in Motorcade

LBJ Sworn In As President

DALLAS—(P)—Lyndon B. Johnson was sworn in as President of the United States at about 2:39 PM CST Friday.

The oath was administered by U. S. District Judge Sarah T. Hughes.

Johnson took the oath aboard the presidential plane at Dallas' Love Field. In one propeller-driven aircraft Air Force One took off immediately to fly to Washington with the new President.

PRESENT AT the swearing-in in the Democratic Party plane were Mrs Kennedy and Mrs Johnson; several congressmen and several congressmen.

Johnson acted as many of the White Mr Kennedy staff, wept. House troops in guards and several people sat to arrive near the crowded scene took the formula into the Love Field as the plane to relieve the situation.

Justice Hughes, who administered the presidential Kennedy's policies. His swore took to Johnson.

Immediately to Washington with Johnson, Mrs Johnson and was a personality in the crowd near Mr Kennedy and poor Mr. When and Mrs Kennedy was changed from one label press release stayed.

THE PLANE carried the new President to Washington was the flew the seat carried a body of President Kennedy's body could not only sweat, whether it to the arrival at the White House.

U. S. Secret Service took President Kennedy's body, the would again when his arrival at the time.

E. S. Hayes Sandler said Post.

First Kennedy's calm with the street mark to arrive at the White House and he climbs the body back.

"We, all kinds of New up proper the bureau of the crusade these until metrow finder...

ALTHOUGH IT was police and funeral policies stayed the lock in Boston, united to the

See JOHNSON on Page 3

Houston Post extra edition from the day JFK died. *Courtesy of the Hobby family.*

the *Houston Post* had published was in 1947 when the French freighter *Grandcamp* blew up Texas City, killing hundreds of people. There aren't many folks in the newsroom of a morning paper at one p.m. Production people—printers, engravers, stereotypers, pressmen, and mailers—are also pretty scarce at that time of day. But under the superb direction of News Editor Ted Welty, the extra started to come together. I put a black reverse bar with four crosses on it across the top.

Printers and pressmen are real newspaper folks. They came in spontaneously so that we were on the street about three hours after the decision to go extra. As far as I know we were on the street before any other central time zone morning paper. I chartered a plane and sent four reporters and photographers to Dallas. I also passed a law that whenever the president was in Houston an assistant managing editor had to be on duty.

Notes on the Wire Copy:

"A206'DN" means this was the 206th story to move on the "A" or main AP, wire that day. The story was filed by the Associated Press Dallas Bureau (DN). Bob Johnson, the bureau chief, was the lead newsman on the story. He wrote an excellent account of the day in *AP World* in 1972. The lead (or "first take") was filed at 12:36 p.m., Central Standard Time. A framed copy has hung in my office ever since.

Justice in the Composing Room

Freddy Young, the composing room foreman at the *Houston Post*, was a gentle giant. One night a printer came to work drunk and pulled a knife on Freddy. Bad career move. Freddy picked him up by his belt and collar and dropped him down a three-story stairwell to the concrete floor below. Ruined his whole day.

The printer filed a grievance under union rules. At the hearing the printer's attorney asked Freddy, "Brother Young, why did you bar Brother Smith from your shop for life without following union rules?"

"I haven't barred Brother Smith for life or for a day," said Freddy. "Brother Smith can come back into my shop any time he wants, and the same thing will happen." End of hearing.

Plaintiffs, Beware the Magic Wand!

In 1965, when I was managing editor of the *Houston Post*, reporter Gene Goltz wrote a Pulitzer Prize-winning series about municipal corruption involving the mayor of Pasadena, a Houston suburb. Because the series had enormous potential for libel, Jack Binion, the *Post*'s lawyer and my godfather and mentor, had read and approved each story.

The mayor's lawyer called me. He and his client wanted to see me that afternoon. I, of course, desperately wanted Jack to be at that meeting, but he was unavailable for several days. Jack, of course, had also expected the call. He assured me that there was nothing to worry about and gave me a magic wand to wave if the meeting got unpleasant.

So Gene and I met with the lawyer and the mayor. The meeting did indeed get unpleasant. Gene, who lived in Pasadena, had stopped by a bar while the series was running and had a few drinks on the way home one night. The bartender, a friend of the mayor, had asked Gene what his problem was with the mayor.

When Gene started to tell him, the bartender pulled out a tape recorder and asked Gene to speak into it. The bartender said he would play the tape for the mayor. Gene, who displayed better judgment at the typewriter than he did in the bar and who was a little the worse for wear, spoke into the recorder.

The tape scared this managing editor mightily, so I waved the magic wand. I said to the lawyer "If your client thinks he has been libeled, you know where the courthouse is. Jack Binion will begin discovery Monday morning."

I never heard from them again. The last thing a crooked public official wants is to give subpoena power to a newspaper. Potential libel plaintiffs, beware the magic wand!

Marlene Johnson

As a newspaperman I have always been very concerned about lawsuits against newspapers. Because what they print is out there for hundreds of thousands of people to see, newspapers have always been very vulnerable to libel suits. But sometimes newspapers get what they deserve.

One case involved my friend Marlene Johnson when she was running for lieutenant governor of Minnesota in 1982. Dan Cohen, who was working for the Republican candidate for governor, tried some pretty sleazy campaign tactics against her. The case is a sordid one that reflects no credit on anybody involved. There are no heroes in this story.

Cohen worked for an advertising agency representing the Republican candidate for governor. He told four reporters covering the campaign that, some years before, Johnson had been convicted for shoplifting. Cohen asked the reporters not to identify him as the source of the information, and they foolishly agreed. Two of the reporters ignored the story. The other two, without checking the public records where the arrest was duly recorded, reported the matter to their editors.

The editors of the two papers—the *Minneapolis Star Tribune* and the *St. Paul Pioneer Post-Dispatch*—then made a decision even more irresponsible than the one made by their reporters. They decided to use the story without checking the facts and to identify Cohen as the source. As it turned out the story was correct, though incomplete. Had it not been correct, they would have exposed their papers to a libel suit from Johnson.

After the stories ran, Cohen was fired. He sued the papers for damages, saying that the papers had violated a contract with him not to reveal that he was the source.

Cohen won a $700,000 judgment in the trial court. The jury had decided that Cohen had suffered $200,000 in actual damages, and then went on to order each newspaper to pay him $250,000 in punitive damages. In other words, the jury was saying that not only was Cohen somehow damaged to the tune of $200,000, but that the papers had committed a crime sufficiently evil that they deserved to be fined a quarter of a million dollars each.

If Cohen's employer wanted to use a teenage conviction for shoplifting $6 worth of sewing materials against Johnson, that was, of course, his privilege. Such tactics are tasteless and demeaning to those who use them, but they are permissible. We Texans have certainly seen much sorrier tactics used by Jim Mattox and Clayton Williams in the 1990 race for governor, not to mention the swift boat campaign against John Kerry in the 2004 presidential election.

But there is a right way and a wrong way for candidates to make fools of themselves if they want to. The right way is to produce the arrest record in public and take full responsibility for doing so. That way the voters can make their judgments both about the candidate who made the information public and the candidate who was arrested for a teenage indiscretion.

There is a right way and a wrong way for news media to handle such a story. The wrong way is to promise confidentiality to someone who is passing out information that is a matter of public record. The right way is to check the record itself and report what the record says.

What was the result of these tactics in Minnesota? The same as in Texas—the voters elected Marlene Johnson. Cohen's candidate, Wheelock Whitney, was buried in a landslide of votes.

In fact, the whole episode turned out to be a blessing in disguise for Johnson. She had anticipated that the conviction would come up in the campaign but had not yet decided how to deal with it. Cohen, of course, had not bothered to mention, even anonymously, that the conviction was later vacated.

In fact the incident generated sympathy for Johnson that was an asset in her campaign. She became a fine public servant of the people of Minnesota, who used the judgment that their journalists lacked. She was lieuten-

Hobby in front of the Houston Post building in 1972. *Courtesy of the Hobby family.*

ant governor from 1983 to 1991, then served in the General Services Office under President Clinton and as executive director of NAFSA: Association of International Educators.

The newspapers appealed. The Minnesota Supreme Court upheld the reasoning in the case—Minnesota law requires that those making promises keep them—but denied any monetary relief, saying it would infringe on the newspapers' First Amendment rights to publish accurate information of public concern. But the U.S. Supreme Court reversed that decision, finding no offense against the First Amendment, so Cohen was entitled to the money.

Bad judgment can be expensive.

A Requiem for the Houston Post

The *Houston Post* died in 1995, which caused me to grieve. Newspapers are special institutions. The death of a newspaper is not like the death of a grocery store or a bank or a movie theater. However noble grocery stores are, they do not entertain, enrage, or challenge people the way newspapers do. They do not have the personality that newspapers do. Grocery stores are not usually staffed with characters as colorful as those who populate newsrooms. But newspapers can fail just like grocery stores. When people don't shop at the grocery store, the store dies.

Newspapers are outrageously expensive to produce. The business is labor intensive. It takes a lot of people to cover the news, to sell the advertising, and to print and distribute the paper. The presses on which the paper is printed cost scores of millions of dollars and can be used only a few hours a day. The raw material (newsprint) is a commodity just like pork bellies. At the same time, newspapers are virtually free to their readers. The subscription and single-copy prices bear little relation to the cost of putting the paper on subscribers' doorsteps.

Ironically, the *Post* was the victim—not the beneficiary—of a booming economy. When the economy in Houston (and the nation) was depressed, merchants didn't buy much advertising, and consequently newspapers didn't buy much newsprint. So newsprint prices were stable. When the economy began to recover, retailers bought more advertising, newspapers bought more newsprint, and the newsprint producers began to raise prices.

Newsprint prices went up about 40 percent in the year before the *Post* died. For a newspaper the size of the *Post*, newsprint is about 40 percent of all expenses. (The more circulation a newspaper has the larger the newsprint factor.) And 40 percent of 40 percent is 16 percent. In other words, the *Post*'s operating costs went up by one-sixth.

The *Post* was the "second paper" in town. Its circulation was substantially smaller than that of the *Chronicle*. Therefore, its advertising rates had to be higher than those of the *Chronicle* on a per reader basis. The *Post* was already a less efficient "buy" for an advertiser and so was in no position to raise its rates to cover costs.

If a business is only marginally in the black even on a cash-flow basis and its costs go up by one-sixth and its revenues don't, it goes broke. The *Houston Chronicle* was the only possible purchaser. So much for the grim arithmetic of prosperity.

When all the numbers were added up, the *Post* was dead. Not just a business, but a voice, a personality that was a vital part of Houston for more than a century was gone. My family and I were involved with the *Post* for most of that century. My father went to work there on March 2, 1895, shortly before his eighteenth birthday. Our association ended in 1983 when we sold the *Post* to the *Toronto Sun*.

Please forgive the lump in my throat.

8

RUNNING FOR LIEUTENANT GOVERNOR AND OTHER POLITICAL STORIES

I ALWAYS WANTED TO RUN FOR OFFICE. From the time I was parliamentarian for Lt. Gov. Ben Ramsey in 1959 I knew that lieutenant governor was the office to which I was best suited.

Though I had not held office I knew something of the workings of state government. I had been a University of Houston Regent (1965-1969), appointed by Gov. John Connally, and a member of the Texas Air Control Board (1969–1971) appointed by Gov. Preston Smith. I had covered the legislature as a reporter for the *Houston Post* and supervised coverage as editor. Also, I knew a good deal about Texas's welfare system because Lt. Gov. Ben Barnes named me chairman of the Senate Interim Committee on Welfare Reform, which studied the system for two years and recommended changes. And I grew up in a family that had been part of state government for a couple of generations.

Several factors made 1972 look like the year to run:

1. The job was open because the incumbent was not running. My friend Ben Barnes was running for governor.
2. The Sharpstown scandal had tarnished incumbents (rightly or not) and made it a good year for new faces.
3. In years ending in "2" all (not half) the Texas Senate seats are up for election. I hoped, wrongly, that the absence of mid-term "free rides" would reduce the number of senators running for lieutenant governor.

Steve Oaks was my campaign manager. Steve was a lawyer at Butler, Binion, Rice, and Cook in Houston. He recruited coordinators across Texas, mainly from his law school buddies. Among them were Kent Hance, the West Texas coordinator who later became a state senator (1973-1978) by beating an incumbent who had supported my opponent Wayne Connally. Kent was then elected to Congress (1979-1985) by defeating a Republican named George W. Bush. Kent was a railroad commissioner from 1987 to 1990. At this writing he is chancellor of Texas Tech University.

Another coordinator was Helen Farabee, wife of Ray Farabee. Ray was later elected to the Texas Senate, from which he retired to become general counsel of the University of Texas System. Helen became my key advisor on health and human services and later chaired a very important commission on welfare reform. Helen died in 1988.

Other key supporters and field lieutenants were David Chappell, Ron Kessler, Lee Godfrey, and Don Rives, who ran my campaign in Tarrant, Dallas, Travis, and Harrison counties, respectively. All were successful and influential attorneys. With their help I carried every major metropolitan area. Don Rives succeeded Steve Oaks as my chief of staff.

Sharpstown was by far the biggest factor in Texas politics that year. In 1971, the legislature passed two bills that led to a U.S. Securities and Exchange Commission (SEC) lawsuit and what became known as the Sharpstown scandal. The SEC accused several Texas lawmakers of taking bribes to get the bills passed. The alleged bribes were loans from the Sharpstown State Bank of Houston, which the lawmakers used to buy stock in the National Bankers Life Insurance Company and then quickly sold for large profits. The bank and the insurance company were owned by Frank W. Sharp of Houston. The SEC filed a civil suit, not a criminal one, that named Gov. Preston Smith, House Speaker Gus Mutscher, state Democratic chairman and state banking board member Elmer Baum, Rep. Tommy Shannon of Fort Worth, and Mutscher's aide Rush Mc-Ginty. Mutscher, Shannon, and McGinty were indicted for conspiracy to accept a bribe and found guilty in early 1972. Governor Smith was named an unindicted co-conspirator.

In the Democratic race for governor, the "old faces," Smith and Barnes, ran third and fourth. The "new faces," Dolph Briscoe, a Uvalde rancher, and Frances "Sissy" Farenthold, a Houston state representative, ran first and second.

In the Democratic race for lieutenant governor, the "old faces," Senators Wayne Connally, Ralph Hall, and Joe Christie, ran second, third, and fourth. A "new face"—mine—ran first.

Half those elected to the legislature that year were "new faces." As Ben Barnes put it in his book *Barn Burning, Barn Building*, "Even Texans who didn't have the stomach for reading long articles about stock tips, loans, and banking legislation could understand headlines that screamed 'fraud' and 'Democrats.'"

Ben was a fine lieutenant governor—the third best we ever had (the first two were named Hobby). Ben was not involved in Sharpstown, but he was in the wrong place at the wrong time.

Hobby with Ben Barnes and Preston Smith, c. 1987. *Courtesy of the Hobby family.*

Voters were angry with just about everyone in office that year. My "new face" slogan was "Bill Hobby will make a good Lieutenant Governor. Honestly."

My runoff opponent was Sen. Wayne Connally, brother of former Texas governor John Connally, who served from 1963 to 1969. In 1972, John Connally was secretary of the treasury, appointed by President Richard Nixon. The treasury secretary is, of course, the boss of the Internal Revenue Service. That relationship didn't hurt Wayne Connally's fundraising at all. And, somehow, the Internal Revenue Service started auditing me.

The campaign was long and nasty. The first clue that I would win came the week before the election. I made a campaign trip to Amarillo, an area I had expected Wayne to carry. When Sen. Max Sherman met me at the airport and introduced me at the event—the first senator to do so in the campaign—I knew that was a good sign. Max became one of my closest friends.

Bill and Diana Hobby at inauguration, 1987. *Courtesy of the Hobby family.*

Early in the afternoon of election day I had another good sign. My campaign manager in a large county that I thought was also Connally country called to tell me I would carry that county by a few votes.

"That's wonderful!" I said. "But how do you know? The polls won't close for hours yet."

"Bill," said my friend, "Marilyn is the county clerk here. I got her divorce for her years ago, and we have maintained a close personal relationship." I carried the county by a few votes.

That campaign was part of a learning process for me. I ran again in 1974, 1978, 1982 and 1986 (in 1974 the legislature changed the terms of most statewide offices from two years to four). One of the campaign truths was that, at that time, there were about twenty counties in Texas that were "one-stop shops," meaning that politics in the county was pretty much up to "the man." If "the man" was for you, you would get about 75 percent of the vote. If he was against you, you would get about 25 percent of the vote. In Fayette County, the man was Sheriff Jim Flournoy of *Best Little Whorehouse in Texas* fame. Jim liked me, so I was golden in Fayette County. He had the ladies of the Chicken Ranch address postcards endorsing me, and I got about 100 percent of the vote every time.

Debating George Strake

I had no Republican opponent when I first ran in 1972. I didn't waste any time announcing for re-election—I did it in August 1973. My opponent in the 1974 Democratic primary was Gaylord Marshall, a commodities futures broker from University Park. He called me a liberal—pretty much the standard charge from my opponents. He raised $8,000. I won with 70.9 percent of the vote.

I was re-elected in 1978 without significant opposition from either party. But in 1982 the Republicans decided my free ride was over. My opponent was George Strake, a Houston oilman who had been appointed secretary of state by Gov. Bill Clements.

This was not to be a walk in the park. Strake had some name identification from his work for Clements, and he was well-known in Houston. His campaign was well-financed and professionally run.

Strake came after me with the usual Republican stuff—I spent too much state money, and I was soft on illegal aliens. Worse than that, the state budget had grown! It certainly had, but not by enough. Texas, then as now, was one of the fastest growing states and trailed the nation in public education and public services. Strake didn't want undocumented workers to go to public schools. I guess he wanted them to go on welfare or to prison.

In the fall of 1982, I had a fifteen-minute debate with Strake on KERA, the public television station in Dallas. George Christian, Sen. Don Adams, and my campaign staff had prepared a briefing book with answers to every conceivable question and accusation. I left the briefing book on the plane.

During the debate, Strake went first. What a shame, he said, that we have only fifteen minutes to this debate. It would be impossible to fully air all the great issues of state in that brief time! He offered to pay for a longer debate.

"George, keep your money. Fifteen minutes is more than enough time for you to tell us all you know about state government," I responded. "I will use my time to ask for support for the constitutional amendment to raise the ceiling on welfare expenditures, which is also on the ballot this year."

Afterward, people compared the non-debate to a scene from the movie *Raiders of the Lost Ark* when Indiana Jones is confronted by a Turkish bad guy wielding a scimitar. The bad guy whirls and twirls and tosses his scimitar around for the crowd, and, while he is showing off, Indiana Jones shoots him.

Strake is a wealthy Roman Catholic. He made a television spot emphasizing his ties to the pope. The spot was intended to run in South Texas. His campaign probably wasn't helped when it somehow ran in East Texas.

The 1982 election turned out to be a good day for Democrats. Mark White was elected governor. I was re-elected lieutenant governor, and Democrats got elected to every statewide office. U.S. Sen. Lloyd Bentsen and I got credit for creating a unified and well-funded Democratic effort run by Bentsen's savvy political strategist Jack Martin. I provided about half the funding, and the combined effort pulled some of the weaker candidates across the line.

When I was running for re-election in 1986, Strake was chair of the Texas Republican Party. He said that I would not be a target for the Republican Party. "We will focus our resources on other races," he said.

Term Limits—Bad Idea

I served eighteen years as lieutenant governor—five terms. When I left office, I was a far better public servant than when I was first elected in 1973. Governing is a complicated business, and on-the-job training is all most of us get. Therefore, I have never been much of a fan of term limits on state and federal legislators. The idea was in vogue in the 1990s when Republicans had trouble electing legislators. When that changed, their interest in term limits declined.

In the 1930s and 1940s, when the GOP could not elect a president, but could occasionally muster a majority in one house or the other of Congress, Republicans supported and enacted our two-term limit on presidential terms. The idea of legislative term limitation is cynical because it assumes voters are not smart enough to know who is good for them, their state, and the nation.

Term limitation also has an effect that its advocates presumably do not like. People who like to call themselves "conservatives" (however radical they are in fact) generally seem to dislike and distrust what they call "the bureaucracy" even more than they do the elected officials they are trying to get rid of. But constant turnover among elected officials means more reliance on staff members (the bureaucrats).

The fact is that public officials, like intelligent people in responsible positions in any walk of life, learn from experience. That's why legislatures work on the basis of seniority. Seniority has good points and bad ones. One of the good points is that committee chairs and others in policy-making positions tend to have the judgment that is at least partly conferred by experience. There's an old saying that sums it up pretty well:

"Good judgment is the result of experience. Experience is the result of bad judgment."

Occasionally people get elected to office who want to save the world. Seniority at least attempts to ensure that such folks can't do any real damage until they have had time to observe that the world has stubbornly resisted saving for several thousand years.

That is not to say that every longtime legislator is an effective, contributing member of the body in which he or she serves. In any case, that's up to the voters to decide, and they decide by re-electing many legislators, stubbornly ignoring the best efforts of elitists to tell them what is best for them.

This country would doubtless not have had the services of Sam Rayburn as Speaker under a term-limitation scheme, and thank goodness that Lyndon Johnson was not term-limited in Congress.

Surprisingly, the first President Bush, a veteran of twenty-four years of federal service, endorsed term limitation. Where did he think we should get our future presidents? Well, now we know. Not from a group of men and women seasoned, like himself, by years of public service.

Waiting for Dukakis

There weren't that many more good days for Democrats in Texas. In 1988, the Democratic and Republican national presidential tickets re-matched Houstonians. The Democratic ticket consisted of Gov. Michael Dukakis of Massachusetts for president and Sen. Lloyd Bentsen of Houston for vice president. The Republican ticket consisted of George H. W. Bush of Houston and Sen. Dan Quayle of Indiana. Houston businessman Bentsen had defeated Houston congressman Bush for the U.S. Senate in 1970.

The day after the Democratic convention in Atlanta, Dukakis and Bentsen began their campaign in Texas. They spent the morning in Bentsen country—South Texas. Lloyd had been elected Hidalgo County judge in 1946 when he was twenty-five years old and to Congress (where he served six years) two years later.

Lloyd had just been re-nominated for a fourth term in the U.S. Senate and so was running for re-election to the Senate as well as for vice president. Lloyd served in the Senate until he resigned in 1993 to become President Clinton's treasury secretary.

The candidates ended the day at a rally in front of Houston City Hall, where I introduced them. The rally was televised so timing was crucial. As the motorcade neared I began my spiel. When my friend and campaign manager Barbara Stanley signaled that Dukakis and Bentsen had actually arrived on the stage, I concluded: "So now please welcome the

Hobby with Lloyd Bentsen during Hobby's first campaign for lieutenant governor, 1972. *William P. Hobby Sr. Family Papers, Dolph Briscoe Center for American History, di_05749.*

next president of the United States, Michael Dukakis," as he came to the microphone.

It was a hot day, so most of the men on the platform had taken off their coats. Governor Dukakis took off his and handed it to me. That was the first of several occasions when I played my true role in the campaign: holding Dukakis's coat.

One night during the campaign my daughter Laura called to say that she had just seen Dukakis campaigning in Ohio on the evening news. John Glenn was holding his coat. "Papa," said Laura, "Senator Glenn had the same expression on his face that you do when you hold the coat."

The low point in the campaign was a ludicrous Republican TV spot showing Dukakis riding in a tank. There were, however, two high points in the campaign, both provided by Texans. One was at the Democratic convention in Atlanta when governor-to-be Ann Richards said that Bush had been born with a silver foot in his mouth. The other came in the vice presidential debate when Quayle invoked President Kennedy's name. Lloyd paused ominously and replied, "Senator, I served with Jack Kennedy, I knew Jack Kennedy, Jack Kennedy was a friend of mine. Senator, you're no Jack Kennedy."

Election night was a death watch. Dukakis carried only ten states. I was with Lloyd at the Driskill Hotel in Austin where he was waiting to concede. The Democratic and Republican campaigns had agreed that neither would claim victory nor concede defeat until after the California polls had closed. Finally the call came from Dukakis. The campaign was officially over. The nightmare had ended. Bentsen was re-elected to the Senate.

Several months later I was having lunch at the faculty club at the Kennedy School of Government at Harvard. Dukakis, a former Kennedy School faculty member and still governor of Massachusetts, appeared in the doorway obviously looking for an invitation to lunch. None came. The governor walked away.

The Late Great Jake Pickle

One of the things you learn in Texas politics is who the good guys are. As lieutenant governor, I got to campaign for lots of other people, ride in parades, and go to prayer breakfasts, goat ropings, and groundbreakings. The good guys can make it fun to be there. One of the good guys was J. J. "Jake" Pickle. He was born in 1913 in Big Spring, Texas, and died in 2005. He served the 10th Congressional District of Texas, which included Austin, well for thirty-two years. He was one of the best arguments I know against term limits. He was also one of the best campaigners I ever knew because he genuinely liked it and because he knew hundreds of funny stories.

Jake's father was the longtime publisher of the *Big Spring Herald*. When Jake was first elected to Congress in 1963, his father wanted to go to Washington to see his son sworn in. Jake took his father to the store to get a new hat. Since his father was a notorious tightwad, Jake had gone to the store ahead of time and asked the salesman to show his father the best hat and tell him it would cost five dollars. Jake, of course, would pay the difference. Mr. Pickle was so delighted with the bargain that he bought two hats.

Jake and I used to campaign together at the Fourth of July parade at Round Top. Jake would chide me for riding a horse in the parade. He thought horses were dangerous. So Jake mounted a pickup truck, placing his hands on the truck's cab. Somebody slammed the door, breaking two of Jake's right fingers. Give me a horse every time.

In 1941, just before World War II, the air force said it needed a base in Austin. The city of Austin bought the land and presented it to the air force. In the early 1990s, the air force announced that it would close Bergstrom Air Force Base in 1995 and sell the land.

"Whoa," said Jake. "That land goes back to the city." The deed from the city of Austin provided that should the land cease to be used as an air force base, it would revert to the city. Today that airfield is the Austin-Bergstrom International Airport.

I hoped they would name it for Jake. The terminal, however, is named for the late Barbara Jordan, who, as the first African American woman elected to the Texas Senate and as a powerful congressional voice for justice, certainly deserved it. The University of Texas at Austin named its North Austin research facility the J. J. Pickle Research Center in recognition of the fine work Pickle did in obtaining federal grants.

For many years Jake represented the 10th Congressional District, which included Austin and some surrounding counties. Tom DeLay changed all that. DeLay was the Republican majority leader of the U.S. House, until he was forced by corruption charges to resign from office. DeLay wanted to make sure that the Texas congressional delegation contained as few Democrats as possible. The 10th district, since it included Austin, was one of the most reliably Democratic in the state. After Jake left office in 1995, it was represented by Lloyd Doggett, who had been in the Texas Senate when I served as lieutenant governor.

DeLay's redistricting plan, adopted by a Republican-dominated legislature and endorsed by Gov. Rick Perry in 2003, essentially dismembered Austin. It is now represented by three congressmen. The 10th district now runs from North Austin to the Houston suburbs and has a Republican congressman. The 25th district extended three hundred miles from Austin to the Rio Grande Valley. The 21st district cuts into Austin on the west, but the bulk of voters are in San Antonio and the conservative Hill Country. Forget compact and contiguous, forget community of interest, the time-honored rules of redistricting. Austin voters had to pay for their Democratic tendencies.

Lloyd Doggett got re-elected anyway, moving from his old 10th district into the new 25th and campaigning heavily in the Rio Grande Valley. The 2003 Texas redistricting proved to be too much even for the conservative U.S. Supreme Court. In 2006, the court ruled that Hispanics had been deprived of representation. The lines of five districts were redrawn, including District 25. Doggett regained most of his old voters in Austin and picked up some southeast suburbs, and he has been handily returned to office ever since.

A Puff of Black Smoke

I had to run for office five times, and even without serious opposition it was a major effort because of the size of the state and the money required to run any kind of campaign. Later on, others were luckier.

When Texas Gov. George W. Bush resigned in December 2000 to become president, Lt. Gov. Rick Perry became governor. That created a vacancy in the office of lieutenant governor for the first time since the constitution was amended in 1984 to address such a circumstance.

A note on legislative history: Before Sen. Grant Jones of Abilene amended Article III, Section 9, in 1984, the pro tem automatically became lieutenant governor if the job was vacated. The pro tem is the most senior senator who has not already served as pro tem. Ordinarily, the pro tem's most serious duty is planning his Governor for a Day celebration—an occasion when both governor and lieutenant governor politely absent themselves to allow recognition for the pro tem.

The constitution now provides: "If the office of Lieutenant Governor becomes vacant, the President pro tempore of the Senate shall convene the Committee of the Whole Senate within 30 days after the vacancy occurs. The Committee of the Whole shall elect one of its members to perform the duties of the Lieutenant Governor . . ."

Sen. Rodney Ellis, an African American from Houston who began his political career on my staff, was the president pro tem. As a result, in the interim between Perry's accession to the governor's office and the election of a lieutenant governor, Rodney was lieutenant governor—the first African American to hold that office.

It was his duty to convene the Senate, and, this being the first such vacancy in the lieutenant governor's office, the Senate had to adopt new rules. Rodney showed me the proposed rules for the election, which had been drafted by Senate parliamentarian Walter Fisher. The rules provided for closed sessions and a complex balloting system that required as many roll calls as there were senators who had declared their candidacy. After each roll call, the senator with the fewest votes would be dropped.

"Rodney, when the cardinals meet in conclave to elect a pope, they don't have to go through this much stuff," I observed. When the cardinals vote for a new pope, the ballots are burned and a puff of smoke appears above the Vatican. White smoke means that a pope has been elected. Thereafter Rodney would remark, "If you see a puff of black smoke, it's me."

There was no puff of black smoke. Sen. Bill Ratliff, a civil engineer I had appointed to head the Senate Education Committee, was elected lieutenant governor. Ratliff was a moderate Republican. "I am a Republican because I agree with the Republicans at least 51 percent of the time," he told reporter Dave McNeely. "It's the same reason I'm a Methodist. I agree with the Methodists 51 percent of the time."

Ratliff, who had represented Senate District 1 in East Texas, was one of the finest lieutenant governors ever to serve Texas. Called "Obi-Wan Kenobi" by his colleagues in the Senate because of his wisdom, Ratliff was a pragmatist who devoted time and brainpower to helping the state find ways to fund education and health and human services.

Of course that made him unacceptable to the state Republican party. After a brief attempt to run for lieutenant governor in 2002, Ratliff withdrew from the race. Still serving his term as state senator, he opposed the punitive Republican redistricting in 2003 because he felt it would underrepresent rural voters.

As for Rodney Ellis, he is still my state senator as of this writing. At his invitation I was privileged to participate in the ceremonial hanging of his portrait in the hall behind the Senate chamber.

9

How the Texas Senate Works

THE MOST IMPORTANT TITLE THE LIEUTENANT GOVERNOR of Texas has is president of the Texas Senate. The Texas Senate has thirty-one members, each of whom serve a four-year term. It is a legislative body rich in traditions of civility, courtesy, and respect for one's colleagues.

I served my apprenticeship in 1959 as parliamentarian for Lt. Gov. Ben Ramsey. Governor Ramsey was then in his fourth term of six, having started public service in 1930 (two years before I was born) as a member of the Texas House from San Augustine. He had served four terms as a state senator and had been secretary of state under Gov. Beauford Jester. After he was re-elected in 1962, Ramsey resigned to accept a seat on the Texas Railroad Commission to which he was appointed by Gov. Price Daniel. He was a railroad commissioner, regulating oil and gas production, until 1977, serving Texas a total of forty-one years. Perhaps his best moment came when he refused to join the "Shivercrats" who were deserting the Democratic Party to vote Republican in the 1952 and 1956 contests between Dwight D. Eisenhower and Adlai Stevenson.

Ben Ramsey exemplified the Senate traditions. He was my role model as lieutenant governor. Governor Ramsey needed a parliamentarian like a boar hog needs tits. Senate rules and traditions were engraved in his brain, as they came to be in mine. You can read the rules until you have them virtually memorized and learn the traditions as you go, but it takes a session or two for them to become instinctive.

At that time, a half-century ago, there were so few bills on the Senate calendar that the parliamentarian kept them in a file box at the rostrum. Then, as now, senators came to the rostrum during the morning call (the routine business period), to seek recognition on their bills.

Ramsey knew everything. Occasionally when he saw a senator on his way he would tell me to lose Senate Bill XYZ. I put the bill in my coat pocket. When the senator asked Ramsey to recognize him on the bill, somehow I couldn't find the bill in the box.

"Senator, are you sure it's out of committee? I can't find Senate Bill ZYX here," I would ask, deliberately misstating the bill number.

"OK, Ben," the senator would usually say, "I'll vote for your damned old so-and-so bill." I suddenly found Senate Bill XYZ.

I met with Governor Ramsey before the session each morning to get instructions on what bills to refer to what committee. Occasionally he would refer a bill to the Committee on S—t by tossing it in the lower left-hand drawer. Talk about final disposition!

Late in the session, when the Senate began to hold afternoon sessions, Ramsey would rarely preside in the afternoon, preferring to play poker with his friends. He left me the telephone number for where he could be reached, with instructions that if a senator wanted to reach him in a real emergency I should dial the number and hand the phone to the senator.

Sure enough, what I thought was an emergency arose, and I followed instructions. The next day Governor Ramsey told me that there had been no real emergency. There were no more emergencies.

Filibuster Etiquette

When the filibuster season began late in the session, Sen. (later Congressman) Henry B. Gonzales from San Antonio announced that he was going to filibuster a bill amending the election code.

The session seemed sure to go through the night when Governor and Mrs. Ramsey were planning to come to dinner at our house. I knew that Governor Ramsey would not preside during the filibuster, but felt I should be there. The parliamentarian really earns his or her pay when somebody other than the lieutenant governor is in the chair.

Governor Ramsey asked me to ask Dan Moody Jr., my predecessor as parliamentarian, to work that night. Dan's sister, Nancy, was my successor. Ramsey had a weakness for gubernatorial offspring. Dan found time in his busy schedule to work that night, and the Ramseys came to our house for dinner.

Just as we were finishing dinner, Dan called. Senator Gonzales was ready to sit down. Knowing that Governor Ramsey wanted to resume the chair, pass the bill, and adjourn the Senate, I asked Dan to ask Senator Gonzales to hold the floor another half hour until Governor Ramsey got there.

Governor Ramsey resumed the chair about nine p.m., well after his usual bedtime. Senator Gonzales sat down, and the Senate passed the bill. Ramsey then recognized the dean of the Senate, R. A. Weinert, for the motion to adjourn.

But Senator Gonzales got back on his feet, apologizing to the Senate for talking so long and asking Governor Ramsey to let him pass a bill about veterans loans.

So Governor Ramsey—and the Senate—passed Gonzales's veterans bill. If gentlemen are involved, filibusters need not be rancorous affairs.

The Role of Cleavage

Before 1959, the investment of state funds, including the Permanent University Fund, was restricted to what were thought to be "conservative" instruments. "Conservative" meant "don't conserve your money. Lose it as provided by law." Sen. Hubert Hudson from Brownsville sponsored a bill to modernize the investment policies. Hubert's best friend in the Texas Senate was Grady Hazelwood from Amarillo. Friendship notwithstanding, Grady was bitterly opposed to Hubert's bill and planned to filibuster it.

One day Hubert had a convivial luncheon for his beautiful sister Caroline Lynch (as in Merrill Lynch) at the Headliners Club. Hubert invited several senate friends and included me. By some remarkable coincidence Grady was seated next to the beautiful Caroline. The wine flowed freely. Grady had an enjoyable lunch, falling in love while looking down Caroline's low-cut sundress.

When the Senate went back in session that afternoon, Grady had Caroline as his guest, and she was sitting next to him on the Senate floor. Ramsey recognized Hubert, who moved to bring his bill up. Hubert explained his bill briefly. There was no objection. Grady was still in love. I asked Governor Ramsey if I should tell Senator Hazelwood that Senator Hudson was up with his bill. Ramsey shook his head.

Hubert's bill passed, much to the benefit of the University of Texas. Cleavage is not always divisive. It can be unifying as well. There are worse ways to make policy.

Considering Executive Nominations

One of the Senate's most important jobs is approving or rejecting a governor's nominations to the scores of boards and commissions that run the state government.

Winifred Small Jones was the wife of John T. Jones, the publisher of the *Houston Chronicle*, and the daughter of Clint Small, longtime state senator, one-time candidate for governor, and Ben Ramsey's friend. An alumna and regent of Texas Woman's University, she had been re-nominated to the TWU board by the governor.

Sen. Bob Baker from Houston was serving his first term. During his campaign he had been bitterly opposed by the *Chronicle*. Baker said he was going to "bust" Mrs. Jones's appointment. This was his privilege as the hometown senator under Senate tradition, although the privilege is rarely invoked because governors usually clear appointments with the hometown senator.

Ramsey held the appointment in committee until late in the session. Probably because I was from Houston and worked for the *Houston Post*, Ramsey twice sent me to dissuade Baker from his ill-advised intention. After I reported my second failure Ramsey told me to ask Baker to come to the rostrum and then get lost.

Ramsey had a come-to-Jesus session with Baker. Jones was confirmed. Ramsey remarked under his breath "I'll be damned if I was going to let Clint Small's daughter get busted."

As Sen. A. M. Aikin frequently advised his colleagues: "Never vote against a nominee except for reasons of character." The *Chronicle*'s boorishness was no reason to vote against the publisher's wife, a fine woman, admired by all who knew her. Senator Aikin, longtime dean of the Senate, was another of my role models.

Nominees who have been busted never forget.

In 1971, when I started running for lieutenant governor, I went to see Judge St. John Garwood, a longtime family friend. Judge Garwood, a former Texas Supreme Court justice, was one of our state's most distinguished citizens. Nevertheless, the Texas Senate, in one of its inglorious moments, had busted his appointment to the UT Board of Regents because he was "too liberal."

When I asked for his support, Judge Garwood took a tattered clipping from his wallet. The clipping contained the Senate roll call on his nomination. "Young Hobby," he said, "of course, I'd be for you anyway." But it didn't hurt that one of my opponents was Sen. Ralph Hall, who had voted against Judge Garwood.

When Gov. Preston Smith nominated Bob Bullock to be Insurance Commissioner, the Senate busted the nomination, using Senator Aikin's standard. Senators Barbara Jordan and Max Sherman voted no. Max was later dean of UT's Lyndon B. Johnson School of Public Affairs and Barbara a professor there. Bullock never liked the school. Max later had to kiss Bullock's ring to be confirmed as chairman of the Commission on Human Services, but Barbara never did.

Rules Fight, 1973

I presided over the Senate for the first time on Wednesday, January 17, 1973. The first item on the agenda was adopting the Senate rules. The previous year, during a summer special session, the Senate had amended its rules to provide that every returning senator would have the right to

Hobby with gavel at Senate podium, c. 1984. *William P. Hobby Sr. Family Papers, Dolph Briscoe Center for American History, di_05734.*

continue serving on each committee he or she was on as long as he or she remained in the Senate. Obviously, that would seriously have weakened the lieutenant governor's power as president of the Senate. Only two appointments would have been available to me that year, for example, on the Senate Finance Committee.

In the course of interviewing senators concerning their assignments, I expressed my concerns about this rule. I was able to gain substantial support for a compromise proposal. The compromise proposed that three members of each Senate committee of less than ten be returning members and four be returning members on the committees numbering more than ten. This proposal was adopted by the Senate on January 17, the day after I was sworn in.

During the previous week I had worked on committee assignments with my parliamentarian, June Hyer, whom I had "borrowed" from her position at the University of Houston-Clear Lake, and my executive assistant, Steve Oaks. One of the senators disappointed by his failure to get a chairmanship was Sen. H. J. "Doc" Blanchard of Lubbock. He had strongly supported my opponent Wayne Connally and had been one of the sponsors of the effort to strip the lieutenant governor of his powers.

The three principal committee chairmanships were Sen. A. M. Aikin of Paris, Finance; Sen. Bill Moore of Bryan, State Affairs; and Sen. Charles Herring of Austin, Jurisprudence. I reappointed them. Jack Hightower enjoyed the Administration Committee chairmanship and did it well. More of a dilemma was Sen. Oscar Mauzy of Dallas, who was chair of the Education Committee and a prime candidate for non-reappointment.

Mauzy had been a prime mover, with Blanchard, in the effort to make the office of lieutenant governor of Texas the kind of glorified clerkship it is in many other states. He also had opposed the appointments of former governor Allan Shivers and former ambassador Ed Clark to the University of Texas Board of Regents. He lost both of these fights overwhelmingly, as he knew he would. That did not match my philosophy. I don't like to lose, which means that I pick my battles pretty carefully. I reappointed Mauzy because he was the most knowledgeable member of the Senate in the area of education finance. Because the Rodriguez case had just been decided, I knew the case would be a major area of concern for the next several years. *Rodriguez v. San Antonio Independent School District* was a 1971 lawsuit claiming that the Texas system of school finance was unconstitutional because there was such a vast difference in the amount expended in different school districts. Edgewood, where Demetrio Rodriguez lived, could raise only $37 per pupil despite a high tax rate, while Alamo Heights, a nearby San Antonio district, could raise $413. A three-judge federal court agreed with Rodriguez, but the U.S. Supreme Court found that the Texas system did not violate the federal constitution and should be resolved by the state. The state's effort to resolve school finance was in fact a major area of concern for all eighteen years I served and the subject of my last special session in 1990.

The Committee on Economic Development is where the banking and insurance bills go. For that chairmanship, I wanted the senator with the beadiest eyes. That was Tom Creighton of Mineral Wells. He was a good lawyer, a former prosecutor, and not owned by any lobby. Creighton didn't want the job at first. The first good thing that happened in my relationship with Creighton was one of those things that I could never have planned, it just happened.

On a snowy night a few days before the inauguration, I had finished work but couldn't go home because I had a taping of the *Capital Eye* program at the KTBC television station. About six p.m. I happened to run into Ben Barnes in the hallway, and he invited me to come with him to Creighton's office for a drink. Barnes, Sen. A. R. "Babe" Schwartz of Galveston, Creighton, and I were there. It was a very fruitful meeting, not in terms of anything decided, but because of the beginning of a fine personal relationship.

During the fight over the rules, Creighton offered an amendment tightening up the requirements for bringing out bills on minority report. The vote was tied 15-15, so I voted for Creighton's amendment. He came up to the rostrum afterward to confer his highest compliment: "Man, you've got brass balls."

How Betty King Became Secretary of the Senate

The Senate has a number of officers who are elected by the whole Senate. These include the secretary of the Senate, the sergeant-at-arms, the calendar clerk, the doorkeeper, the engrossing and enrolling clerk, and the journal clerk. The parliamentarian is also an officer of the Senate, but generally the Senate concedes all authority to the lieutenant governor in choosing who will fill this position. These officers are non-partisan, highly competent, and endlessly patient professionals whose willingness to work long hours during the sessions are what make the Senate work. When I presided during my first session, I chose June Hyer as my parliamentarian, but did not consider recommending any changes in staffing the Senate. Instead, I tried to learn more from the current staff about making the Senate work.

When I became lieutenant governor, the secretary of the Senate was Charlie Schnabel, who had held that job since 1955. The job description

Hobby with Betty King, c. 1977. *William P. Hobby Sr. Family Papers, Dolph Briscoe Center for American History, di_05744.*

for the secretary of the Senate is basically "whatever it takes." The most visible job is standing at the front of the Senate chamber to call the roll for votes, but the real job is done in the office behind the chamber, tending to the needs of senators. A good secretary makes for a happy, smooth-working Senate.

I didn't have a particular complaint with Charlie Schnabel, but in late 1975 he got himself in trouble. He later pled guilty to a misdemeanor connected to misuse of Senate staff to work on University of Texas at Austin track and field events. He resigned from his job on November 8, 1976.

When the Senate convened in 1977, the election of Senate officers was one of the first things on the agenda at the beginning of a regular session. It is usually so pro forma that no one realizes it has happened. Not so in 1977.

As chair of the Senate Administration Committee, Sen. Don Adams of Jasper was handling the election of the secretary of the Senate. Sometime before the election, he had asked me if I had a candidate for the job. I said no, which was a lie, because I very much wanted Betty King, the Senate journal clerk, to be elected. It was pretty clear others felt the same way because when Donny came back to me after his poll of the Senate, he told me that he wanted to nominate Ms. King. He did, and she served with distinction for twenty-four years.

When Betty retired in 2001 after fifty-four years in state government, she had served with eleven lieutenant governors. The Senate declared Betty King Day. They named a committee room after her and declared her the first winner of the Betty King Public Service Award. They hung her portrait in the committee room named after her. Senators talked about her steadfast public service, her "den mother" attitude, and her ability to solve problems. But I think I summed it all up when I said, "She makes everything happen right."

As for Charlie Schnabel, I think we did him a favor. He became administrative assistant to "Timber Charlie," Texas Congressman Charlie Wilson, who became the biggest factor in the U.S. funding the Afghanistan mujahideen's war against the Soviet Union and the subject of a book and a film titled *Charlie Wilson's War*. Charlie Schnabel spent time in the barren mountains of Afghanistan with the mujahideen rebels transporting American-supplied missile launchers to their strongholds. He had a great deal of fun doing it.

Budget Blues

The main business of the legislature is passing the appropriations bill—the rest is poetry, as I said frequently. The biennial budget bill sets the spending priorities for the state. It determines the direction for the future and, if well done, balances the many needs and demands of a big and growing state. Passing the bill takes all 140 days of the session and sometimes more to get done, and the process is fraught with peril.

As all Texas school children learn, Texas is a Reconstruction state that has a long ballot, meaning that a large number of state officials are elected by the voters rather than being appointed by the governor. Moreover, almost all of those elected officials have important duties outlined in the state constitution. One of those officials is the state comptroller, who is the tax collector. He must certify that the budget passed every two years by the legislature is not larger than the revenue the state is expected to generate. At the beginning of each session the comptroller makes a revenue projection—his best guess for how much revenue can be collected over the next two years. This projection is made in January. The budget bill is usually certified in June, and the budget year starts in September.

Bob Bullock, who was elected comptroller in 1974, had a reputation for being volatile, not to mention intimidating. Near the end of the 1975 session (when I was still a baby lieutenant governor) Comptroller Bullock called and told me he couldn't certify the appropriations bill.

I panicked. "But Mr. Bullock, why not? It's within your revenue estimate." I said, in a terror-stricken voice. Not "Bob," mind you, but "Mr. Bullock." Actually, the bill wasn't within the official estimate, but it was within our private agreement. Bullock and I had an agreement that gave me about $400,000 "walking around money"—money that I could put into the bill during conference. (A conference committee consisting of five members of each house is convened when differing House and Senate bills need to be reconciled.)

"Governor, a page is missing, and I can't certify a bill that doesn't add up."

"Well, Mr. Bullock, what page is it?"

"Page so-and-so. It has the Board of Hearing Aid Examiners appropriation on it." Actually I could conceive of a state without a Board of Hearing Aid Examiners. But, Bullock said, the appropriation for next agency in alphabetical order, the Highway Department, began on the alleged missing page. Pretty hard to imagine Texas without highways.

I couldn't conceive of what might happen. It was certainly too late to pass another appropriations bill. As they say in the navy, it was time for "ALL HANDS, MAN YOUR BATTLE STATIONS. SET CONDITION ABLE THROUGHOUT THE SHIP."

I called Budget Director Tom Keel, still in a panic. Tom assured me that no page was missing, that Bullock was pulling my leg. "We sent him four copies of the bill, all wrapped up in a red ribbon so that he can split it up among his people who work on certification," said Tom. "But I know where he drinks his lunch, and I'll take some extra pages over to him." Problem solved. Bullock had his fun, but my right leg is still about an inch longer than my left one.

Secretary of the Senate Patsy Spaw, who was then an assistant enrolling clerk, later told me about even more fun and games on that occasion. When she was told that a page was missing, she located the printing error and called her contact at the comptroller's office to ask when she could deliver the missing page, something that seemed routine. But she didn't know Bob Bullock. She was told that they would have to get back to her.

She later learned that Bullock had sought an attorney general's opinion about whether the comptroller could certify the bill with a page missing. The AG opined that the comptroller's job was to certify that the amount appropriated was within the amount of revenue estimated to be available.

The missing page was only a recapitulation page and not critical to the amount appropriated.

Meanwhile, Patsy was told that she would not be allowed to deliver the bill. She assumed—cavalierly and unwisely, she said—that she could insert it when the bill came back from the comptroller. At that time, the practice was to seal the original document with wax so no one could tamper with it—extra copies were sent unsealed so they could be reviewed. The enrolling clerk, Mary Hobart Key, had an etched topaz ring used to seal the melted wax around the clasps of the large document.

But when Patsy went to pick up the bill, it looked different. Added to the melted red sealing wax was wiring all around the document soldered closed at the clasps—a little message from Mr. Bullock. Somehow, they slipped the missing page into the correct spot without taking apart the wiring. Patsy said it aged her ten years.

Actually, passing the budget bill doesn't end the fun and games. Although the Texas governor may not play a large role in drafting or debating the budget, he gets the last word. He can veto the entire bill (not likely) or he can exercise his constitutional right to the line item veto and strike individual items that he deems unnecessary.

One of my greatest friends—and worst critics—when I was in office was Ann Richards. I first knew her when she was a member of Rep. Sarah Weddington's staff, then as a Travis County commissioner, and later as state treasurer and governor. Her lightning wit transformed the good ol' boy world of county politics. One story she liked to tell was about visiting her precinct maintenance barn (one of the main responsibilities of a county commissioner is repairing the potholes in the county roads). Making conversation with the road maintenance men, Ann noted a dog hanging around the barn. "That's the ugliest dog I have ever seen," she said, "What's its name?" "Ann," the road boss told her.

Ann was a champion for women and a tireless advocate. One of her causes was increasing the protection available for abused women. As a county commissioner, she was relentless in lobbying me to include state funding for a center for abused women in Travis County. It wasn't an easy sell, but I told her I would do all I could. Nevertheless, the 1979 appropriations bill reached the conference committee stage without funding for the center (I remember that the Senate had it in the bill, and the House took it out).

Just as we were reaching the hard-choices time in conference committee, a wreath of roses arrived in my office. It was a giant display on a metal stand like a funeral display. There was a gold banner across it inscribed, "A promise is a promise." The card was signed: Ann Richards.

Hobby with Ann Richards, c. 1977. *William P. Hobby Sr. Family Papers, Dolph Briscoe Center for American History, di_05747.*

I did what it took—calling in some chits, making some trades—and funding for the center for abused women reappeared in the appropriations bill conference committee report, which was duly accepted by both houses. But the story wasn't over. Gov. Bill Clements, always looking for ways to cut the budget, vetoed that item.

I still had the roses in my office, but they had died and turned black. I scratched out the inscription, wrote in "A veto is a veto," and sent them back to Ann.

The following session, in 1981, we funded the center for abused women by combining it with one of Governor Clements's favorite items, a sewage treatment plant in Nuevo Laredo, so he could not veto it.

10

The Constitution of 1876: Still Standing Despite My Best Efforts

WHEN I TOOK THE OATH AS LIEUTENANT GOVERNOR in 1973, we were in a reform era. The voters had spoken out about corruption and bad government, and those of us elected that year got the message. The 1973 session included a lot of "sunshine" legislation, including state open records and open meetings laws and some ethics bills. Speaker of the House Price Daniel Jr. was the main champion of these bills. I had some reservations and took some hits in the media for slowing down Daniel's legislative freight train. The bills that passed were better for more scrutiny.

One of the good government initiatives I embraced wholeheartedly, however, was constitutional revision. At the same time that voters elected me in 1972, they overwhelmingly approved convening a constitutional convention to revise the unwieldy, outdated, and highly restrictive state constitution.

The Texas Constitution was adopted in 1876, right after the Civil War. It was a Reconstruction constitution, adopted, like those in many southern states, after the Confederate states had fared badly at the hands of carpetbaggers and scalawags. In Texas, the Reconstruction governor was Edmund J. Davis, a radical Republican who opposed secession, unlike another radical Republican, Gov. Rick Perry, 140 years later. Governor Davis had been a Union general and got elected in 1869 after he returned to Texas.

Among other things, Davis intimidated and institutionalized the opposition, muzzled newspapers, disenfranchised voters, raised property taxes, and, when he was defeated for re-election in 1873, barricaded himself in his office in hopes President Ulysses S. Grant would intervene to keep him in office. That didn't happen. It would be 105 years before Texas had another Republican governor, and it was my misfortune to be lieutenant governor at the time.

When Texans convened to write a new constitution in 1876 they were fed up with arbitrary governors. They wrote a very long, very detailed document that created an intricate system of checks and balances that was designed to keep both the governor and state government weak. According to constitutional scholar George Braden, the 1876 constitution had 218 amendments (there are now at least 456). In 1973 the constitution contained almost 64,000 words. Three-fourths of the states have constitutions less than half this length, and two of those constitutions contain only about 8,000 words.

I believed that we could create a document more appropriate to governing a populous state in the twentieth century. I was wrong. In fact, I got sidelined rather early in the process. The constitutional convention was to consist of Texas legislators, and Attorney General John Hill ruled that a non-legislator could not be chair. That pretty much left the job to Speaker Daniel, for whom I did not have the greatest respect.

I hoped the convention would build on the work of the Constitutional Revision Commission, a highly representative panel of capable, high-minded citizens chaired by former Supreme Court Justice Robert Calvert. The commission had tackled tough issues, from taxation to metro government, and produced a thoughtful, middle-of-the-road document.

When I spoke to the delegates to the convention in January 7, 1974, I warned them about special interests. "The people want a constitution for everyone, not just special interests," I said. "They will not be confused by oratory or sidetracked by sham. They want results. They want a constitution for tomorrow as well as today." Any attempt to draft a constitution to serve such interests would be "futile and also dishonorable," I added.

Rewriting the constitution, since it set the framework for government and covered every aspect of government, was a fat target for special interests. All the lobbyists in town wanted their interests protected.

Sadly, it was the specific special interest of the Republican Party in enshrining the state's right-to-work law in the constitution that derailed the convention. Texas is one of about twenty-two right-to-work states that do not permit union shops—workplaces where all employees are required to join a labor union. On July 30, 1974, with time running out, the proposed constitution was five votes short of approval, and the holdouts were fighting the right-to-work provision. Tempers were hot. The "Duke of Paducah," Bill Heatley, chair of the House Appropriations Committee, physically kept Rep. Elmer Tarbox of Lubbock from voting yes. Dallas Rep. Jim Mattox, a strong union supporter who later would serve as attorney general, called Speaker Daniel a liar from the floor. Sen. H. J. "Doc" Blanchard collapsed near the podium and needed medical attention.

I tried to persuade my representative, Craig Washington of Houston, to vote "yes" with a note passed to him on the floor. "The [expletive deleted] doesn't have a vote," Washington said, not knowing I was standing behind him. When I tapped him on the shoulder we both started laughing.

Governor Briscoe, who didn't much like the proposed constitution because it would allow the legislature to call itself into session, said it would be immoral to intervene.

I thought the proposed new constitution was an improvement over the 1876 constitution, but there wasn't much I could do. The proposed constitution failed to pass by three votes.

After the convention failed, a lot of time was wasted on blame. I was more concerned about salvaging whatever was possible. Given that the convention composed of legislators had failed to get the job done, I favored convening a citizens' convention to tackle revision. That idea proved to be not very popular. Rep. Ray Hutchison, a Dallas Republican who headed the House Constitution Revision Committee, said that would be a waste of money. The convention had turned out a good product, he said, the people had already paid for it, and revision needed to be accomplished as soon as possible.

The next regular session succeeded where the convention had failed. To speed the work along, we decided to work with a joint House-Senate committee. One senator, Walter Mengden, a Houston Republican known as "Mad Dog," tried filibustering the vote for a joint committee, but that ended when I told him he was "making an ass of the Senate."

It took the Senate exactly one day to pass the revision proposal with a four-fifths vote. The new document stripped out right-to-work and other more controversial provisions but was still a substantial improvement over the present constitution. The House followed suit, and Speaker Billy Clayton and I signed a resolution sending it to the people for a vote.

The eight amendments that went to the ballot would have made some changes in Texas's way of doing business.

- It would have permitted 90-day legislative sessions in even-numbered years. Now legislative sessions are limited to 140 days in odd-numbered years.
- It would have merged the Supreme Court, which handles civil cases, with the Court of Criminal Appeals.
- It would have abolished the state's right of appeal in criminal cases.
- It would have allowed local voters to add or delete local offices (like the examiner of hides, which still existed in some areas) and to vote for county ordinance-making power.
- It would have set a debt ceiling for cities and counties.
- It would have allowed the governor to name commission chairs and remove appointees.
- It would have contained a commitment to equal educational opportunity.

We thought we had a better chance of approval by splitting the proposed constitution into eight separate amendments. That way voters would not have to reject the entire document if they only objected to one provision. Speaker Clayton, Attorney General Hill, and I, as well as many legislators, immediately began to campaign for adoption.

Comptroller Bob Bullock, never one to back away from a fight, jumped in with a study claiming that the proposed constitution would cost the state between $1 billion and $11 billion a year. The booklet he published was called *Fiscal Implications of the Property Tax Constitution*. The Legislative Budget Board did its own fiscal implications report and determined it would cost a total of $36 million a year with $711,000 to $817,0900 more for annual sessions.

In October, Governor Briscoe, who had been largely silent on the subject, came out against all eight amendments. He told a press conference that a new constitution could vastly increase state expenditures, perhaps even triggering an income tax. There were good things in the amendments, but the bad outweighed the good, he said. That pretty much doomed our effort. All eight amendments failed at the polls. It wasn't even close.

As a wise columnist, Jon Ford, wrote in the *Waco Tribune-Herald* after the election, "You cannot rile the courthouse crowd, the oil industry, real estate men, environmentalists, the Civil Liberties Union, influential trial judges, small and large taxpayers, school officials and the Governor and still expect to win . . . . They didn't like some of it, didn't understand most of it and were mighty suspicious of the whole bundle."

In retrospect, it was incredible that such substantive change got as far as it did. I attributed the defeat to "fear of change and innovation." Texas voters will accept change in small increments when they are convinced of the need for it. But multiple changes with strong and credible opposition is going nowhere in a deeply conservative state.

Or as columnist Lynn Ashby wrote in the *Houston Post*:

"Dolph and Bill went up the hill
To fetch a constitution
Dolph backed down
The plan was drowned
So much for our solution."

Nevertheless, Governor Briscoe and I worked together well for another three years, until he was defeated in the primary.

11

Kinder, Gentler Days

P EOPLE WHO INTRODUCE THE LIEUTENANT GOVERNOR at speaking events often say that the office is the most powerful in Texas government. In a good many states, lieutenant governors run as a team with the governor and mainly serve as a stand-in when the governor is out of state or indisposed. Lieutenant governors joke that they don't have much to do except phone the governor and ask about his or her health.

In Texas and some other southern states, the lieutenant governor has additional duties. As lieutenant governor, I presided over the Legislative Budget Board, which writes the first draft of the state budget. I served as co-chair of the Legislative Council and the Legislative Audit Committee. I appointed committee chairs and named committees, and I decided, within limits prescribed by the rules, which bills came up for debate and which did not.

Those were powers that the senators voted at the beginning of each term when they adopted the rules. In fact, even when the lieutenant governor was a Democrat and the Senate largely Republican, they did not change this arrangement.

There's a temptation to think that we lived in kinder, gentler days between 1973 when I took office and 1991 when I left. Perhaps, perhaps not. When I was first elected in 1972, the governor, sworn in on the same day, was Dolph Briscoe. Governor Briscoe was a cattle rancher with vast holdings in South Texas. Briscoe had some business connections to my family. His father had been in business with Ross Sterling, governor of Texas, a founder of Humble Oil, and publisher of the *Houston Post* before my father acquired it. My father went on hunting trips on Briscoe's Chupadera Ranch.

Governor Briscoe and I were both Democrats, but our backgrounds were very different. He was from Uvalde, and as a rancher and former president of the Texas and Southwestern Cattle Raisers Association, he was an effective proponent for agriculture—a huge industry in Texas then and now.

I was a newspaperman from the state's largest city. I didn't have a single ranch to my name. In spite of our differences, we worked together very

Janey and Dolph Briscoe greet Bill and Diana Hobby before the 1973 inauguration.
Courtesy of the Hobby family.

well. In my first inaugural speech I pledged that I would stand "at the right hand of Dolph Briscoe, whom we principally honor here today." Then we stood together at a reception in the Capitol rotunda. We had invited to the reception those who had elected us, the Texas public, and shook hands until there were no more to shake. Dolph and I didn't agree on everything. I had reservations about some of his proposals, such as higher highway funding and rural property tax relief, and he opposed adoption of a new Texas constitution, which I supported. Nevertheless, we got along well. He respected that it was my responsibility to lead the Senate and never interfered with the will of that body. I am proud that in his memoir, *Dolph Briscoe: My Life in Texas Ranching and Politics,* he referred to me as a "steadfast friend," and we remained so until his death on June 27, 2010.

When Briscoe and I were first elected, Texas was pretty much a one-party state. Liberal Democrats and conservative Democrats duked it out, but they were all members of the same party. Election to office meant winning the Democratic primary. There were Republicans, most of them from Dallas and Houston, but, as they joked, they could hold their caucus in a phone booth.

The Texas Legislature was famously known for rowdy, if not downright bizarre, behavior. This reputation is perhaps because Texas has had better writers, such as Molly Ivins, as chroniclers than other states. It just may be that lawmakers in, say, Fargo, North Dakota, did not have a Molly Ivins to bring them national attention when they failed to act like good girls and boys.

I had standards for decorum in the Senate—mainly, that we would have fewer instances of fisticuffs than in the Texas House. It was not a high bar. Senators are elected by a large group of voters, and they have big

Family portrait, 1975. Diana and Bill Hobby, seated. From left standing, Kate, Paul, Laura, and Andrew Hobby. *William P. Hobby Sr. Family Papers, Dolph Briscoe Center for American History, di_05748*.

personalities. Sometimes, under the pressure of the momentous decisions, tempers flare.

One of my unwritten rules was that the Senate would not meet at night if at all possible. We rarely met in the afternoon until we reached that point in the session when scheduling afternoon meetings became necessary to finish the people's business. Earlier in the session it makes sense and is more productive for committees to meet in the afternoon. Sometimes, when leaving the building for dinner, senators would have a drink or maybe even two, and that tended to make it harder to do constructive work.

As presiding officer, I rarely left the podium and even less often left the building when the Senate was in session. From time to time, however, the duties of state outside the Capitol could not be ignored. It was on one of those mornings in March 1979 that I left the Capitol. When I got back shortly after lunch, I had several urgent messages from Betty King, the secretary of the Senate.

Turns out this was the day when the running feud between Sen. W. T. "Bill" Moore of Bryan, dean of the Senate, and Sen. A. R. "Babe" Schwartz of Galveston, erupted on the floor.

Bill Moore was called the Bull of the Brazos for good reason. He was a big man who didn't have much truck with those who disagreed with him—a good man to have on your team and a bad one to have as an enemy.

Babe Schwartz likewise earned his nickname—he was as quick as a featherweight boxer, razor-tongued, and prone to keep punching long after the battle was won or lost.

Both were Democrats, but Moore was a staunch rural conservative and Schwartz was an urban liberal. It wouldn't have mattered much. Moore couldn't stand Schwartz, and Schwartz couldn't stop taunting Moore.

The issue that blew up on the Senate floor (I am relying on Betty and newspaper accounts here) was a bill that Moore was carrying to absolve contractors of liability for their workmanship on public projects once a city, county, or other division of local government had accepted the project. There were a few exceptions—proving fraud, if a warranty was in effect, etc.

Sen. Lloyd Doggett of Austin, who could be just as annoying as Schwartz, attacked it as "unthinkable." Schwartz jumped in, saying, "That means that when one of our buildings falls on some innocent soul, the taxpayers are liable."

They wanted Moore to tell them the bill was written by the Association of General Contractors, but when they asked Moore where he got the bill, he got mad and said, "I don't know where I got the bill. Maybe I found it on the floor. I carry so many bills."

Doggett produced a point of order that the bill had no fiscal note (a statement of its cost to taxpayers), and the point of order prevailed, so the bill was pulled down.

It didn't end there. Moore, understandably burned up, then found that Schwartz had taken up residence in the State Affairs Committee, where he was preparing to question witnesses about a bill on public accountancy. Moore was chairman of the committee, and Schwartz wasn't a member. "You're out of order," Moore roared. "You're not going to take over my committee."

Quoting from the *Dallas Times-Herald*: "Schwartz suggested that if he didn't like it, Moore could eject him. Moore said that would be an undue burden for the sergeant-at-arms. 'Senator, as obnoxious as you may be to me . . .' Schwartz said. 'Senator, you're repulsive to me,' Moore interrupted."

By this time they had drawn a crowd. Schwartz said he had outlived many of Moore's contemporaries and even they had permitted non-committee members to speak. Moore said, "You haven't outlived me, and I'll be here when you're gone. And don't come to my funeral because it would be a sacrilege." Moore was wrong. He died in 1999 at the age of eighty-one. I don't know if Schwartz went to his funeral.

Moore gaveled the committee adjourned in a huff and headed for Schwartz. They stood toe to toe for a moment before Moore stalked out of the chamber, muttering that he would have clobbered Schwartz "if he wasn't so small."

"I've been hit before, and I've known Sen. Moore a long time, and I'm not afraid of either one," said Schwartz, who was neither intimidated nor repentant.

After hearing Betty's account of the altercation, I called Moore and Schwartz into my office—separately—and expressed my displeasure at their conduct. It never got quite that out of hand again.

Gov. Bill Clements, the first Republican elected governor since Reconstruction, was elected in 1978. His election was an upset—Democratic Attorney General John Hill had been considered the frontrunner. Clements was first inaugurated January 18, 1979.

During Clements's first term there was a reasonably good working relationship among the governor, myself, and House Speaker Billy Clayton. As George Christian said in Carolyn Barta's book *Bill Clements: Texian to his Toenails*, "They cut him some slack early." Clements's second term was a different story. After he defeated Mark White in 1986, the mood was surly.

I invited Clements to a meeting of the Senate committee chairs at the beginning of his second term, early in 1987. Clements usually spent weekends in Dallas, and on Mondays he was full of ideas from his friends at the country club. The chairmen's meetings took place on Monday evenings in the Ben Ramsey Room right off my office. Refreshments were served. Clements arrived in a jovial mood, eager to talk about his great programs.

He left in an ugly mood, sliced and diced by a buzzsaw of powerful senators with strong opinions. He told his biographer that I insulted him, but the fact was senators disagreed with him. One of his plans was to build more prisons. That aroused a spirited response from Sen. Ray Farabee, who thought there were better ways to spend taxpayer money. Some of the other senators joined in because it was good sport. Because of that session, the governor's second term didn't get off to a great start. The meeting did accomplish one worthwhile purpose: Clements never came back to the Senate side of the Capitol.

It didn't really get better. Clements's programs were traditional Republican programs, although they seem pretty reasonable in comparison with the ideological and ridiculous proposals we get today. He wanted to "scrub the budget." Some of us had scrubbed the budget several times before. In 1975 Governor Briscoe had named me chair of the Joint Advisory Commission on Government Operations, which was called the "Hobby Commission." Our job, Briscoe told us, was "to stop the unbridled growth of state government," and I directed the commission to "keep your eyes on the big dollars and chase as few rabbits as you can." The commission targeted duplicative agencies, unnecessary regulation, and categorical funding. We had some successes.

During his first term, which started in 1979, Clements wanted to cut taxes by $1 billion by reducing a teacher pay raise and state aid to education, both of which we had proposed in the Legislative Budget Board budget. He called our budget "a letter to Santa Claus." There was not $1 billion available for those reductions and not much reason for them. At that time, Texas ranked forty-fifth among the states in state and local tax collections and lowest among the top industrial states. It was and is one of only seven states with no income tax. There were critical unmet needs in mental health, education, prisons, and the state police. The state of Texas is as big a tax break as there is.

In my opinion, Texans wanted better government—not less. I saw no big groundswell of public support for reducing or eliminating services. "I don't think anyone is more for cutting taxes than I am," I said, "but when you talk about cutting taxes responsibly you've got to talk about where you can reduce expenditures. Education, welfare, transportation and criminal justice constitute 85 percent of the budget so if you're talking about a $1

Gov. Bill Clements signing property tax repeal with Hobby, House Speaker Billy Clayton (second from right), others. *Photograph by Bill Malone, Texas Governor's Office, copy in William P. Hobby Sr. Family Papers, Dolph Briscoe Center for American History, di_05953.*

billion tax cut you're talking about major program reductions, and I haven't heard anybody say where those major program reductions ought to be."

Clements's inaugural address included the line "You will hear voices during my administration expressing doubts about some of my proposals. But, I will persist, I will prevail." He looked at me. I smiled. He didn't prevail.

Clements did talk about increasing the gasoline tax, which funds highways and education. That incident irritated me a little bit. Clements had a couple of meetings in his office, and House Speaker Billy Clayton and I were there. He talked about increasing the gasoline tax and the severance tax and so forth—all this was his idea. Clayton and I just never had any enthusiasm for any of these projects at all. Finally, Clayton said, "Governor, all those bills have to originate in the House and pass out of Rep. Bob Davis's Ways and Means Committee, and Davis [a Republican and Clements's campaign chairman] is a good friend of yours. Why don't you

Hobby with Mark White, 1986. *William P. Hobby Sr. Family Papers, Dolph Briscoe Center for American History, di_05728.*

call Bob Davis and ask him if you could get it out of his committee?" Anyway, I picked up the paper one day and saw that Clements had put out a press release. It said that, after long study of the matter with the lieutenant governor and the Speaker, he had decided there would be no tax increases. He was the only one who ever had any interest in the idea.

Clements and I also had a disagreement about wiretaps in 1980. It will sound preposterous today, but back then there was some respect for privacy and civil rights. I commented to a reporter that, "the governor wants to wiretap the dope dealers, but that's OK—he's only going to tap the guilty ones." Had I been a member of the legislature I would have voted against wiretaps because it makes it easier for government to spy on citizens. As it was, I was in the minority, so I did the best I could to make the bill less invasive. Since then, of course, we have had a president who thought he could eavesdrop on anyone anytime without the benefit of a court order. Those were kinder, gentler times.

Mark White was elected governor in 1982, defeating Bill Clements's bid for re-election. Mark had been Governor Briscoe's secretary of state and was elected attorney general in 1978. Mark and I agreed on most things, and we managed to make some real legislative progress, most notably in public education. Some of my friends, former senator Max Sherman and UPI reporter Ann Arnold, were on Mark's staff. But Mark was a much more partisan Democrat than I, and one of the first things he was urged to do was ask the Senate to return to his office the names of the appointments made by Governor Clements after he was defeated. White did so, and it caused a bitter, bruising battle. In one four-hour session, the heavily Democratic Senate took up nominees one-by-one and voted to send back 59 of the 102 names. Among those "busted" were former Gov. John Connally, named to be a UT regent, and former Speaker Billy Clayton, appointed to the A&M System Board. Merit was not considered, only political party. It was a mistake and was done over my objections.

As presiding officer of the Senate, I did not consider that I had authority to kill bills that I disliked. Under Senate rules, if a senator can persuade two-thirds of the senators to vote to bring a bill up, the senator is entitled to run with the bill. Ron Kessler of Dallas was quoted as saying: "Hobby's most commendable characteristic is he does not thwart the will of the Senate."

I was more concerned that a truly contentious bill, one with dozens of potential amendments, could stall Senate business. In the 140-day legislative session Texas has, such a bill can doom many less controversial bills. A bill that will be filibustered is worst of all. I presided over the longest filibuster in Senate history in 1977. Sen. Bill Meier of Fort Worth was fighting a bill because it would deny access to the names of people who received workers' compensation benefits. He talked for forty-three and a half hours, which is still a Texas record and a national record, longer even than U.S. Sen. Strom Thurmond's fifteen-hour tirade against a 1957 civil rights bill. Like most filibusters, this one didn't accomplish anything except to delay other bills.

There were contentious bills every session, and, in my time in office, we twisted arms aplenty on tax bills and on workers' compensation.

Perhaps the most contentious issue, because it dealt directly with political ambition and survival, was redistricting, both Congressional and legislative. We respected incumbency, Democratic and Republican. We gained a seat for our party if we could, but we didn't redistrict in the middle of a decade to get partisan advantage. And we didn't think we could violate the Voting Rights Act with impunity, as the Texas Legislature did in 2003 at the direction of U.S. House Republican Majority Leader Tom DeLay.

Did we sometimes float out hugely complex, lengthy legislative substitutes at the last moment when legislators had no way of studying them or knowing what was in them? Yes, sometimes the appropriations bill came back from conference committee at the eleventh hour before the mandatory adjournment of the legislative session, and we tried our very best (usually successfully) to pass it. On one of those occasions when the school finance and education appropriations bill came back to the floor, the very opinionated Sen. Oscar Mauzy of Dallas filibustered it to death, causing a special session. Thereafter, I kept a sign on the desk saying "Do not recognize Mauzy on the last day for ANY reason!"

Later, as a Supreme Court justice, Mauzy was a member of the court that overturned a very similar school finance law and paved the way for a more equitable system than the various systems we were able to craft during the 1970s and 1980s.

There is one key difference between then and now that I think is important to consider. During those days, we tried to solve problems in the best way for the future of the state. That was more important to us than checking off a win on a partisan agenda.

The name of the game was compromise. Even if we started out with an ideal bill (defined as the best possible remedy for a particular barrier in the path of public progress arrived at after careful study by a blue-ribbon interim committee) we knew it would have a long and torturous path. Various interests would weigh in. Different constituencies would try to work their will.

And then there was the Texas House of Representatives. House members are elected from smaller districts and run every two years, so their views are different from senators. House members represent the barbers. Senators represent the bankers.

At every session there was a contentious issue that went by a different name but looked suspiciously familiar. Some of its aliases were medical malpractice, tort reform, products liability, no-fault insurance, and workers' compensation. The underlying issue was that business wanted more limits on lawsuits and plaintiffs wanted fewer. This pitted the plaintiff's bar against the defense bar.

Those bills were usually hammered out in the lieutenant governor's conference room by prominent lawyers on both sides. Frequently that meant Morris Atlas of McAllen for the defense and Joe Jamail of Houston for plaintiffs.

The negotiations were aided by the fact that I could say "If you guys don't agree, there won't be a bill." An even worse threat was "If you guys don't agree, I'll just throw it out there, and who knows what will happen."

When I ran for re-election in 1982, the *Corpus Christi Caller-Times* was kind enough to editorialize that "His gifts of conciliation and compromise are apt to be much needed in the coming legislative session as newly assertive Republicans seek to stake out new claims and worried Democrats struggle to regroup."

I'm not sure I worked any magic on the "newly assertive Republicans." They eventually took over the state and now have things all their way. The Democratic Party contributed amply to its own demise. Certainly at the national level and to a lesser degree at the state level the party has shot itself in the foot a few times. During some disastrous political conventions in the 1970s and 1980s, party rules on delegate selection and other matters moved the party to the left of the mainstream of American political thought. I objected to the delegate quota system, which specified that you have to have so many minorities, so many women, and so forth.

I always named Republicans to leadership roles. These appointments were based on talent and not political party. For example, Sen. Bob McFarland of Arlington chaired the Senate Criminal Justice Committee when we were required to remedy the faults found by the federal courts in our state prison system. Sen. O. H. "Ike" Harris chaired the Senate Economic Development Committee.

J. P. Bryan, former president of the Texas State Historical Association, compared my diplomacy to that of Stephen F. Austin, when awarding me a totally undeserved honor for philanthropy at the association's 2006 gala. Bryan said that both Austin and I were better known for other qualities, but that diplomacy was our most important contribution.

In 2008, diplomacy was missing at both the state and federal levels. In the case of former Republican House Speaker Tom Craddick, the *Austin American-Statesman* noted that his negotiating style consists of saying "No." The goal, as the late political advisor Tony Proffitt described it, is to win, not to work out problems. Harvey Kronberg, editor of the *Quorum Report*, described it this way: Speaker James E. "Pete" Laney, a Democrat from Hale Center who served in the House for thirty-four years, ten of them as Speaker, legislated from the center. Major bills started as middle-of-the-road proposals and floor leaders "crawfished to the right to pick up some votes and crawfished to the left to pick up others," Kronberg said. The result was a bill with broad support. With the big Republican majority, Kronberg noted, Craddick followed the Tom DeLay example of starting with a bill that had been drafted by a socially conservative Republican think tank. There was as little compromise as possible—votes were often down straight party lines.

The result was a lack of civility, bad legislation, unmet needs, and partisan divisions between the factions that are too deep to bridge. It is a poor way to govern. House members evidently thought so too, because in 2009 they ousted Craddick and elected Joe Straus of San Antonio, a moderate Republican.

Poor Tom DeLay

It is one of the pleasant ironies of politics that Republicans lost the Fort Bend County seat occupied by Majority Leader DeLay in 2006 because of a law of their own making. DeLay was not only one of the most abusive majority leaders of the U.S. House in history, he was also one of the most corrupt. He was forced to resign his position because of indictments and charges against him. Understandably, Republicans wanted to also remove his name from the ballot in the next election.

In the early 1980s, both parties sometimes ignored their own voters in the primaries and replaced candidates whom the voters had nominated ("stalking horses") with candidates more acceptable to the party leadership. In 1983, when I was presiding over the Senate, the legislature passed Senate Bill 122 to stop this practice. After the 1980 primaries, seven candidates from both major political parties, including four state representative candidates, two district judge candidates, and one court of civil appeals candidate, declined their nominations. In 1982, ten winning candidates declined nominations.

In explaining his bill, the sponsor, Sen. Kent Caperton, said it would end the practice of replacing nominees who decide not to run "not through ineligibility, not through unavailability to serve, or not through any other reason than political considerations."

Needless to say, the brief filed by the Democrats to keep DeLay on the ballot in 2006 cited this bill. They won. DeLay's name was on the ballot, and Democrats claimed the seat.

12

Artesia Hall

O N January 13, 2004, I picked up a voicemail.
"My name is Beth Warren," the voice said. "I have been
doing some research on the Internet and found that Pat Smith
and Joseph Farrar sued you as lieutenant governor back in the 1970s or
80s over an academy and some schools that were closed down in Liberty,
Texas, and Houston. I was sent to Dr. Farrar when I was sixteen years
old, and was beaten, thrown around, threatened and given a gun and told
to kill myself."

Warren then explained that she now lived in Midland and was the mother
of seven children, one of whom was getting a doctorate at Texas Tech.

"I grew up and out of that after I nearly lost my life. After all that
happened to me, life drifted by, and I tried to set it all aside and get it out
of my mind. I nearly lost my life. I know that they tried to come back and
say that the schools were wrongly closed. I'd like to get some information
about what went on and why they sued y'all."

It was a fairly dramatic reminder of my attempt thirty-one years earlier to prevent harm to children incarcerated in an East Texas institution
named Artesia Hall. It was just one of the unregulated "schools" at that
time at which the owners applied their own primitive ideas of discipline
and sanitary conditions. Eventually the legislature would completely over-
haul childcare institutional licensing.

It also resulted in lawsuits against me, seventeen years of litigation,
and a split decision by the U.S. Supreme Court.

I remember hearing about Artesia Hall in vivid fashion from an East
Texas undertaker after a speech I gave in Anahuac. In fact, I think I first
heard of it from news accounts in June 1973, when the owners of the institution were indicted for murder.

Artesia Hall was a private school for emotionally disturbed children,
some of whom were referred by juvenile courts. It was a collection of mo-
bile homes and temporary buildings in the East Texas piney woods near
Liberty. The school was used by columnist Molly Ivins as an example of
why Texas is the "National Laboratory for Bad Government."

At Artesia Hall, children were punished by midnight marches, duck walking, ditch digging (with beatings), confinement in a 4' by 4' chain link cage and cold water "GI baths" where they were scrubbed with wire brushes until they bled.

Joseph D. Farrar, who ran Artesia Hall, was a monster. On June 15, 1973, he was arrested and put in the Liberty County jail. He was accused of willful failure to administer proper medical treatment and to provide timely hospitalization for seventeen-year-old Danna Annette Hvolboll, who had swallowed insecticide. Hvolboll's schoolmates said that when Hvolboll started shaking, she was slapped, forced to sing and vomit, and marched around the grounds. The next day, they said, she was kept strapped to a bed to restrain what appeared to be convulsions. Too weak to dress for church, she was taken away in a car by Dr. Farrar. Hvolboll died in Houston at Ben Taub Hospital on November 13 or 14. Farrar was charged with murder.

My chief of staff, Steve Oaks, had known Farrar from the days when Steve was a student at the College of William and Mary, where Farrar was dean of students. Steve told me that Farrar was bad news, that Farrar had been fired from William and Mary and later fired as headmaster of a school from which he stole money. When Steve learned that Farrar had set himself up as headmaster of a school in Harris County, he warned some Harris County judges about Farrar, and they stopped sending youngsters there.

The murder charge put Artesia Hall in the headlines once again, but the school was no stranger to the news in Liberty County. On May 8, 1971, for example, a game warden picked up three escapees from the school. They described beatings, hair pulling, a wire cage called "the cooler," and wire brush baths. They begged not to be returned, but Farrar apparently prevailed, and the three were returned to his custody at Artesia Hall.

Soon after that, however, Liberty County Attorney A. J. Hartell filed suit to close the home for operating without a license. But just three days before the hearing to close Artesia Hall, the state Department of Public Welfare granted it a license (that turned out to be an interesting story— more about that later).

I think that John Whitmire, a young state representative from Houston, also talked to me about Artesia Hall. He said there was an "atmosphere of intimidation and repression that suffused the whole place."

When I saw the news stories in June 1973, I asked Oaks to find out what he could from Commissioner of Public Welfare Raymond Vowell. By June 19 welfare department staffer George Campbell was traveling to East Texas.

The next day, I asked Vowell to come to my office to explain what he was doing to protect the children at the school. We got on the phone with Campbell. He reported that the atmosphere was repressive and that abuse was likely still going on.

I told Vowell to use all available resources, including the Attorney General's Office, to take decisive action.

The same day, I put out a news release that said: "I am appalled and deeply distressed that this facility ever operated with the approval of the Department of Public Welfare in view of the serious charges that have been made about this operation over the last several years, charges that are a matter of public record.

"If there is no clear evidence of infraction of the licensing regulations, then we can only conclude that there has been serious dereliction of duty to see to it that the licensing regulations were drafted strongly enough to protect the wellbeing of those unable to protect themselves. This problem is part of a larger failure of DPW to establish effective regulations governing licensing of child care and foster care facilities."

I then asked Sen. Chet Brooks, D-Houston, chairman of the Senate Human Resources Committee, to review the state's licensing responsibilities. "As Lieutenant Governor of the state, I assure you that I am going to exercise the authority of this office to whatever extent is necessary to achieve and maintain the integrity and accountability of the institutional program licensing by this state."

That same day, I asked my staff assistant Harry Ledbetter to go with John Whitmire on a fact-finding mission to Liberty County. They left the next morning, June 21, on a state plane with two assistant attorneys general and welfare department staff.

I followed up with a letter to Vowell asking that the department immediately make sure that all the children were accounted for. I wanted him to contact the children's parents, advise them of the situation, and see if they wanted their children returned home. In addition, I asked that Vowell work with Attorney General John Hill to revoke the license at Artesia Hall and guarantee the safety and well-being of the children.

That night, after giving a speech to a Trinity River Authority awards dinner in Anahuac, Jim Sterling, a Dayton funeral director, came up to talk to me. He was foreman of the grand jury that had investigated Artesia Hall. Sterling was more than a little frustrated. According to Sterling, local efforts had failed to close the school. Local requests for an investigation by the Texas Department of Public Safety had resulted in a relatively clean bill of health for the institution. As for the misdemeanors discovered, Sterling said later, the DPS investigator "told me it was just trivia we are bothering them with."

Sterling was a friend of Gov. Dolph Briscoe (he had managed Briscoe's campaign in the area), and he wanted me to tell the governor about the abuses at Artesia Hall. I was listening to a funeral home operator who was accustomed to scraping bodies off the pavement, and he was horrified by what was happening at Artesia Hall. He told me about children who were forced into cold water baths and scrubbed with wire brushes, who were "disciplined by being stripped, bound in chains, and then put on the end of a long lever of some sort and being repeatedly dipped into a septic tank."

Next morning, I got in touch with Governor Briscoe, who convened a meeting in his office. Janey Briscoe was there, and she was horrified. We decided to go immediately to Artesia Hall for a first-hand look and to ask Attorney General John Hill to investigate.

Briscoe was usually a mild-mannered fellow, but this made him angry. He ordered Vowell to come his office with Hill's first assistant, Larry York. When Vowell got there, Governor Briscoe asked him why Artesia Hall was still operating. He wanted immediate action to save the lives of children still in the institution.

Briscoe also wanted the commissioner of Mental Health and Mental Retardation to go immediately to Artesia Hall to start the process of putting MHMR staff from Rusk State Hospital in charge of the children.

That afternoon, June 22, I went with Dolph and Janey to Liberty County.

The attorney general and his team were already on the ground and asking State District Judge Clarence Cain for a temporary injunction to close the school and evict Farrar's staff. While we sat in the courtroom, Hill argued that the fifty students at Artesia Hall faced "a clear and present danger of physical and mental intimidation" if the state did not take control. A resident, Joy Whitman, seventeen, testified that Farrar punished her by holding her by the hair and shaking her—"like shaking out a rug." She also detailed other physical punishments that the teenagers were forced to endure.

Cain granted the injunction, and staff from Rusk State Hospital took over operation of Artesia Hall. We left the courthouse and drove out to visit Artesia Hall to talk to the children. While I was there, more students told me about being shaken by the hair.

Janey Briscoe said "The thing that was so bad was the stark fear on those little ones' faces. It was worse than I expected. I had expected a school. It was more like a trailer park."

I mentioned an interesting story about how Artesia Hall got a license just in time to avoid being closed by a Liberty County judge. The House Subcommittee on Human Resources, headed by Rep. Lane Denton of Waco, got to the bottom of that. It turned out that a Houston supervisor of licensing, Ruth Urmy, had refused to license the place. She had visited there in May 1971 because of abuse reports and had gotten permission to start proceedings to close the operation.

At that time Artesia Hall wasn't licensed. In fact, Farrar didn't apply for a license until June 1971. But then he hired W. Kendall Baker, a former member of the State Board of Public Welfare. Baker hired Rep. Price Daniel Jr., son of Gov. Price Daniel and soon to be Speaker of the House, as co-counsel. Next thing, Urmy was removed from the case. Later she was demoted and reprimanded.

Sue Keeney, regional director of social services for DPW's Houston region, took control of the case. She hired a private psychiatrist, Dr. Charles E. Hauser, for a fee of $1,100. Hauser testified that he first reported that Farrar was "uniquely unqualified to operate such a facility." Later he submitted a second report in which he said that, based on Farrar's promises to change his policy on the physical and mental treatment of students, the school could meet "minimum standards."

During his testimony to the House Committee, Hauser stated that he was upset to learn that the second report was the basis for licensing Artesia Hall. Sue Keeney testified that she was instructed by her supervisor to accept the license application after her supervisor met with Farrar.

Kendall Baker, who served on the Public Welfare Board from 1953 to 1971, told the committee he "may have been sold a bill of goods" by Farrar. He acknowledged that "in all probability if it had been someone else besides me, it never would have been licensed."

Artesia Hall was not an isolated case. State welfare officials released the names of thirty-nine unlicensed childcare institutions, and legislators and the media immediately began to compile horror stories about other institutions. A former employee at Kendall Woods Ranch Academy near Boerne said beatings, solitary confinement, and unsanitary conditions were permitted. Whitmire and Rep. Emmett Whitehead of Rusk described Dyer Vocational Training Center near Centerville as a "human warehouse." House investigators visiting the Mary Lee School campus in Travis County found it "dirty and fly infested," with children who said they were fed Spam, crackers, and water and subjected to a 4' by 4' lockup closet for discipline. Meanwhile, the state of Illinois was committing children to the Wimberley Children's Center, where some lived outdoors in tents year-round.

These sorry circumstances developed because some children didn't fit in the niches the state had. They weren't mentally ill enough for a mental hospital and not criminal enough for juvenile detention. Artesia Hall flourished because state licensing standards were ambiguous and largely unenforceable. George Butler, the chairman of the State Board of Public Welfare, had suggested that staff offer aid to unlicensed homes so the welfare department would not appear "so tough." Commissioner Vowell told the committee that "we do not have the expertise to license these kind of places. . . . We don't have the people with the knowledge to handle this."

After Artesia Hall, the welfare department pledged more oversight. They sent a task force to investigate conditions at the Mary Lee School in Travis County. The task force was led by a former DPW regional administrator who had served on the Mary Lee Advisory Board and who may have intervened to help the school get a license. Not surprisingly, the report showed no serious compliance problems. *Houston Chronicle* Bureau Chief Bo Byers wrote that the inspection "borders on the farcical."

A report from former Deputy Assistant Commissioner of Mental Health/Mental Retardation Dr. Len L. Kerr recommended that all state admissions to childcare facilities be halted and that the state establish rigorous standards to enforce regulations.

The House Subcommittee on Human Resources concluded in its report that Artesia Hall did not meet state standards and would not have been licensed without the help of Speaker Daniel and the "subtle pressure" from former welfare board member Baker.

General Hill asked for a special legislative session to address the state's licensing process. Governor Briscoe appointed a task force on Youth Care and Rehabilitation headed by his executive assistant, Charles Purnell.

When the legislative session opened in 1975, a comprehensive reform bill was high on the agenda, but something new had entered the mix. Brother Lester Roloff was in trouble for operating unlicensed homes in the Corpus Christi area. He said the Bible made him do it. Because of him, evangelical Christians opposed any oversight of their institutions.

The House passed a reform bill, but the Senate balked. Sen. Bill Moore of College Station was carrying the bill. He was a lukewarm sponsor at best, and once again lived up to his reputation as one of the more outrageous members of the legislature. When the bill came to the floor for consideration senators were divided, and the vote to suspend the rules (so debate could move forward) failed.

Moore threw the bill in the wastebasket. "I don't want to hear about it any more. I'm through with it," he stated. Moore contended that his bill satisfied everyone "except Brother Lester Roloff and Ron Clower." Senator Clower of Dallas wanted to exempt church-related institutions.

I broke a tie and defeated Clower's amendment. The bill, as passed, made all residential childcare facilities subject to licensing by the state Department of Public Welfare, including those with religious affiliations.

In 1975 Joseph Farrar sued me. Judge Cain, County Attorney Arthur J. Hartell III, and the director and two employees of the Department of Public Welfare were also named defendants. Farrar alleged we had deprived him of his liberty and property without due process by means of conspiracy and malicious prosecution aimed at closing Artesia Hall. He requested $17 million in damages. The trial started in federal district court in Houston on August 15, 1983. Joseph Farrar was dead, but his son, Dale Farrar, and Pat Smith, co-administrators of his estate, were substituted as plaintiffs.

When I took the stand, the attorney for the plaintiffs, former Attorney General Waggoner Carr, worked hard to convince the jury that my actions were political grandstanding by a powerful politician. Carr's constant badgering prompted the judge, Robert O'Conor Jr., to repeatedly sustain objections against argumentative and repetitive questions.

I told the truth—I went to Artesia Hall because I was concerned for the safety of the children living there.

The jury found that all defendants except me had conspired against the plaintiffs but that this conspiracy was not a proximate cause of any injury suffered by the plaintiffs. In my case the jury found that I had "committed an act or acts under color of state law that deprived Plaintiff Joseph Davis Farrar of a civil right." But the jury also determined that my conduct was not "a proximate cause of any damages." The judge ruled that the plaintiffs would take nothing and the parties would bear their own costs.

Zeke Zbranek represented the county sheriff in this trial. He was the dominant lawyer in the trial. By that time he was a legendary lawyer in Liberty County. In legal circles he became known as "the Liberty Lion." I first knew Zeke Zbranek when he represented Liberty County in the legislature in the 1950s. After famed Houston defense attorney Percy Foreman lost four cases against Zbranek, Percy said, "If Patrick Henry had ever gone to Liberty, he would have taken death."

In 1985, the Fifth Circuit Court of Appeals affirmed the failure to award damages, noting that the plaintiff had not proved any actual deprivation of a constitutional right. Because the jury had found that I had deprived Farrar of a civil right, however, they remanded the order for a judgment against me for nominal damages.

The plaintiffs wanted me to pay the attorneys' fees, which had been adding up as the case dragged along. In 1987, fourteen years after Artesia Hall was closed, a district judge ruled that I owed $280,000 in fees, $27,932 in expenses, and $9,730 in pre-judgment interest. The Fifth Circuit reversed this ruling in 1991, declaring that the Farrars had failed to achieve their goal, winning only $1 in damages instead of $17 million, and that this "technical victory" was so insignificant that they could not be considered prevailing parties who could collect attorneys fees.

The case was appealed to the U.S. Supreme Court. I had depended on the attorney general to represent me before this, but now I hired my own counsel, former U.S. District Judge Finis Cowan.

The high court ruled in my favor. The decision was a complicated one, but basically it turned on the definition of "prevailing party." The court found that a plaintiff who wins nominal damages is a prevailing party (Farrar) but that nominal damages also may highlight the plaintiff's failure to prove actual, compensable injury. Furthermore, a test of reasonableness must be applied, based on the amount and nature of damages, so that the court may lawfully award low fees or no fees.

The court determined "When a plaintiff recovers only nominal damages because of his failure to prove an essential element of his claim for monetary relief . . . the only reasonable fee is usually no fee at all." The Fifth Circuit judgment that no attorneys' fees be awarded was affirmed.

In her concurring opinion, Justice Sandra Day O'Connor remarked: "If ever there was a plaintiff who deserved no attorney's fees at all, that plaintiff is Joseph Farrar. He filed a lawsuit demanding 17 million dollars from six defendants. After 10 years of litigation and two trips to the Court of Appeals, he got one dollar from one defendant. As the Court holds today, that is simply not the type of victory that merits an award of attorney's fees." I have always liked Justice O'Connor. The legal nightmare took seventeen years to resolve and was set to rest long after many people had forgotten Artesia Hall. It was expensive, time-consuming, and worrisome, but I'm quite sure I would do the same thing over. That phone call in 2004 was a heartwarming reminder that some had not forgotten.

"God bless whoever closed down those schools," Beth Warren said thirty years later. "I think I was one of the ones who survived."

13

Déjà Vu All Over Again

THE MOST PERSISTENT AND PERHAPS THE MOST IMPORTANT ISSUE in state government is how to pay for public schools and public universities. In both cases the cost is partly paid for by money appropriated by the legislature, and partly paid for by somebody else. In the case of public schools "somebody else" is the school district property taxpayer. At the universities it is the students (or their families) who pay tuition with pre-tax dollars.

When "somebody else" complains loudly enough, the legislature listens. It tells the school districts they can't raise taxes and the universities they can't raise tuition. But then it doesn't appropriate state aid to make up the difference. That would be extravagant!

Never mind that people with more education make more money and pay more taxes. Never mind the quality of life of the minimum-wage earner. Never mind that neglecting education today increases prison and welfare costs tomorrow. Some future legislature will have to worry about that. Education is an expensive labor-intensive enterprise that gets caught in the middle and starved. But as expensive as education is, it's cheaper than ignorance.

When I took office in 1973, the *Rodriguez v. San Antonio Independent School District* case had raised serious questions about the educational finance problem. Later, the state Supreme Court threw out school finance laws in 1989 and 1992. As University of Texas at Austin Law School Dean Mark Yudof (later University of Texas chancellor and now University of California chancellor) and I once wrote "School finance reform in Texas is like a Russian novel. The story line runs across generations, the plot is complex, the prose is tedious, and everybody dies in the end."

I spent a good deal of time when I was lieutenant governor trying to work out a way to pay for public schools that would pass the legislature and please the courts. The legislature was the easy part. After the bill passed, the lawsuit was usually filed before the ink was dry on the governor's signature.

During the 1970s and 1980s the challenges came from property-poor schools, doomed to fall behind their wealthy brethren because the state did not appropriate enough money to close the gap. Edgewood, a property-poor school district in San Antonio, was usually the lead plaintiff. When the state Supreme Court ruled in *Edgewood Independent School District v. Kirby* in 1989, it noted that Edgewood had $38,854 in property wealth per student while Alamo Heights, also in Bexar County, had $570,109.

In the 1990s there was a new twist. *West Orange-Cove v. Neeley* was brought by wealthier school districts watching their tax dollars siphoned off to poorer districts under what was called the state's "Robin Hood" plan. With their taxing capacity maxed out, these districts faced a growing fiscal bind.

A trial court judge decided in 2004 that the state support was so inadequate that it violated the state constitution's requirement for an "adequate" system of public schools. The Supreme Court declined to go along, determining that the amount paid by the state per student was constitutional. But since most local school districts tax property at or close to the state maximum of $1.50 per $100 of valuation to "provide a general diffusion of knowledge," the court ruled that the state had created an unconstitutional statewide property tax.

The Texas Constitution makes the state the equalizer of educational opportunity. Given the notorious complexity of school finance and the fierce emotions that naturally surround the subject, the task of equalizing is not easy.

Our system of paying for public schools combines state dollars with local property tax dollars and, by its very nature, gets out of balance from time to time. That is why the legislature has had to change the system about every four years during the last two decades.

Jobs we once had that could be done with a high school or associate degree have been outsourced, generally moved to Asia or elsewhere where labor is cheap. Even those high-value jobs we thought we owned have gone to countries with highly educated, low-wage talent.

But we can't outsource education.

Add to that the great shift in our population that has been documented so well by former state demographer (later director of the U.S. Census) Steve Murdock. Hispanics are the fastest growing ethnic group in Texas. Statistically, Hispanics and African Americans do not do as well in school as the largest minority group—Anglos. The smallest group, Asians, tend to do well. In 2005, the Texas Higher Education Coordinating Board reported that the percentage of Hispanic high school graduates going to

Hobby with Bill Ratliff when Ratliff was sworn in as lieutenant governor in 2000.
Photograph courtesy Senate Media Services.

college was not increasing despite a concentrated effort called "Closing the Gap" begun in 2000.

Hispanics, again statistically speaking, tend to be concentrated in property-poor school districts. As Ross Perot said in 1984, when he headed a school finance commission, "What are we going to do with those people—send them to Arkansas?" His point was that we had better figure out how to close the performance gap between demographic groups or suffer the consequences. Twenty years later we still hadn't figured it out.

When State District Judge John Dietz found the school finance system unconstitutional in September 2004, he noted that the state's share of school funding had dropped from 80 percent in 1949 to 38 percent in 2004. Under the "Robin Hood" system, wealthier districts were helping to pay to educate children in poorer districts, and the state's share appropriated by the legislature continued to decrease. That is called saving the taxpayers' money.

School finance is pretty simple. Either the state pays or local districts pay. If the state pays less, local districts pay more. The question is whether you want to pay for schools with the state sales tax or local property taxes. If the state pays less and prohibits districts from paying more, the schools are likely to be inadequate. But it is possible to have a high degree of equity that will not impact local taxes if the state pays its share. In recent years, as with higher education, the state did not pay its share, and school districts such as Austin started shipping one-fourth of their tax revenue ($136 million in 2004–2005) to poor districts. Out of whack? You bet.

Former state senator and lieutenant governor Bill Ratliff, one of the best public officials Texas has ever had, wrote the 1993 school finance bill. This was the bill that became known as "Robin Hood" and was challenged in the courts in later years. "I don't see anything wrong with the current school finance system, had the state continued to fund its proportionate share," he said in August 2004.

When I was in office, school finance occupied a lot of time and effort and cost a lot of money, but rarely did our product last more than a year or two.

The modern history of school finance begins with the Gilmer-Aikin Act of 1949. Gilmer-Aikin created what was called the Minimum Foundation Program, a system to fund schools with a combination of state and local tax revenue, most of which was to come from the state. That act remained in place for nearly twenty-five years. But Texas changed a lot in that quarter-century. It became an urban state, and urban real estate is a lot more valuable than rural land. Energy prices increased greatly. The tax base and revenues in urban and energy-rich rural districts soared.

In 1975, the legislature passed a $638 million bill that increased state school funding and attempted to bring about more equity. It created an enrichment fund for poor school districts and a very limited guaranteed yield. Guaranteed yield is a means of balancing local tax effort with state funds to create a set amount of funding for each student. In 1977 we passed a property tax bill that gave us a uniform way to look at property values across the state. That year we were able to add $1 billion to schools. That bill increased state aid to most school districts and allowed up to 800 districts out of 1,100 to decrease taxes. But Texas had become so diverse that it was impossible to create a system that could serve a huge metropolitan district like Houston (my home) and a small rural district like Spring Lake (House Speaker Billy Clayton's home) equally well.

School finance was a major task for the 1984 school reform effort. I appointed Comptroller Bob Bullock to the Select Committee on Public Education, which was headed by Ross Perot. Bullock loved a challenge, and he designed a dramatically different plan. Commissioner of Education Raymon Bynum immediately told the legislature that Bullock's plan would mean a tax increase in half of the school districts.

The Mexican-American Legal Defense Fund (MALDEF) filed suit against the school finance system in May 1984, mainly to support Bullock's plan. In June, the legislature increased aid to poor schools and passed a $4.6 billion tax bill to pay for it.

The next year, MALDEF sued again, calling the legislature's 1984 effort "intolerably illegal." In 1990, after the state Supreme Court finally agreed with MALDEF and overturned the existing school finance system, the legislature met in four acrimonious sessions before increasing state support to public schools by $528 million. MALDEF was already on the way back to the courthouse. In 1991, the state Supreme Court also decided the new law didn't pass muster because it didn't fix the property tax system.

And on and on. After a 2004 ruling, the legislature again labored and came up with a plan to cut property taxes but not improve education. As we said, the prose is tedious, and everyone dies in the end.

14

No Pass, No Play

YOU NEED A GOOD SENSE OF IRONY TO ENJOY POLITICS. Consider this: The most extensive education reform bill in Texas became law because Gov. Mark White had promised a teacher pay raise and didn't have the money to pay for it. But after he gave teachers the pay raise he had promised—and a tax bill to pay for it—they campaigned against him, and he was defeated for re-election.

Mark White was state attorney general when he beat Republican Gov. Bill Clements in 1982. It was a banner election year for Democrats. U.S. Sen. Lloyd Bentsen and I teamed up to finance a massive get-out-the-vote effort that was credited with electing not only White but a whole slate of promising Democrats, including state Treasurer Ann Richards.

White promised a number of things during his campaign, including a teacher pay raise. He wanted a two-year 24 percent increase but no new taxes. Even before the legislature came into session, I told Mark that there couldn't be a teacher pay raise without new taxes. In fact, the 1983 session ended with neither. The Senate was willing to support a pay raise and the tax increase it would take to pay for it, but the House, which has to originate tax bills, was opposed, and White was not at all excited about endorsing a tax bill.

It's possible that the idea for the Select Committee on Public Education came from Comptroller Bob Bullock, who suggested a study of school finance. Speaker Gib Lewis, who balked at the teacher pay raise, liked that idea. But White expanded that idea into a thorough study of the state education system. He found exactly the right man to head it: Ross Perot. Understand that in 1983, Perot had not yet run for president twice or become a not-entirely-complimentary household word. He was still just a Dallas billionaire, a Republican, and a successful entrepreneur who had created Electronic Data Systems.

As head of the Select Committee, Perot's charge was to write a plan to insure that Texas schools were up to the demands of a technology-based economy. He was expected to tackle not just teacher pay but merit pay, plus teacher competence, curriculum, classroom discipline, equitable

Bill Malone

Hobby swearing in Ann Richards as state treasurer, January 1983. *Photograph by Bill Malone, copy in William P. Hobby Sr. Family Papers, Dolph Briscoe Center for American History, di_05737.*

finance, school finance, the dropout rate, and more. And when that was done, he needed to tell us how to find the money to pay for everything.

I served on the committee, and I appointed some distinguished educators, Comptroller Bob Bullock, and state Sen. Carl Parker, who, as chairman of the Senate Education Committee, would have to carry the legislation the committee recommended.

The committee did a superb job. Select committees have huge advantages in paving the way for controversial bills—they study issues, build support coalitions, ferret out the opposition, and work out some of the rough spots.

Perot was a standout leader. His charge was broad, and he made it broader. He was fearless, and he was quotable. He was a technology leader, and he knew that Texas's oil and gas prosperity was fading fast. The state needed to spend more on the minds of its people.

Ross Perot, Mark White, and Bill Hobby, 1984. *William P. Hobby Sr. Family Papers, Dolph Briscoe Center for American History, di_05952.*

He took on high school athletics, hammer and tongs: "If the people of Texas want Friday night entertainment instead of education, let's find out about it," he said at a public hearing in Austin. Carl Parker backed him up. He told the principals that the legislature "is scratching to put the funds together to keep our school system from being declared unconstitutional, and you're out there saying, 'Keep sending that state money because we need to spend our local money on sixteen football coaches and matching shirts for them so we can be the big boy in the district.'"

Perot said there were little schools with sixty teachers and twelve coaches. When a principal objected that such a situation was "rare," Perot retorted, "So is a one-legged tap-dancer, but it happens."

The committee came in with a list of recommendations that covered the waterfront—school organization and management, electing the State Board of Education, state funding, alternative schools and discipline management, teacher education and testing, class sizes, the curriculum, textbooks, vocational and special education, and, of course, extracurricular activities. Mark White, to his everlasting credit, strongly supported its recommendations.

The special session of 1984 began on June 4. That gave us thirty days to both reform education and pass a tax bill. Hardly anyone thought we could do it, much less produce a bill that Milton Goldberg, chairman of the national education task force that produced the "Nation at Risk" report called the "hallmark for the nation."

Teachers groups, principals groups, coaches, school district coalitions—you name it—were opposed. It was a miracle of sorts that all of us from the governor on down could pull together so effectively.

Perot set the stage and then left town. But he had hired several adroit lobbyists to represent the committee—Rusty Kelley, Jack Wheeler, and his very capable attorney Tom Luce were on hand day and night.

I had the easy job. The Senate at that time was remarkably united, with a substantial Democratic majority and seasoned leaders like Carl Parker, Ray Farabee, and Kent Caperton. I referred the bill to the Committee of the Whole Senate, a strategy well suited to complicated issues in short, single-issue special sessions when things have to move fast. I had done the same with redistricting in 1981.

In the House, Gib Lewis had a harder job. He had 150 members, and legislators don't like voting against their school districts and they don't like voting for tax bills. "No Pass, No Play" was hard enough, but that was resolved in a sensible fashion by requiring students to get a passing grade on all their courses in each six-week period in order to be eligible to play sports or to participate in other extracurricular activities.

The issue that threatened to derail the train was the teacher competency test. (I took the test—it was about junior high level.) The four teachers groups in the state first signed on to the bill, but three of them came off the train, supposedly over the pay raise mechanism. One of them, the Texas State Teachers Association, held a news conference and the president-elect, Becky Brooks, said, "Even a dog knows the difference between being stumbled over and being kicked."

Bear in mind that the bill was adding $3 billion to public education and increasing teacher salaries substantially. Brooks took issue because that wasn't enough money to completely fund the career ladder created by the bill.

Days before the clock was going to run out on the session, I called the teachers groups into my office and asked for an apology. They declined. I told them to leave and not come back, ever. "Don't forget your briefcase," I told one of them. Sen. John Montford, who was at the meeting, described it as "like the Alamo, but without the blood." Betty King remembered hearing me in her office down the hall. "We could hear him shout in our offices—scared us to death. Never before or since have I heard him explode that way," she said.

The bill passed fairly easily in the Senate, but only after a fourteen-hour session in the House. Speaker Lewis demonstrated firm leadership with every blow of his gavel.

That left a tax bill, a $4.8 billion tax bill, the first in thirteen years and the largest in state history at that time. It included money for education reform as well as highway improvements.

It took an eleventh-hour crisis, all-night meetings, and the threat of a last-minute filibuster to finally pass the bill. About twenty-four hours before the session would end, the House unanimously rejected the bill the Senate had passed. The bill the House sent us taxed a number of businesses, advertising, repairs, amusements, and other services. The Senate substituted a broader-based solution—a one-fourth cent increase in the sales tax.

Not only did the House reject this tax bill, it refused to create a conference committee to resolve differences. The Speaker and I created a "non-conference committee" that would hold "non-meetings." White called people into his office, and we worked nearly all night to find something acceptable to both sides. In the end we reduced the sales tax to one-eighth of a cent and extended the sales tax to newspapers. And I was a lifelong newspaperman!

Then Sen. John Leedom, a Republican, threatened to filibuster it to death. I finally found a way to dissuade him by finding $32 million in surplus at the Texas Department of Corrections, which allowed us to eliminate the proposed tax on car and truck repairs. There was applause in both houses when the tax bill passed.

House Bill 72, the education reform bill, was historic legislation. But in some respects it didn't move the ball very far. In the end, Texas still had the shortest school year of all the states, and our students spent fewer hours in class than students in other states.

But that bill set statewide standards—uniform testing in the third, sixth, and twelfth grades. It tested teachers and beefed up teacher education. "No Pass, No Play" set academic requirements for students who wanted to participate in sports or other extracurricular activities.

Remarkably, most of the reforms initiated in House Bill 72 persist to this day. The teacher test was never repeated, but the statewide student tests are a hallmark of Texas education. They also served as the model for President George W. Bush's "No Child Left Behind" federal legislation.

Limits on class size are still in effect, with only twenty-two children permitted in kindergarten through fourth grade classes. Teachers will argue that the limits have been watered down with a generous waiver policy granted by the Texas Education Agency, but the law remains unchanged.

The state-funded preschool classes that we started for four-year-olds were extended to three-year-olds in the 1989–1990 session. This program is still available now, as it was then, to those who are economically disadvantaged or non-English speaking. However, school districts are not required to offer pre-kindergarten to three-year-olds, and they are exempt from offering pre-kindergarten to four-year-olds if fewer than fifteen children qualify.

The extraordinary thing is that "No Pass, No Play," one of the most contentious provisions of House Bill 72, continues to exist in Texas law and practice. There were early attempts to unravel it in the legislative sessions after 1984, but, by and large, school districts learned to live with it. The world did not end, and Friday night football did not perish from the earth.

In fact, in 2007 the legislature closed a loophole in the law that allowed school districts to exempt courses from those included in the "No Pass, No Play" requirement. A *Dallas Morning News* investigation had discovered that some districts were exempting elective and vocational courses such as professional baking, jewelry-making, photography, choir, and theatre production from "No Pass, No Play." The 2007 bill limited exemptions to advanced placement and honors courses in core subjects such as mathematics and English.

In 2009, *Austin American-Statesman* political columnist Gardner Selby called the special session of 1984 one of "life-changing significance." "I'd suggest no governor since has called such a meaningful session, though there might be opportunities ahead to act in realms where Texas lags and leaders get a firm bead on what to do," he wrote.

The praise came too late for Mark White. His education reforms were popular, but the tax increase wasn't. To make matters worse, in 1986 the state's economy was going south in a hurry. The Texas State Teachers Association opposed him. Bill Clements, who got a drubbing from White in 1982, resurfaced with deep pockets and a yen for revenge. White lost the election.

Governor White's education reforms have had a lasting impact on Texas public education. But teachers, who were among the major beneficiaries of those reforms, made it their mission to defeat the man responsible. They succeeded.

15

The Capitol Makeover

THE TEXAS CAPITOL IS A MAGNIFICENT BUILDING, grand in size, handsome in proportions, and ideally located on a rise of land at the head of Austin's Congress Avenue. As most Texans know, it is taller than the U.S. Capitol. In fact, it is the largest state capitol in the nation.

This imposing edifice was begun in 1881, at a time when Texas was not particularly prosperous. It was paid for not in dollars, but in land—the 3 million acres in the Texas Panhandle that became the XIT Ranch. The structure was completed eight years later, a monument to the grand dreams of Texans for their seat of government.

My grandfather, Edwin E. Hobby, was a state senator when the legislature voted to build the Capitol. Later, he worked in the building as a commissioner of the state Supreme Court.

I love the details of the Capitol. For example, the stairway that leads from the first floor to the hallway behind the Senate chamber has a first flight of thirty-two steps, one for each senator and the lieutenant governor. The second flight has eight steps representing the statewide constitutionally elected officials: the governor, attorney general, land commissioner, comptroller, treasurer, and three railroad commissioners.

By the time I served as lieutenant governor, the grand old building was showing its age. Our Capitol was, in fact, a firetrap.

At that time, the Capitol had apartments for the Speaker of the House and the lieutenant governor. Diana and I did not live in the apartment. We occasionally allowed guests to stay there and used the dining room for entertaining. On one of those occasions, on February 7, 1983, my daughter Kate was in Austin to accept two championship awards from the Texas Hunter and Jumper Association. Kate was one of the best young riders in Texas (still is, but she isn't quite so young). After the banquet, she and some of her riding friends stayed in the lieutenant governor's apartment.

That night, a fire started in the apartment. The blaze was detected at 5:25 a.m. by a heat sensor, and four Capitol security officers responded immediately. One of them, Joel Quintanilla, tried to kick open the door to the apartment library when it exploded out at him. He was burned on his arms, hands, and face. Officers Arthur Patterson and Wilfred V. Spinks got him into the Senate chamber and later to a hospital.

Meanwhile, Officer James Mitchell beat on the hallway door and woke Kate up—she recalls that she couldn't breathe. She first tried to reach the others who were sleeping in the apartment. Kate was forced back, first by a wall of heat, then when she opened the outside door to the library and saw the whole room engulfed in flames. The officers took her downstairs by elevator.

Meanwhile, Joan and Jim Waterman, who owned the New Caney farm where we kept our horses, were sleeping in a back bedroom. They managed to escape down the back stairs. Matt Hansen, a talented rider and trainer for the Watermans, did not escape. He was found dead of smoke inhalation.

Diana and I were staying in our duplex in West Austin, and we learned of this catastrophe when Kate and the Watermans showed up at the door in their nightclothes, transported there by a passerby. "The Capitol's on fire and Matt's dead," Kate said. I hurried to the Capitol, which was surrounded by fire trucks, police, and emergency crews.

Gov. Mark White came over from the Governor's Mansion. We watched the Capitol burn from the sidewalk outside the east wing. The fire turned the back corridor into an inferno and was barely contained before it got into the Senate chamber. Acting Austin Fire Chief Brady Pool told us, "If I can't control this fire in the next five minutes we'll lose the whole building."

The chief said he had been expecting something like this for a long time. He later told reporters, "We came close to losing the whole complex—I mean the whole shooting match."

Austin firefighters were heroes that morning. They saved the Capitol. "I have never witnessed a more professional performance," I said at the time. "To them goes the credit for saving a historic and irreplaceable building."

I called Senate Secretary Betty King, who came immediately. It looked as if we might lose Senate records. We were back at work in the Senate chamber the next morning. We had no heat, no lights, and no sound system because there was no electricity, and there was a strong smell of smoke. Betty King called the roll wearing a suede coat, and most of the senators wore their overcoats.

I moved my office to the third floor. The Senate staff, whose offices had been on the second floor, moved into offices elsewhere in the building—Secretary of State John Fainter found us space in his offices. The ten senators whose first- and third-floor offices had been damaged took up temporary digs in a state office building on Barton Springs Road. They stayed there only as long as it took to move some small state agencies out of the Capitol. No senator wants to be that far from the action.

We soon learned that the fire was caused by defective wiring in a television set. Zenith, which manufactured the set, settled for $1.3 million after Attorney General Jim Mattox sued the company.

We didn't miss a day of work. In less than three weeks the House and the Senate approved $7 million for fire damage repairs. The fire was a gigantic wake-up call. The dangerous condition of the Capitol could no longer be ignored. It had cost one life and very nearly others.

Texas lost its first two capitols to fire, one in 1881 and one in 1899 (when the second one burned, the offices had already been moved into the present building). We came dangerously close to losing another because we had ignored the warnings. One of them came from Sen. George C. Purl in 1931, who said: "That the Capitol of Texas is a firetrap is obvious to any casual observer." He was just one who tried and failed to get appropriations for repairs.

The Capitol originally housed all of state government and about 350 people. When I was in office, state government was a lot bigger. Most of its offices and staff were located outside the Capitol building, but there were more than 1,300 people working in the Capitol itself. To house them, the building had been subdivided, double-decked, and partitioned. The open basement, passageways, restrooms, and even the 1930 State Treasury vault had been converted into warrens of offices. False ceilings had been built to carry wiring and air conditioning ducts. Many of the original firewalls, well-designed to stop the spread of fire and smoke, had been removed or drilled through. Safe passage out of the building had been heavily compromised by the haphazard renovations. Much later we discovered that the sprinkler system was useless; the main valve had been shut off at some time in the past. Furthermore, stately and significant architectural features had been buried under twentieth-century ticky-tack.

Governor White wanted to proceed immediately with a complete Capitol restoration, hoping to have it completed by 1986, when Texas would celebrate the sesquicentennial of its independence from Mexico. His plan ran into opposition, not just because of its hefty price tag, but because legislators feared being permanently moved out of the Capitol. A great deal of the double-decking and partitioning accommodated more offices for legislators and staff.

White's proposal emerged from the legislature stripped of his restoration plan, but the bill did create a State Preservation Board headed by the

Hobby gives a tour of the Capitol reconstruction, January 12, 1986. Sen. J. E. "Buster" Brown is to Hobby's left and Pete Snelsen is on the right. *William P. Hobby Sr. Family Papers, Dolph Briscoe Center for American History, di_05955.*

governor. The board was given the authority to hire an architect and a curator responsible for the care, preservation, and restoration of the building and grounds. These steps were important developments in professionalizing the maintenance of the Capitol.

The first architect of the Capitol was Roy Eugene Graham, who had directed historic preservation at the University of Virginia and been resident architect at Colonial Williamsburg. The curator, Bonnie Campbell, had been curator at the California State Capitol.

Graham directed the restoration of the east wing. I was determined that the work would respect this cultural landmark. I was even more convinced of this course when construction uncovered four beautiful original arches in the east corridor. I had decided early on that this corridor would contain a reception room, a committee room, and my staff offices. There would be no lieutenant governor's apartment. The arches, enclosed with glass, became a central feature of this majestic space. We searched for and found authentic American Renaissance antiques to furnish the new rooms. The restoration, most of it done while the Senate was in recess, was completed by 1985. The new meeting room was named for my mentor, Lt. Gov. Ben Ramsey.

As I had hoped, the restoration of the east corridor became the model for the entire Capitol restoration. In 1988 we appointed a new architect, Allen McCree, and charged him with finalizing a restoration plan. McCree turned out to be a good P.R. man. He took legislators on weekly tours to show them the dangers lurking behind the pink granite façade: faulty wiring, toxic asbestos insulation, and leaky plumbing, to name a few. During one tour, an obliging rainstorm demonstrated just how badly the roof leaked.

The master plan developed by Ford Powell & Carson and other firms produced an inspired solution to the space problem. The plan called for the construction of a large annex to house offices, committee rooms, support services, and even parking. But, unlike the other pink granite government buildings that sometimes impair the view of the Capitol, this structure would be underground. What came to be called the Capitol Extension freed up space in the original building for modern heating, plus electrical, telecommunication, and plumbing lines.

The plan called for the extension to be constructed first. When it was completed, legislators would be moved out of the Capitol into the extension wing by wing, while the building was restored inside and out.

During this planning process, the governor, Speaker, and I appointed representatives to monitor the planning and keep us apprised. They were Mary Jane Mansford, Becky Perrine, and Saralee Tiede. They did their job well enough to become known as "The Witches." If you look carefully at the pavers over the Capitol Extension, you'll see one dedicated to "The Witches." Then, as we were working on this complicated process, good fortune smiled on us in the person of Dealey Decherd Herndon. Dealey's late father, Ben Decherd, was chairman of the board of the A. H. Belo Corporation, which owned the *Dallas Morning News* and a number of television stations. Her husband, David Herndon, had been secretary of state. Dealey was a genius not only at preservation but at project management. She had been administrator of the group that helped Governor and Mrs. Clements restore the Governor's Mansion. She had been appointed as the citizen member of the State Preservation Board. And she loved the Capitol.

Dealey was the force behind the Capitol restoration and became executive director of the State Preservation Board in 1991. When the Capitol restoration was finished, she started Herndon, Stauch & Associates,

Hobby painting a wall as part of the Capitol reconstruction, 1985. *William P. Hobby Sr. Family Papers, Dolph Briscoe Center for American History, di_05957.*

a construction firm that specialized in historic construction. She sold the firm in 2006 and in 2008 returned to the preservation board to oversee restoration of the Governor's Mansion after it was destroyed by fire.

Most of the actual construction on the Capitol Extension and the Capitol restoration started after I left office in January 1991. The result showed the brilliance of both the plan and its execution. The 667,000-square-foot extension is anything but a dark underground den of offices. Its wide corridors are well lit by skylights, and a two-story rotunda gives a stunning view of the Capitol dome. The architectural features, from pilasters, columns, and railings to a terrazzo depiction of the state seal, echo the historic grace of the Capitol. Yet this very busy and accommodating building is all but invisible to those looking at the original Capitol. Among its amenities is a spacious cafeteria that replaces the dingy, crowded, and dirty eating space in the Capitol called not-so-affectionately, the "Linoleum Club."

When the Capitol Extension was complete, work began to stabilize and retrofit the Capitol itself. Exterior walls were re-mortared, deteriorated metal was replaced, and the dome was repaired. New wiring, plumbing, and security systems were installed, with a fire alarm network high on the priority list. The cost was $188 million. It was worth every penny. The restoration of the Texas Capitol was a magnificent accomplishment, a national model, and a great lesson in how a horrible catastrophe can be a catalyst for good.

16

FROM THIRD WORLD TO WORLD POWER:
A STATE IN TRANSITION

H AVING A ROLE IN GOVERNING TEXAS IS A PRIVILEGE. As people are tired of hearing, the state is larger than many countries, including France, and all other states except Alaska. Its Gross Domestic Product of more than $800 billion would make it a world power. It has counties larger than many states (Rhode Island would fit in Brewster County with room to spare). Texas also has a unique and colorful history—no other state was an independent country. No other state came into the Union with the right to subdivide itself. (Gov. Rick Perry got this one wrong in 2009, when he was entertaining his constituents at an anti-tax rally with talk about seceding from the United States. He told reporters that Texans might get so fed up they would secede. When Texas entered the union, he said, it was with the understanding they could pull out. Wrong. Texas never had that understanding. Texas seceded once, in 1861. It was a bad idea then and now.)

I digress. Texas has been blessed with resources, most notably oil and natural gas, but also with other minerals, timber, grasslands, underground reservoirs, and a seemingly endless sweep of land.

In the 1970s and 1980s when I was privileged to serve as lieutenant governor, Texas began colliding with its limitations. During most of my tenure the biggest issue on the agenda was the state budget. The legislature works on many bills, more than five thousand if you count both Senate and House versions. But the fact is, there is the appropriations bill, which establishes the state budget for the next two years, and all the rest is poetry. The appropriations bill is mainly about three things: education, health and human services, and prisons.

Education includes kindergarten-through-twelfth grade public education and higher education. Heath and human services includes Medicaid, the Children's Health Insurance Program, aid for those with disabilities, and subsistence programs (welfare). So when you hear someone talk about scrubbing the budget, ask them how many teachers they want to cut, how many children they want to go without health care, and how many prison guards they want to cut. How many universities or community colleges does the thrifty legislator want to close in his district?

I scrubbed the budget nine times during the eighteen years I was in office. There is nothing happening on that front now that didn't happen many times in the past and won't many times in the future. Only the names are different. We appointed a commission to reorganize government—the Hobby-Clayton Commission. I appointed a special committee to make health and human services more efficient—the 1980 report was called "The Potential in the Patchwork." I inaugurated zero-based budgeting. We combined agencies, separated agencies, made commissioners elected, made commissioners appointed, imposed hiring freezes, and created budget execution and the bond review commission.

In the end it came down to this: the state of Texas ranks almost dead last in its commitment to every service to its citizens. That is why we are thankful for Mississippi, which usually ranks even lower. For example, according to Texas Sen. Elliot Shapleigh's 2007 report, "Texas on the Brink," Texas ranks forty-sixth on mental health, thirty-eighth on Medicaid, forty-eighth on parks and recreation, forty-eighth on police protection, thirty-eighth on public elementary and secondary education, and forty-second on highways in per capita spending. Ironically, such numbers used to be published by the Comptroller of Public Accounts—"Texas, Where We Stand"—but Comptroller Susan Combs somehow stopped making those numbers available on her website, as the *Austin Chronicle* pointed out.

Shapleigh also noted that Texas ranks forty-sixth in SAT scores. Coincidence? Education is the key to prosperity. Call it a knowledge economy, an information society, or a creative culture—ideas and innovation have kept America strong and productive. Texans may have given lip service to education, but it was not a critical priority in the minds of most Texans during the 1970s and 1980s (or later on, if you keep up with statistics). Many were still caught up in the idea that if you didn't have an oil well you could get one. In many ways Texas was a third-world country dependent on its natural resources and extractive industry, a mindset that does not lead to a sustainable future.

I had some differences of opinion with Gov. Bill Clements on education funding. He hadn't been in office long when he said that higher education had greater waste than any state agency and appointed a committee to look into imposing more financial control. At the time I said "There exists in the Legislature as well a virulent strain of anti-intellectualism that does not reflect well on this state. But it should be the duty of a governor to counteract that sort of thinking rather than to give it redneck reinforcement."

I wasn't very impressed with Bill Clements's knowledge of state budgeting. He had hired businessman Paul Wrotenbery as director of his Budget and Planning Office. Before he had been there long, Wrotenbery invited me over to his office and lectured me about budgeting. I never went to any other meetings with Wrotenbery.

My heroes were Peter O'Donnell, a Dallas philanthropist, and Adm. Bob Inman, former director of the National Security Agency, former deputy chief of the Central Intelligence Agency, then president of the Microelectronics and Computing Corporation (MCC), and later Lyndon B. Johnson Centennial Chair professor at and dean of the LBJ School of Public Affairs. These two men were visionaries who saw a future for Texas built on innovation and knew that innovation depended on a superior system of education. They realized that our future depended not on what came out of the ground or grew on the ground, but what came out of people's heads. They realized, unlike many of our contemporaries, that education required an investment.

The great bust of the mid-1980s was a warning to heed their words. The price of oil plummeted and state revenues with it. At the same time, agriculture—then the second largest component of Texas's GNP—was in a slump. Real estate prices followed the roller coaster downhill. As I write these words in 2009, it all sounds familiar. Déjà vu all over again.

Notice, I said education requires investment. Investment, not contribution. In the 1970s and 1980s we invested in education. When times were good, we invested our surplus and resisted the temptation to cut taxes. When times were bad, we struggled to stay even, at least. It was not easy, because state revenue was headed south along with oil prices (at that time the oil and gas severance tax raised much more money than it does today). Furthermore, Republican Gov. Bill Clements had pledged to cut taxes, not raise them. Speaker of the House Gib Lewis knew he would have a fight with his House members, who feared the political implications of a tax increase. In the Senate we thought it was worth it, and we prevailed.

I passed four tax bills. A tax bill is a terrible thing. There are only three ways to tax. One is to tax money when it comes in. That's an income tax. The Texas Constitution, thanks to an amendment championed by my successor, Bob Bullock, requires that any income tax passed by the legislature be approved by the voters. So we'll never have an income tax in Texas.

You also can tax money while it's in place. That's a property tax, and the constitution prohibits a statewide property tax. The use of the property tax is reserved to local governments, and this tax is plenty high in most places now. About half of property taxes goes to schools. That's why the state's cumulative tax burden kept going up despite Gov. George W.

Bush's $2.5 billion tax cuts in 1995 and 1997. You can also tax money when it's being spent. That's what is called a sales tax. You can call it a sin tax or a motor vehicle tax or a gasoline tax, but it's a sales tax. In Texas, that is the way we raise most of our money for state government—a 6.25 percent sales tax with local option add-ons for home rule cities, community college districts, economic development, or public transit.

When we were faced with the necessity of passing a tax bill in the legislature, we would talk about this idea and that recommendation, and in the end it all came down to the same thing—add a quarter penny to the sales tax. And that isn't all bad, because in Texas we exempt food, housing, and medicine from the sales tax, so the sales tax is not as regressive as in some states. It was always a struggle, down to the last painful vote, but I don't remember any legislator who got beat on the tax issue. Maybe we lived in happier times.

During the 1987 tax fight, when the Senate was holding fast against deep cuts in education, Clements likened Democratic senators to "prairie chickens." "They have a genetic compulsion to thump the ground. And so I think the Democrats have been going through a thumping period that they felt compelled to do. Now hopefully we will get down to serious business." That turned into good fun. We had T-shirts made up that said, "Proud to be a prairie chicken," and senators wore them under their suit coats (with a tie, of course). They also passed a resolution naming the prairie chicken the state grouse and expressing "Heartfelt and sincere gratitude for the contributions of the prairie chicken."

The investment we made in our schools and our universities at that time fueled the technology boom of the 1990s in Austin, Dallas, and Houston. It helped attract biotechnology to Houston and San Antonio and telecommunications to Dallas. Some of our cities, like Austin, became known worldwide for the creative talent of their workforce, their human capital.

Texas rode the boom times up in the 1990s, and then, aided by a state budget surplus, Governor Bush cut taxes. By now we have seen the disastrous impact of his federal tax cuts on the nation. Less well publicized is the impact of Bush's 1995–1997 $2.5 billion tax cut on Texas. Children of working low-income people were cut off from their only access to health insurance. The Department of Protective and Regulatory Service saw caseloads soar, with the result that more children died from violence and neglect, and one grand jury indicted the entire department. Texas's infrastructure, including our once-admired highway system, started—and continued—to decay. And a decade later, in 2007, Texas ranked forty-fourth in expenditures per pupil for public education, according to the U.S. Census Bureau.

But Texas ranked number one in one department. Our public schools lead the nation in the amount of debt, according to the same study.

We need to focus on education. When there is no money, it is a disaster for higher education. In the past ten years the percentage of public higher education funded by the state has declined to about 20 percent. This is because after you fund entitlements, such as health and human services, which are driven by federal funds; after you fund highways, again driven by federal funds; after you fund prisons, which is required since we lock up more people per capita than just about anywhere, the only sizeable pot of money left is higher education. In other words, the budget is balanced on the back of higher education.

In 2003 the state faced a $10 billion shortfall largely because of Governor Bush's tax cuts. Then-Speaker Pete Laney, a Democrat, pointed out that what appeared to be a simple job of cutting $10 billion from a $114 billion budget was actually much more difficult because the legislature has little discretion over dedicated funds or federally matched funds and little desire to cut public safety or public school budgets. Leave those out, Laney reasoned, and the money remaining is only $13.7 billion, and about $10 billion of that goes to higher education. And, in fact, in 2003 the legislature cut just about everything, and the state's share of the higher education budget declined again.

The result has been higher tuition. In other words, those who can afford it will get a college education. I'm not totally opposed to tuition increases—I backed a very unpopular one in 1985 and got mobbed in the Senate chamber by several thousand angry students for doing so. I believe that our very low tuition in Texas deserves a regular review and moderate increases when justified. But in 1999 I also headed the Commission on a Representative Student Body created by all the state universities. Our conclusion was that Texas is in for disaster if we cannot increase the number of Hispanic and African American students who enroll and succeed in higher education. At that time, Texas had 14 percent fewer college graduates in its population than the nation at large. In 1997, only 16 percent of Hispanics were enrolled in higher education (the state is 29 percent Hispanic) and only 7 percent of African Americans (12 percent of the population is African American). These numbers came from the agency that oversees higher education, the Texas Higher Education Coordinating Board. The cost of tuition and books are a major barrier for many of these students.

Meanwhile, the share of the state's contribution to K-12 education declined. In 1993 the state funded 48 percent of the cost. In 2003 it was 38 percent. Does it matter? I think it does. In 2003, Sematech, the semiconductor research consortium located in Austin, decided to locate its next generation research institute in Albany, New York—not because of New York state's lovely climate, but because of a cool $1 billion that the state invested in the State University of New York at Albany's research capacity. Albany studied Austin's success and imitated it. Texas did not compete—could not compete—because Texas was already allowing its higher education system to deteriorate.

In 2004, Texas ranked dead last among the states in the number of young people entering higher education. Will this make a difference? You bet, unless you believe that agriculture and oil wells are going to fuel the state's future.

There is a great philosophical divide on the issue of taxes. Great theories abound on how cutting taxes for the wealthiest 1 percent of the nation will fuel huge economic investment. Unfortunately, we haven't seen that happen. We have seen the public institutions that support our most important resource—educated people—struggle and decline. Our state will decline with it.

But, amazingly enough, Texas does not rank last in tax burden. As the state has reneged on its commitments to schoolchildren, the aged and infirm, and infrastructure, local governments have been forced to pick up the slack. So while the state per capita tax burden is forty-ninth in the nation, the total (state and local) burden is forty-third. Local taxes increase as property values increase.

There are 181 legislators. Almost all of them went to college, many of them to state universities. So it would seem as if higher education would be a slam-dunk, that they would all want to pay for higher education. But it doesn't work that way.

17

THE PRIVATIZATION OF PUBLIC HIGHER EDUCATION

This is my updated version of a lecture I gave at the University of Virginia and at the University of Texas in 2005.

Public support for higher education is declining all over the country. In state after state, support is going down. Tuition is going up.

In 2002 the *Chronicle of Higher Education* reported in an article titled "The Fall of the Flagships" that the University of Texas at Austin and Texas A&M University barely made the *U.S. News & World Report* top fifty. That's right—the top FIFTY. In 2005, UT-Austin was tied for forty-seventh. A&M was sixty-fourth. In 2010, UT-Austin was tied for forty-seventh and A&M was tied for sixty-first.

Mark Yudof, chancellor of the California University System and former chancellor of the University of Texas System, wrote an article for the *Chronicle of Higher Education* in 2002 asking "Is The Public Research University Dead?" In other words, is higher education still a "public good"?

A university degree is worth a lot of money. It is often the difference between a reasonably prosperous style of life and a poor one. So why is education not funded more generously? The answer, I think, goes back to Plato's concerns about democracy. We are now more of a democracy and less of a republic. The political clamor to take care of OUR needs NOW makes investment in the future very difficult and, of course, education is investment in the future. A society can spend all its resources on alleviating poverty, improving health care, and cleaning up the environment, in resolving the human problems of NOW, and invest nothing in the future.

But, in fact, we are even doing less and less about the NOW, much less the future. We are spinning downward. We have already plunged past mediocrity in health care, aid to the poor, and concern for the environment.

Never mind what past generations provided for us in education. What has posterity ever done for me? Education, and higher education in particular, has weak legislative support. That is ironic because virtually all legislators are college graduates, mostly from public universities. Yet public higher and secondary education are being starved.

Let's talk about prestige first. How do we measure it? Never mind whether we should or not, we do.

U.S. News & World Report rankings are eagerly or fearfully awaited, then praised by the winners and criticized by the losers. The bragging rights have value with alumni, regents, legislators, and donors. Universities and political candidates can raise funds more easily when a good poll has just come out. If the poll was bad, well—the sample was biased, or the questions were badly worded, or there must have been a computer error. But the "prestige" issue is really a remnant of elitism or classism that, as a nation, we cannot shake. The early colleges were for the rich, powerful, and connected. There was a class expectation that sons would follow fathers to Virginia, Harvard, and Yale. Virtually no sons (and certainly no daughters) of the poor or the working class went to college.

These early universities had nearly a two-hundred-year head start to create the notion of "prestige" in higher education. Many of those early perceptions remain today. Colleges that catered to the "ruling class," the elite, were prestigious.

In the mid-nineteenth century things began to change. The immigrant population was growing and becoming successful. Immigrants wanted their children to be able to become doctors and lawyers too. They formed Boston College and Fordham and City College of New York, which became, over time, fine universities. But they were not the elite.

Outside of the northeast, large land-grant universities were created and other state universities developed to meet the increasing demand for higher education. These universities tended to focus more on the practical aspects of an education: pre-med, engineering, agriculture, teaching, etc. In regions that had less of a tradition of elite private education (the Midwest and West Coast) public universities quickly developed strong local reputations.

One of the best laws the United States Congress ever passed was the GI Bill of Rights. It remade higher education and, more importantly, the nation. Public universities got a boost when the GI Bill went into effect after World War II and created a great demand for admissions. Soon the measure of prestige became a combination of the old (who went there) and selectivity (how hard it is to get in).

That is pretty much the model we have now, but both personal and institutional wealth have been added to the mix. As demand continued to grow with the baby boomers (and now their echo) and a tremendous increase in the percentage of high school graduates seeking a college education, reputation, money, and demand became the underpinnings of university prestige—money being among the strongest. Many of the parameters used by *U.S. News* are tied to institutional wealth.

Certainly the "Ivies" are great universities, and having them set the standard is a good thing. But the world we live in is much different from the times of the founding of these universities, and our higher education needs are much greater. Then, a few leaders in government, commerce, and religion could guide the efforts of a young country. Now we need a large and highly educated citizenry.

A few state universities came out of the pack. Virginia, Michigan, Berkeley, and North Carolina come to mind. They are viewed as prestigious and are known as the "public Ivies."

Instead of a few hundred college students, today we have 15 million—80 percent in public universities. Is it time to rethink our notions of quality and prestige? At least we should reduce the emphasis on old-style prestige and focus more on updated measures of quality.

For example, the four-year graduation rate is an outmoded measure. That number may have been significant when collegians were usually full-time students, seventeen to twenty-one years old, just out of high school, attending residential colleges, unmarried, and unemployed. But the four-year rate is no longer relevant at urban universities such as UT San Antonio, UT El Paso, and the University of Houston. And it's these schools that educate the most students.

Distinctions are shifting between public and private universities. Early on, state universities and colleges got nearly all their money from state tax dollars with little coming from students or gifts. Private universities were dependent on tuition dollars, benefactors, or "contributed service" from priests and nuns. Now the private universities get more and more public dollars through federal student aid, Pell grants, Perkins grants, Tuition Equalization Grants, and contracts.

At the same time, public universities are growing faster than the legislative will to continue existing levels of public support. The result: students pay more. The perception that state universities are highly subsidized by tax dollars is no longer true. Such universities used to be called "state-supported." Today, "state-assisted" might be a better term. How about "state-located"? After all, they are on state land. Some wags even say "state-molested."

Important differences remain between the public and the private universities, but they are more about governance than financial support.

Interestingly enough there seems to be a negative correlation among the public universities in terms of the percentage of state funding and prestige. Public institutions that get the fewest state dollars have the most prestige. For example, the University of Michigan gets only 10 percent of its budget from appropriated funds. The University of Virginia gets 8 percent.

The greatest difference between private and public universities of higher education is in governance and autonomy. The independents have a great advantage here. Language tells the tale.

Board members of private universities are called "trustees." They see themselves as advocates of the college, supporters of its president, and leaders in fundraising. Board members of state universities are called "regents"—rulers rather than advocates. They see themselves as overseers and representatives of the appointing authority, usually the governor of the state. Occasionally they interfere in educational and social policy matters.

Legislative control of budgets by the legislature and of curriculum by the coordinating board, statewide control of programming and physical plants, tuition-setting authority at the state level, enrollment caps, collective bargaining agreements, and much more differentiate public universities from private institutions, with private universities coming out the winner in most cases. The recent decision of the Texas Legislature to give tuition authority to the universities and their boards is an exception. Or at least it was until regents actually did raise tuition, and the legislature said, "We didn't really mean it. We're going to investigate you." Of course it remains to be seen whether or not the legislature will further reduce appropriations as tuition rises.

Through all of this we are witnessing a dramatic reduction in public support for higher education in both sectors and a shift of the burden to students and their families. Smaller and less prestigious private schools often are totally dependent on tuition for their annual operating budgets. Such dependence affects their admissions and retention policies and threatens to price them out of the market.

Fiscal strategies that encouraged the previously excluded (the poor and what were then called minorities) to attend college no longer have the support they once did. Texas, for example, has—or had—a tuition prepayment program called Texas 2000. Diana and I bought prepayment packages for all our grandchildren—the best investment we ever made. That program has now been suspended because of unprecedented tuition increases.

The shift in support from grants to loans, along with the large increases in tuition and fees at all universities, place a financial burden that may frighten away those students who are the first in their families to seek a college education. The current proposal to raise the federal cap on loans for undergraduate education from $22,600 to $30,000 will scare people off. How many kids in Laredo will want to go $30,000 in debt to become schoolteachers earning $32,000? This may bring a return to classism, which cannot be a good thing for this nation.

Those who will be excluded from college are the growth sectors of our society, the base needed to ensure an educated workforce in the future. If affordable educational opportunities decline, workers will be imported, or work will be exported. Neither action bodes well for the good of our state or country.

Why are our leaders in Austin so determined that Texas be a mediocre state?

18

Boom and Bust

THERE WERE TWO JOKES going around Texas in the mid-1980s.
    1. Sign on an oilman's door in Midland: Oh Lord, please send me another oil boom. I promise I won't piss this one away.
    2. What is the difference between gonorrhea and an Austin condo? You can get rid of gonorrhea.

But it wasn't very funny if you were trying to write a state budget in the midst of one of the state's more spectacular economic train wrecks. I have written budgets in booms and busts. Booms are better.

In 1975, three years after I was elected lieutenant governor, the state had its first billion-dollar surplus. That made headlines, of course, as great good news, but as usually happens with good news, there is a catch. The way the Legislative Budget Board presented it then, the surplus is the amount of revenue that the state will have for the next two-year budget cycle minus the last budget.

It doesn't take into account that there will be more needs that will require more spending than in the past budget—more children in school, more college students, more patients in mental hospitals and, maybe, more inmates in prison. A budget surplus is usually the result of a growing economy, and a growing economy means more people. More people need more state services.

During those surplus years, Dolph Briscoe was governor, a fine one. Dolph was a rancher, the largest landowner in Texas, and he felt strongly that rising property taxes were harming rural Texans. One of his major initiatives was a property tax cut, which established an agriculture tax exemption.

The good years came to an end. Not a screeching halt at first. Comptroller Bob Bullock saw the first signs of the coming bust in 1982 when candidate Mark White was promising a teacher pay raise without a tax increase. The price of oil was dipping to $30 a barrel, and, although that wasn't a really big dip, it was enough to slow exploration.

Texas's oil production in the 1980s was declining—it had been declining for decades. But oil and gas were still a significant part of the economy.

Mark and Linda Gale White with Bill and Diana Hobby on inauguration day, 1983.
William P. Hobby Sr. Family Papers, Dolph Briscoe Center for American History, di_05739.

Even today, Houston is a global supplier of drilling equipment and technical expertise, as well as a major refiner and headquarters for some of the world's largest multi-national oil companies. The entire Gulf Coast has a symbiotic relationship with oil and gas, as does Midland-Odessa. Agriculture (beef and other livestock, grain, cotton, and processing industries) ranked second in its contributions to the economy. Neither agriculture nor the petroleum industry is known for stability.

When we finished the special session of 1984 we felt good. We had improved public education and infrastructure and had passed a $5.5 billion tax bill to pay for it. We thought we had seen the end of the big tax bills for a while.

White, who had been attorney general when he ran against Clements in 1982, had campaigned on a promise of no new taxes. Reality set in during his first session when he learned there wasn't enough money for the teacher pay raise he also had promised. He reluctantly decided to break one promise to keep the other and called the Education Reform Special Session in 1984. When Bob Bullock spoke to that session, he said "When Governor Hobby and Speaker Lewis invited me over here, they asked me to talk about money. That being the case, I could make the shortest talk in legislative history. You don't have any."

The $5.5 billion tax bill in 1984 raised teacher pay, created a more equi-table system of aid to public schools, and supplemented our highway fund. Passing it wasn't easy. The House didn't like the Senate version and rec-onciling the two versions ate precious hours of the thirty-day session. Sen. John Leedom, a Dallas Republican, threatened a filibuster on the last day, which would have meant a special session, but Bullock and LBB director Jim Oliver talked him out of it. I did not reappoint Leedom to the Finance Committee after he voted against a tax bill. If you don't vote to raise the money you don't get to decide how to spend it.

Governor White said that if the legislature passed this tax bill no more taxes would be necessary in 1985. He was wrong. When the legislature convened in January 1985, oil prices were even lower, and the impact was rippling through the rest of the economy.

We had hoped to continue to build on the education reform with a career ladder for teachers and a pre-kindergarten program. Instead, we were looking at cuts. To keep higher education safe from a proposed 25 percent budget cut, I proposed increasing tuition from $4 to $8 a credit hour. At the time, our tuition rates were nearly the lowest in the nation. White didn't like the idea, and the students at the University of Texas at Austin really didn't like the idea. Several hundred marched on the Capitol, demanding a meet-ing. They got it. I spoke to them for nearly an hour in the Senate cham-ber. We passed the tuition increase, raised a lot of state fees, and somehow scraped money together to fund an indigent health care program.

But in 1986 we were staring at a growing deficit. Oil prices were taking a nosedive, the result of OPEC's (Organization of the Petroleum Exporting Countries) 1983 action to increase supplies. Comptroller Bob Bullock told us in February that we were looking at a $1.3 billion shortfall when the legislature met in January 1987. Gov. Mark White responded with an ex-ecutive order directing state agencies to cut 13 percent from their budgets.

In June, Bullock increased his deficit estimate to $2.3 billion. Oil dropped to $15 a barrel. Unemployment in Texas rose to 10.5 percent. Gov-ernor White called a special session. The voluntary cuts had come up $700 million short—but even if all the agencies had come in at 13 percent, the state would still have been $1 billion short.

White called the first special session in August, and thirty days later the problem hadn't been solved. Speaker Lewis and the House balked at another tax hike and wanted to rely solely on budget cuts. The Senate and I believed that budget cuts would undo all of the progress made in 1984 and jeopardize higher education, health care, and other needed state ser-vices. We deadlocked.

White called another session for September 8, right after the first one ended, asking for budget cuts combined with a 1.125 cent increase in the state sales tax. We reduced state agency budgets by $582 million, cutting state colleges and universities by 10 percent, the Department of Human Services by 9 percent, and the Department of Health by 13 percent.

We repealed the state employee 3 percent pay raise and reduced the number of state employees by almost two thousand. We robbed every reserve fund we could find, delayed payments to the state retirement fund, and passed the 1.125 cent increase in the state sales tax.

Meanwhile, there was a hot gubernatorial race, a rematch between Bill Clements, who had been the first Republican governor since reconstruction when he served from 1979 to 1983. Clements had been spoiling for another shot at White, who cost him re-election in 1982. When the economy started to go south, Clements accused White of fiddling while Rome burned, adding that the only difference between Mark White and Roman Emperor Nero was that Nero didn't take a political poll before he started fiddling.

No one likes to pay more taxes, including me. But civic and economic health depend on investments in children's health and education, infrastructure so that our bridges don't fall down, in the research that powers innovation, and in lifesaving measures, such as criminal justice and protective services.

During economic downturns the state keeps growing. The demand for state services doesn't decline when the revenue does.

In November, Mark White lost the election. The media blamed "high negatives" brought on by the recession, tax bills, higher state fees, teachers angry over testing, and what have you. Bill Clements was back in office, and he was a "no tax" governor.

But when the legislature convened in 1987, Texas was still deep in recession. Oil prices were still down and oil production, according to Bob Bullock, had decreased by 5.1 million barrels in 1986, costing us a potential $35.5 million in severance taxes.

Before the session started, Bullock laid out the situation to the Texas Association of Taxpayers. In a nutshell, he said Texas was too dependent on oil and gas and needed to find about $4 to $5 billion in new revenue to finance the 1988-1989 budget. He even told us how to do it: broaden the sales tax to all personal and professional services.

Texas's tax structure then and now rested on the sales tax. There is no income tax. The oil and gas severance tax was declining, and the business franchise tax at that time drew heavily from capital-intensive business such

Dolph and Janey Briscoe, Bill and Rita Clements, Jan and Bob Bullock, Bill Hobby, Ann Richards, Preston and Ima May Smith, 1991. *William P. Hobby Sr. Family Papers, Dolph Briscoe Center for American History, di_04919.*

as utilities and manufacturing. Because the sales tax was largely confined to goods and the franchise tax to investment on the ground, the growing service and technology sectors got off easy. Bullock's plan was a good one, and slowly, painfully, more and more services have been included in the sales tax or in the business tax restructuring of 2004, well after I left office.

But in 1987, no one was in a good mood. Governor Clements started out proposing a budget that didn't add up.

A word here about the Texas budget process. In many states the governor's budget is the legislative starting point. In Texas, not so. An unpleasant experience with Reconstruction after the Civil War caused Texans to adopt a constitution that parcels out powers among the three branches of government and creates all sorts of checks on the executive branch. One of those checks is on the budget process. The governor can and does propose a budget, but the one taken up in the legislature is the one written and approved by the Legislative Budget Board (LBB). Gov Ann Richards simply adopted the LBB budget as her own. When I was in office, the lieutenant governor chaired the LBB. The Speaker and I appointed the other eight members from their respective houses. Clements was not the first or last governor to find this arrangement distasteful.

I said in my 1987 inaugural speech that there should be no cuts in the public education system we had worked so hard to fix and that higher education was long overdue for an increase. Clements recognized the pickle we were in by saying that the temporary sales tax and gasoline taxes we had enacted during the special session should be extended and that broadening the sales tax base might be a good thing.

But the devil is in the details. Clements and I didn't agree on much, and we didn't enjoy talking about it. Speaker Lewis was no fan of tax increases, but he was proud of our progress on public schools, and he could read a budget. We finished the regular session with no budget. *Texas Monthly* was right when it wrote of the 70th Legislature's regular session: "They had

Hobby with Gov. Bill Clements and Speaker Gib Lewis at one of their weekly breakfasts during the legislative session, c. 1988. *Photograph by Bill Malone. Texas Governor's Office, copy courtesy of the Hobby family.*

only one thing to do, and they didn't do it." With no alternative, Clements called a special session. Bullock set the stage with no sugar coating: "The last time you invited me to speak, you asked me to talk about money. I said at the time that I could make the shortest talk in legislative history: You simply didn't have any. Today, I would say you have even less." The hole in the budget was $698 million deep, he said.

We were tired and grouchy. Governor Clements was weakened by charges that as a trustee of Southern Methodist University he knew about illicit payments to football players and a subsequent cover up. Clements later admitted that he had lied, but said "there was no Bible in the room." Gib Lewis wanted to wrap things up and "get out of Dodge." So did I, but I wasn't willing to squander our children's heritage and Texas's future.

Gib and I spent hours talking to Clements—in the end he signed the budget bill. When asked why he signed the bill, he said he "was sleepy and I wanted to get to bed."

In late July, Clements signed tax bills totaling $5.7 billion, a Texas record at that time. The bills made some minor expansions of the sales tax to such services as garbage collection, pest control, and janitorial contracting. Observers correctly joked that anyone who could hire a lobbyist skated. Tobacco taxes were increased, and the temporary taxes extended.

"We did what we had to do. . . . We had to open the schools. We had to continue state government on some reasonable basis, and we had to address the problem of the federal courts on mental health and mental retardation and the prison system," Clements said.

We didn't exactly change the world, but we kept the schools open. We eventually satisfied the courts that we could run our mental health, mental retardation facilities, and our prison system without supervision. As far as I know the widely dispersed tax increases didn't put anyone out of business. In fact, the Texas economy, resilient as always, began to recover.

Some years later, oil sold for more than $100 a barrel and Austin condos sold like hot cakes. And some years after that, oil was cheap again— gasoline cost less than $2 a gallon—and Austin condos sat empty once more. Boom and bust.

19

The Dreaded Two-Thirds Rule and the Killer Bees

I N ANY LEGISLATIVE BODY, many more bills are introduced than can be considered, so there must be a screening process. The process varies according to the customs of the body and the convenience of the legislators. In the Texas House, the Calendars Committee sets the calendar. In the U.S. Senate, the majority leader does so. In the U.S. House, the Rules Committee does so.

The Texas Senate is its own calendars committee, chaired by the Senate president—the lieutenant governor. The Senate itself decides when bills will come up for a vote.

The screening process works like this:

The lieutenant governor first refers each bill to one of the standing committees. This committee will allow witnesses to speak for or against the bill, then vote whether or not to send it to the floor, called "reporting it out." The committee chairman allocates committee time by setting the committee calendar. When a bill is reported from committee, the bill goes on the Senate's Regular Order of Business (ROB) in the order in which the committee report is received. (Senate Rule 5.12).

After a few weeks dozens of bills are on the ROB, many more than can ever be considered or than a senator can be prepared to debate. So there is an Intent Calendar (SR 5.14), by which a senator gives notice of intent to move to suspend the ROB in order to consider a bill the senator sponsors. Each senator may list three bills. That's ninety-three bills, still too many.

At least one-third of the bills are passed on the Local and Uncontested Calendar (SR 9.03-6). Bills that are unopposed in committee may be recommended for the Local Calendar by the committee when it reports the bill to the whole Senate. The Senate Administration Committee decides the order in which bills will come up. The Local and Uncontested Calendar is usually published the night before. Any two senators can knock a bill off the Local Calendar.

If a bill is on the Intent Calendar, the next step is for the president of the Senate to recognize the senator to bring up the bill. In order to bring up the bill, it is necessary to move to suspend the Regular Order of Business. That motion requires a vote of two-thirds of the Senate present and voting—twenty-one if all are present—to consider the bill. (SR 5.13). By custom, at the very top of the Regular Order of Business is what's known as the "blocker bill," some innocuous-sounding bill, such as one to create a monument on the Capitol grounds, that will never be passed.

I recognized senators based, more or less, on the length of time the bill had been on intent and, of course, the importance of the bill. When a senator asks the president for recognition he is telling the president he has his twenty-one votes. If he doesn't, he has wasted the Senate's time, and his bills go to the end of a very long line.

Once recognized, the senator explains the bill and moves to suspend the Regular Order of Business. This is technically a non-debatable motion, but by custom that's when most debate happens. I used to announce about the first week in May that after a senator had explained the bill and answered a few questions I would sustain a point of order against further debate on the non-debatable motion and proceed to the vote on the motion. That, of course, is a judgment call.

Debates don't change votes. When a frustrated bill sponsor says to an opponent of the bill, "Senator, I can explain it to you, but I can't understand it for you," it's time to vote.

Once the bill itself is up, the only the way to end debate is by moving the previous question (SR 6.01). That motion, rarely made, is non-debatable and requires a simple majority.

The biggest mistake I made as president of the Texas Senate was trying to circumvent the Senate's two-thirds tradition in 1979. The bill that set it off would have set an early date for a Texas presidential primary. The idea was to give Texas a stronger voice in the presidential nominating process.

We were in the middle of a contentious session in 1979. There was a well-organized and determined minority of Democratic senators who were fighting what they considered to be anti-consumer legislation. They were using every tactic in the book to block the legislation they opposed. One tactic was the filibuster. They had developed a tag-team variation on filibustering that could keep the talking going for days. I started calling them the "Killer Bees" because no one knew when they would strike next.

There were enough votes in the Senate to pass the presidential primary bill, but not the two-thirds vote necessary to suspend the Regular Order of Business. I had to get the bill to the top of the Senate Calendar so I could lay it out without needing a two-thirds vote. We had already tried bringing up an election bill that could be amended to change the presidential primary, but the "Killer Bees" saw that coming and filibustered until midnight, after which only House bills could be considered without suspending another rule.

I gave notice that I would lay out the Regular Order of Business on Friday, May 18. That meant that the primary bill would be at the top of the calendar. It could come up and pass on a majority vote. Bad idea.

The opponents of the primary bill feared that Republicans would vote in the Republican presidential primary for former governor John Connally, who was running for president in 1980, then vote for conservative Democrats for state and local offices in the Democratic primary that would occur later in the year.

The whole thing was a fiasco. In protest twelve "Killer Bee" senators flew the Capitol to break a quorum. The "Worker Bees," who stayed behind, spent each session haranguing the absentees, since we didn't have the quorum necessary to transact any business. And we were in the very last weeks of the session with lots of legislation in the pipeline.

Before long, the Worker Bees put a call on the Senate. This action required all absentees to return. The Worker Bees sent the Texas Rangers to net the Killer Bees wherever they had flown. The fact was, for several days the Killer Bees had been hived up in Dora McDonald's small garage apartment. Dora McDonald, Sen. Carl Parker's chief of staff, lived only blocks from the Capitol. Her guests passed the time playing cards, arguing, and listening to each other snore. The Worker Bees continued to harangue them from the Senate floor.

One senator, Gene Jones, left the hive—he wanted to see his granddaughter. The Rangers heard that Jones was home in Houston. Photo in hand, they knocked on his door. A man who looked a lot like the picture opened the door. The Ranger asked him if he was Jones. He said yes. They arrested him and took him to Austin. He was Jones all right, but not Gene Jones. They had arrested Gene's brother, Clayton. When the knock came at the door the senator had jumped over the back fence and stayed lost for another day.

After a few days I repented my ways (and still do) and the Bees returned to the hive. The bill never passed. It wasn't a very good idea anyway. Neither was putting a call on the Senate. I can't imagine what I was thinking. John Connally, a former Texas governor who switched parties in 1973, was a spectacularly unsuccessful Republican presidential candidate, netting only one delegate, an Arkansas woman who became known as the "$11 million delegate." That was what Connally's campaign cost.

Hobby, in beekeeper's gear, and Parliamentarian Steve Dial welcome the "Killer Bees" at their ten-year reunion in 1989. *Courtesy of the Hobby family.*

Some years later, the Killer Bees celebrated their anniversary at Scholz Garten in Austin. I sent the Rangers to bring them to a reception in the Capitol. Clad in a beekeeper's hat, I greeted them from the rostrum.

The Senate rules are designed to create an orderly process that respects the rights of individual members. They have lasted this long because they do the job well and consider the need for compromise in the legislative operation. Trampling the rights of the minority is never a good idea, but despite my bad experience, it has happened over and over again.

In 2003, Tom DeLay, who was then majority leader of the U.S. House and a congressman from Sugar Land, Texas, decided that the legislature should again redistrict Texas seats in the U.S. House. No matter that this had just occurred, as ordered by law, in 2001. In 2002 voters had elected sizeable Republican majorities on both sides of the rotunda, and DeLay saw an opportunity to freeze Democrats out for years to come.

The minority Democrats in the state House saw no way to defeat DeLay's redistricting plan on the floor. So fifty-two Democratic representatives took a chapter from the Killer Bees and flew away—this time to Ardmore, Oklahoma, where the Texas Rangers had no jurisdiction. The absence of more than one-third of the House broke a quorum, and business stalled. This earned the absent Democrats the nickname "Killer D's." The regular session ended in stalemate, but Republican Gov. Rick Perry called legislators back in a summer special session to redistrict. This time, the Senate Democrats took flight for Albuquerque, New Mexico. They had to come back, however, and the redistricting bill passed into law.

DeLay got what he wanted. Of the ten Democratic congressmen he had in his sights, only three were re-elected. Four were defeated, one decided not to run again, one lost the primary, and one switched parties.

Frequently, people criticize the Senate's two-thirds rule. There is no rule called the two-thirds rule and never has been. In 2007, a freshman senator, lacking in manners as well as sense, inveighed against the custom at length on his first day in office. The Senate voted 30 to 1 against changing the custom. New members of the club shouldn't try to change its traditions. Anything that doesn't have the support of two-thirds of the Senate is seldom a good idea anyway.

Two years later, in 2009, the issue came up again, specifically as a way to overrun the Democrats and pass a bill requiring Texas voters to have photo identification in order to vote. The Senate, with its Republican majority, adopted a rule that suspended the two-thirds tradition for just that one issue. Democrats lost the rules fight, 18 to 13, with only one Republican joining them to uphold Senate tradition. Remember, legislative rules are adopted at the beginning of the session by a simple majority, but, once adopted, it requires a two-thirds or four-fifths vote to suspend a rule.

Texas Republicans obviously considered the voter I.D. bill the most critical item that could come up during the 2009 legislative session. Forget health care for children and adults, the needs of higher education, and the prospect of a $9 billion drop in revenue. Forget that despite Attorney General Greg Abbott's best efforts and a $1.4 million study, he could only come up with twenty-six cases of voter fraud, of which eighteen were legal votes that were somehow improperly handled after the ballots were cast.

Apparently Texas Republicans lack any sense of irony. When the same silly voter I.D. issue came up in 2007, the House of Representatives distinguished itself by fraudulently voting to prevent fraudulent voting. As I said, there is little evidence of fraudulent voting in the state, but there is ample evidence of fraudulent voting in the House. News footage by an Austin television station caught Texas House members pushing the buttons on their absent colleagues' voting machines. The video quickly went to YouTube and was viewed more than a million times.

In the House, each member's desk has a set of buttons on which a member can vote aye, no, or present not voting. When a member is away from his or her desk, the member can lock the buttons to prevent fraudulent voting. They almost never do.

The fraudulent voting to prevent fraudulent voting has become so notorious that on November 29, 2007, Speaker Tom Craddick asked the House Administration Committee to "study and make recommendations for alternative voting devices in the Texas House chamber and make recommendations before the next session." The proposed solution, as decided by Speaker Craddick, was to spend approximately $128,000 on ten fingerprint-activated voting machines that House members could use if they wanted to. That's right, according to the *Austin American-Statesman*, use of the expensive new gadgets would be strictly voluntary. Fortunately this was an idea that disappeared when Joe Straus became Speaker of the House.

During the Senate rules fight, Sen. Tommy Williams, who sponsored the Republican-backed rules change, cited "precedent" for his motion, naming a number of instances that occurred during my term in office. One, of course, was the bill that incited the Killer Bees—I've already explained what a bad mistake I made then. A few of the other bills he cited had come up during special called sessions, when the situation is different from that in regular sessions. In special sessions, the governor controls the agenda, deciding if and when to add subjects that can be considered. Thus, the Regular Order of Business may be very short, with no "blocker bill" and no need to suspend the rules. And some of the bills Williams cited were set for special order, which requires a two-thirds vote, just as it does to suspend the Regular Order of Business. Sometimes major legislation is set for special order—at a specific date and time—so that members know in advance and can be present to vote.

Another precedent cited by Senator Williams was a resolution granting permission to hang a portrait of Gov. Dolph Briscoe in the Capitol rotunda along with those of previous governors. There was no opposition. I probably never even sent it to committee. No one seemed to mind. I explained this all in a memo to Sen. Rodney Ellis, who was opposing the rules change, signed, "Your respectful parliamentarian, Bill Hobby."

20

FAMILY FEUDS

WHEN I WAS PRESIDING OVER THE SENATE, my favorite days were predictable, bland, and boring. If there was debate, I liked it courteous and brief. Bills came up for consideration and were approved in orderly fashion with regular thuds of the gavel. In other words, I favored the kind of session designed to frustrate a press corps primed to report on color and action.

With thirty-one members, the Senate is small enough, and usually collegial enough, to work out conflicts in a civilized way, either in committee or in my office. When a bill was both major and controversial, it might take several meetings in my office, but this was more likely to produce good legislation than a floor fight with many amendments drafted on the fly and without careful consideration.

In the House, with 150 members, business is transacted differently. With lengthy debate and a host of untested amendments, it may take long hours, even days, to pass a truly difficult piece of legislation.

But, despite my best hopes, there were times when senators couldn't agree on a compromise, and the fights spilled out of the back corridors onto the floor. Some of those were bitter battles.

As I have mentioned before, most often these battles were over issues that pitted the defense bar, employed by the business community, against the plaintiffs bar, representing those with grievances. These issues often were characterized as fights between the big guys and the little guys, business and consumers, doctors and patients. But, in fact, they were fought between the different sides of the bar. The issues had different names, but there was at least one every session. Likewise, you could classify senators conservative or liberal, but they were listening to the lawyers.

Medical malpractice was one of the first major struggles during my tenure. By 1975 the cost of medical malpractice insurance rates had gone from approximately $80 to $100 per hospital bed to $500 to $600 a bed, about a 400 percent increase in five years. Doctors, hospitals, and the insurance industry wanted to limit liability, reduce the time for filing lawsuits,

Hobby with gavel at Senate podium, late 1970s. *William P. Hobby Sr. Family Papers, Dolph Briscoe Center for American History, di_05735.*

and give rate control to the State Board of Insurance. That year, we managed to give the insurance board rate approval, set up a joint underwriting pool for high-risk coverage, and authorize a two-year study of the issue.

I thought we had made considerable progress, but Texas doctors wanted more limits on their liability, and they were vocal about it. In my opinion they had helped bring about the situation when they had insisted some years before that malpractice rates not be state-regulated. I appointed Page Keeton, former dean of the University of Texas School of Law, to head the study panel on medical professional liability. In 1977, with Sen. Ray Farabee of Wichita Falls again as author, a bill passed that satisfied everyone and laid the issue to rest for the rest of my time in office.

The following session, in 1979, was a particularly contentious year for the defense/plaintiffs issue. One of the issues in dispute was the Texas Consumer Protection Act. At that time the Republicans were a small minority in the Senate. But combined with the conservative Democrats, they were a majority and were highly successful at passing legislation that more progressive Democrats considered bad for consumers. That same session also featured the political antipathy that created the Killer Bees, as previously noted.

Workers' compensation was by far the most contentious issue I faced the whole time I served as lieutenant governor. The issue appeared to be rather mundane, even tedious, all about how workers are compensated for on-the-job injuries. In fact, it became a three-year-long pitched battle with moments of betrayal, heart-sinking reverses, and emotional personal attacks—exactly what I hoped to avoid in my daily job presiding over the Senate.

It began, as these things always do, with a crisis. In January 1987, after a year-long study of workers' compensation, a House Select Interim Committee on Workers' Compensation Insurance concluded that the existing law needed to be abolished. Workers' comp insurance premiums had gone up 48.7 percent in 1986 and another 17 percent increase was on the horizon. Business wanted cost containment measures and ways to streamline disputed claims. Labor said the current system was working pretty well.

In just a month, the workers' compensation fund for state employees was broke and required emergency appropriations. The session ended without passing any comprehensive workers' comp legislation—there were too many other pressing issues.

Governor Clements decided to create another study—the third in five years. This one was called the Joint Select Committee on Workers' Compensation, and, like the previous one, it was headed by Rep. Richard Smith, a Bryan Republican. His goal was to provide "the best benefits we can afford at the lowest possible cost." It sounded great, but Joe Gagen, chair of the Industrial Accident Board that resolved disputes, warned that there would be no easy answers. He knew what he was talking about.

At the time it appeared to me another of the defense bar/plaintiffs bar issues that could be solved easily enough by calling in Morris Atlas, a respected defense attorney, and Joe Jamail, a respected trial lawyer. Both men had the stature in their profession to pound out a workable compromise.

This issue was different. It had the usual warfare between business, which regarded the system as far too generous to workers and the lawyers who represented them, and labor, which wanted employers penalized for their failure to maintain a safe workplace. Added to the mix were insurance companies, which kept demanding higher rates, and lawyers, who found workers' comp cases a reliable source of income.

I had appointed a good cross section of Senate opinion to the Joint Committee, including Sen. Kent Caperton, a Bryan Democrat and a trial lawyer, and Bob Glasgow, a more conservative Democrat from Stephenville, whom I appointed vice chair. There was trouble on the horizon when Caperton said he would not be bound by the committee's recommendations. The committee report, issued in December 1988, had a laundry list of recommendations, including higher weekly benefits to injured workers, self-insurance for large employers, and a tracking system to determine which businesses had excessive comp claims.

But the real fight was going to be over the recommendation that the Industrial Accident Board become the major arbiter of claims, dramatically limiting trial de novo and the lump-sum settlements. Trial de novo allowed courts to begin their work without regard to the administrative determination that had already occurred at the Industrial Accident Board. With trial de novo, the jury was not limited to the "substantial evidence" rule, which required only deciding whether the board had followed state law in making its ruling. Another hot issue was lump-sum settlements. This was an option for workers, which, incidentally, made it easy for lawyers to collect their contingency payments.

I was most impressed by the committee's findings that the system "doesn't work and it doesn't compensate" (as I told the Texas Association of Compensation Consumers in March, after the session had started). The study noted that despite a 148 percent increase in premiums in five years, Texas ranked high in the number of workplace injuries, and benefits for injured employees were low. The House introduced the committee's recommendations as House Bill 1. In the Senate we agreed to have a bill out in the beginning of May, leaving us about thirty days to resolve any differences.

Once again, I was much too optimistic. By late April, I was out of patience, so I set a deadline for the senators who had spent endless hours talking instead of producing a bill. I said we would have a bill on the floor of the Senate in the next week, and I would remember whoever blocked it for a long time. At the time, I said there was plenty of blame to go around—insurance rates were high because many employers operated unsafe work places and there were no rewards for the safer employers. I also noted that the plaintiffs' attorneys were insisting on a system of justice that suppressed evidence, since the Industrial Accident Board proceedings could not be admitted in court.

By mid-May I called out the big gun—Joe Jamail, trial lawyer extraordinaire, who had succeeded in resolving some of these disputes in the past. Jamail, famous for winning a $10.5 billion judgment against Texaco, Inc., when he was representing the Pennzoil Co., had brought compromise to the tort reform battle in 1987. I thought he could do it again. My plan backfired. Someone—Jamail?—apparently let reporters know about his mission, and his photo showed up in the newspapers. The trial lawyers who had been working for months on a solution just got mad.

We did not have a bill on the floor the next week, but on May 22, with only a week to go in the session, we passed a Senate bill. It was a substantial improvement in that it set up a two-tiered claims dispute structure and stricter rules of evidence for cases that reached a jury trial. But trial de novo was the battle cry, and the Senate bill did not eliminate trial de novo or jury trials. The House accused the Senate of dragging its feet until the last moment. The conference committee failed to reach agreement before adjournment sine die May 29.

I told the *Houston Post* that I was disappointed that "there was so much misinformation in the minds of the leadership of the House as to what was in the Senate bill" that they did not give it proper consideration. Rep. Richard Smith, who headed House conferees, blamed "too many players," including business, labor, doctors, insurance companies, and lawyers. He had a point.

Governor Clements set June 20 as the date for a special legislative session on workers' comp. He said it would be "therapeutic" for legislators to go home and listen to their constituents. Special legislative sessions are generally an effective way to pass contentious legislation. The subjects are limited to what the governor puts on the agenda. This focuses the attention of legislators, the public, and the press. And the thirty-day lifespan of a special session deters foot dragging.

But the first called session of 1989 did not work as planned. When the session opened on June 20, I was tired of attacks on the Senate by the Texas Association of Business, which seemed to think that though jury trials may be a sacred right for everyone else, they should be denied to injured workers. I pointed out that it is insurance carriers who appeal to the courts 57 percent of the time, yet "the idiots who represent the business community say we don't want a trial by jury. You know that is really kind of silly."

Sen. Kent Caperton and Sen. John Montford, a former prosecutor from Lubbock, were co-sponsors of the Senate bill. They ably represented both factions in the Senate—those who sided with labor and trial lawyers and those who favored business and the defense bar. They pledged to come up with a system that would include both arbitration and jury trial, but the scope of the jury trials would be more limited than in the previous proposal.

We weren't really making a lot of progress when an incident occurred that pretty much scuttled any chance for agreement. On July 5, Lonnie "Bo" Pilgrim, a big Republican contributor and founder and chairman of Pilgrim's Pride Corporation—once the largest chicken processing firm in the nation—showed up on the Senate floor handing out $10,000 checks. I remember being in my office in the afternoon when Sen. Hugh Parmer of Fort Worth came in. He told me he had been bribed by Bo Pilgrim—or rather that Pilgrim had handed him a check (which he quickly returned) while remarking something like "we need some help." I said he needed to report the incident to the Travis County district attorney. Parmer asked me to go with him to see Ronnie Earle, who was then D.A. He had his lawyer, Sen. Craig Washington, come along—I remember we were late getting there because Craig was late.

It turned out that Pilgrim had given checks to nine senators—five Democrats, who later returned them, one Democrat—John Montford— who immediately refused the check and escorted Pilgrim out of his office, one Republican who said he probably would keep it since Pilgrim was a longtime friend, and two other Republicans who had trouble making up their minds. Ronnie Earle called it "an outrageous act." Pilgrim freely admitted that he wanted to influence the votes on workers' comp. It turned out that the chicken-plucking industry is a dangerous one, and Pilgrim's Pride had an unsavory record of job safety. The company had paid $8 million to injured employees in five years. In one incident a worker drowned in a pit that had not been covered; in another a worker lost both legs after crawling into a bin containing a motorized auger while the machine was operating. Pilgrim's Pride declared bankruptcy in December 2008, but to this day, the factory in Pittsburg, Texas, features a thirty-seven-foot-high likeness of Bo Pilgrim in a pilgrim's hat.

I called the Pilgrim incident "a ludicrous episode" and predicted it wouldn't affect passage of the bill, but that was whistling in the dark. The whole affair dealt a serious blow to the business side's credibility and gave the opposition all the ammunition they needed to run the clock on the thirty-day session. At that point, the House and Senate had adopted separate bills, the conference committee was scheduled to meet, and there was still more than a week left in the session. Before long it got personal. Sen. Ted Lyon, a Mesquite Democrat, accused Richard Smith, the House floor leader, of planning to run against Senator Caperton. Smith responded that the trial lawyers never wanted a bill in the first place. The usually patient

Senator Montford said he had never "been up against such a brick wall before in terms of negotiating—just absolutely no flexibility at all."

The first called session of 1989 ended July 19 in failure. There was lots of finger-pointing and not much hope of a quick solution. The governor came in for editorial blame for opening the session agenda to such non-pertinent issues as a bill banning the burning of the U.S. and Texas flags, one making the University of Texas at Dallas a four-year school, and one creating a four-year university in Killeen. In all, Clements added fifty-two more issues to the session.

I asked the governor to call the legislature back in the next few weeks, but he had planned a summer trip to Africa and decided to delay the next session until November. Working with key senators and the best advisors I could find, I decided on a different strategy. This time there would be a "Hobby bill." It would be my best attempt to come up with a bill resolving the thorny issues of workers' comp. On October 25, I gave a briefing in the Senate chamber on the bill, using charts and a pointer to sum up the issues. The system, I said, was inequitable, undercompensating serious injuries and overcompensating lesser injuries. Texas employers paid premiums 34 percent above the national average, and insurance premiums had increased 148 percent in four years.

The proposal was well received. The *Dallas Morning News* thought it brought "hope for real reform. . . . The Lieutenant Governor still holds enormous personal clout in the body over which he has presided for the last 16 years. If anyone can gain the handful of votes necessary to pass meaningful reform, it's Bill Hobby." The *Austin American-Statesman* opined that it was a "reasonable proposal" that "should serve as basis for agreement."

I submitted my bill, with Senator Montford as sponsor, before the session opened on November 14. Almost immediately, Speaker Lewis and his floor leader, Representative Smith, said they could back the "Hobby Plan." When the session opened, they stood back so that the Senate could pass its bill. Likewise we had assurances that Governor Clements wouldn't interfere with unhelpful comments. I referred the bill to the Economic Development Committee, where I could get speedy, favorable action.

Senator Caperton and Sen. Carl Parker of Port Arthur had introduced an opposing bill, and Caperton immediately cried foul. "The fix is in (in) Economic Development," he told a press briefing. Parker said I was "doing serious harm to people that he will be sorry for in years to come."

We went to war with actuarial reports. Mine showed that the Caperton-Parker bill would increase the cost of the workers' comp system by 205 percent, compared to 13 percent for my bill. Caperton said he had an actuarial forecast showing his bill would reduce rates by 12 percent. Parker called my report "grossly incomplete and inaccurate." Meanwhile, Parker and Caperton used their parliamentary expertise to good advantage, tagging my bill to slow it down.

The process was painful. Caperton was one of my go-to senators. He had carried the 1984 education reform package with great competence and grace. Parker, for all his sharp tongue and quick temper, was chair of the Senate Education Committee and a valuable lieutenant on education and other matters. It wasn't easy to hear and read their comments about my bill and my motives. The lights were burning late in the Capitol as we prepared for the floor fight.

When my bill came to the Senate floor on November 20, it was immediately clear we lacked the votes to get it passed. On an 18 to 13 vote, the Senate refused to table Senator Parker's substitute for a critical part of the bill dealing with workers' benefits. It took twelve hours on the floor, and, when it was over, the Senate approved a bill that, as one news account said, "riddled, ripped and repudiated" my workers' comp plan.

"The legislative process isn't over," I told the news media. It wasn't. The House rather quickly revived my original bill or something remarkably similar and sent it back to the Senate, 122-23. Once again, the Senate balked, refusing 17-14 on December 1 to concur with the House. I appointed a Senate conference committee, which set off another firestorm. Caperton and Parker contended that the committee had four members favoring my bill and only one favoring the bill that actually passed the Senate. They based their argument on the eighteen senators who had voted days earlier to adopt their substitute. I argued, quite truthfully, that all the senators on the committee had supported the bill that passed the Senate.

Senators fumed that I would fail again. "I don't care how many times they put our backs to the wall . . . whenever they come back there will be 17 people waiting on them that are going to trash whatever they come back with," said Sen. Craig Washington of Houston—the senator who represented my home. "There are the votes in this Senate right now to kill the sorry bill that came over from the House. Deader than hell," said Sen. Chet Brooks of Pasadena.

Time was running out and we were exhausted. On December 8, I brought the conference committee report to the floor, and it was voted down. It was Friday afternoon. I was still holding out some hope when the House adjourned to go home. It appeared that the cause was lost. But at this dark moment there were some signs of a breakthrough. Sen. Chet Edwards, a Waco Democrat, offered some changes he said he could live with. Speaker Lewis said he would call the House back if there was a compromise, and I vowed to work over the weekend.

During the previous weeks the pro-reform coalition, led by Gene Fondren, president of the Auto Dealers of Texas, had been targeting the senators they thought were most likely to change their votes. Each of those senators had been hearing from business owners and others in their districts. At one point a crowd of small businessmen and women had picketed Edwards's Waco office. The work paid off.

On Sunday, December 10, Edwards and two other senators, Judith Zaffirini of Laredo and Chet Brooks of Pasadena, announced a compromise. It consisted of seven amendments that they said would create "a more meaningful appeals" process, but retain the American Medical Association impairment schedule that would set compensation regardless of occupation. The impairment schedule had been the hottest subject in Senate debate, but I considered it the only way to take some of the judgmental slack out of the system. The three senators said they would support the compromise only if it were acceptable to the House. It was.

On December 12, we passed the compromise bill, sent it to the governor—who said he would waste no time signing it—and adjourned sine die one day before the session would expire.

We could have adjourned a bit earlier, but I had to be in New York the night before to represent my mother at a dinner honoring former members of President Dwight D. Eisenhower's cabinet. The dinner was on Ike's one hundredth birthday. It was organized by a bunch of original Eisenhower supporters and took place on an aircraft carrier tied up at a naval museum. Colin Powell made a great speech. The whole thing felt like the launch of a Powell-for-President campaign.

I could not get back to Austin in time for the Senate session the next morning, but workers' comp was a done deal by that time, with one last roll call remaining. I put Montford in the chair and asked him to recess, rather than adjourn, the Senate after the roll call. After the workers' comp vote Montford recessed until the next day. I made it clear that no business would be transacted the next day and that I didn't care if a quorum was present. I was not running for re-election, and I just wanted to adjourn the Senate sine die one last time. As it turned out, I would have another chance. But I didn't realize it then.

21

Texas Prisons and the War on Drugs

URING MUCH OF THE TIME I WAS IN OFFICE we didn't have to worry much about running the prisons because the federal government was doing it. The reason was *Ruiz v. Estelle*, a case brought against the state of Texas in 1972 for prison overcrowding, inadequate security, sorry health care, and many other things that plaintiffs claimed violated the constitutional prohibition against cruel and unusual punishment.

After a 129-day trial, Federal Judge William Wayne Justice pretty much agreed. He pointed out that Texas didn't have enough prisons to house its inmates adequately (they were double- and triple-bunked and housed in tents). He also found that there were not enough guards to manage the inmates, so the guards had deputized some inmates to do their jobs and given them weapons. The building tender system resulted in considerable brutality, and Justice ordered it stopped. Building tenders were inmates designated by staff to control and discipline other inmates—a practice that in several other states had been outlawed in the 1970–1971 *Gates v. Collier* decision. Judge Justice determined that prison health care was so bad that inmates were dispensing drugs, setting bones, and doing sutures.

His court order was appealed to the Fifth Circuit, which changed some of it, but upheld most of it. Judge Justice appointed a special master, and from 1980 through 1994 he was pretty much in charge—he actually exercised more limited control through 2003.

Having a special master is a lot like having a kid in college—his communications were very often translated as "just send money." One of the judge's orders was that prisons be operated at 95 percent of capacity as a remedy to overcrowding. We weren't doing a great job of complying with that, since it required backing up prisoners in county jails. The counties had taken to suing the state, since the backlog put them in violation of state jail standards. The other solution was to turn inmates loose faster, sometimes with bad outcomes.

The court orders presented unusual challenges. As a state, we had no choice but to follow the directions. In fact, most of us wanted to end the sorry situation that had led to the lawsuits in the first place.

As the 1981 session began, I set out a game plan to deal with the *Ruiz* court order. "We have a very overcrowded prison system," I told the *Dallas Times-Herald* on February 1. "We need, just as quickly as possible, to eliminate triple-celling. We would be two years down that road but for a Clements veto of something over $30 million in prison construction funds." (Governor Clements had vetoed our prison building item in 1979.)

I also recommended that there be increases in corrections officers, but not to Judge Justice's specifications—he wanted staffing at the national average of one officer to five inmates—Texas then had one officer to eleven inmates.

"There are some conditions, his criticism of medical care of inmates, I think are justified," I added, pointing out that in 1979, the legislature had authorized the construction of a four hundred-bed prison hospital in Galveston. Meanwhile, the Legislative Budget Board had approved an 80 percent increase in medical staffing.

The *Ruiz* decision was 118 pages long, and it covered just about every aspect of prison operation. Plotting a responsible course for the state was a full-time job. It involved communicating with the governor's and attorney general's criminal justice experts, the special master, and the Texas Department of Corrections, as well as the ability to gauge what the legislature could be persuaded to pass. My man was Sen. Ray Farabee, who probably wished the cup would pass from him. Ray was a skillful lawyer, a compassionate and practical man, and the chairman of the State Affairs Committee, which handles much major legislation. I had complete confidence in Ray to choose the right path. It was tempting to try to build our way out of the crisis—Gov. Ann Richards later tried to do that. Ray, instead, tried to meet the obligations the court set on us. Since he had to deal with the court-appointed master, Vincent Nathan, both on the budget and prison administration, he met with him and observed that he did not have horns and a tail and seemed fairly reasonable. Ray suggested that I meet with Nathan also, and I recall that I did.

Ray had to carry some unpopular legislation, including one bill authorizing private prisons. Only three other states at that time permitted private prisons. Prison reform advocates, state employees, and the Texas Department of Corrections were all opposed to them. It did provide for new prisons, which were not constructed at state expense, and by and large, they have been run well.

Texas has the largest prison system in the United States—in 2009 there were about 155,000 prison beds. Why? Because Texans are tough on crime. At every new session the legislators create new crimes, which are new ways to send people to prison, and longer sentences, which keep them there longer. When you are always busy finding new ways to send people to prison, you need a lot of prisons. Whether sending so many people to prison works to reduce crime, rather than just costing lots of money, is debatable. The 2000 study, "Texas Tough, an Analysis of Incarceration and Crime Trends in the Lone Star State," by the Justice Policy Institute of Washington, D.C., found that one in twenty adult Texans were then under criminal justice supervision, and that 54.8 percent of those incarcerated were convicted for non-violent offenses. And the study didn't see much correlation with crime rates. Texas had only a 5.1 percent drop in crime, while New York, which has the third-slowest-growing prison population, had a decrease of 21 percent.

In 1981 Texas had a war on drugs. This was basically President Reagan's federal war on drugs replicated at the state level. Its leader was Ross Perot, who was then a technology billionaire and a staunch Republican. Republican Gov. Bill Clements was a big supporter of ending drug use once and for all.

Wars on somethings don't work. Think alcohol, poverty, drugs, terror. Prohibition of alcohol was tried in the United States, Russia, Finland, and Norway with uniformly disastrous results. Liquor consumption and crime famously went up, not down. Even though President Lyndon Johnson declared war on poverty in 1964, we still have a lot of poverty in the United States.

The Texas war on drugs made it easier for police to wiretap people, created new crimes, set higher penalties for old ones, and made it harder to get parole. Just like Prohibition, the idea was to reduce crime. Laws don't prevent crime. People have been making laws for about four thousand years, and we have more crime than ever. There's no such animal as a law that reduces crime.

I have not noticed a strong correlation between the increased number of wiretaps and success in the war on drugs. When the issue came up in 1977, I told the *Marlin Democrat* "Despite the fact that we have the highest number behind bars of any state, despite the fact that they serve longer sentences than any state, crime in our streets continues to increase. I will continue to oppose the unwarranted intrusion of government into the private lives of the citizens of this state."

I lost the wiretap battle in 1981. I sent the bill to the Senate Criminal Jurisprudence Committee, which was chaired by Sen. Oscar Mauzy, an unrepentant Dallas liberal who thought wiretap was a very bad idea. He wouldn't hear the bill. Most of the Senate (not to mention the House and the governor), however, wanted the bill passed. So I pried the bill out of Oscar's committee and sent it to another committee where it would be heard and sent to the floor. I'd like to think we made some good amendments during the time it spent in the Senate.

Along the same lines, in 1995 Congress thought it would be a great idea to decide what we could and could not see on the Internet. As usual, the people who had promised to take government off our back decided to put it in our living room. They wanted fines and jail terms for people who transmitted material that was "obscene, lewd, lascivious, filthy or indecent" over the Internet. The Internet opened the way to the wonders of cyberspace. We've learned to pull up reproductions of paintings in the Louvre, reference material from the Library of Congress, and bills up for consideration in the Texas Legislature. We are travelers in a fantastic new world of knowledge and information. So naturally our Big Brothers in Congress couldn't leave us alone.

Eventually Congress passed the Child Pornography Prevention Act of 1996 that set mandatory prison sentences of at least fifteen years for production and distribution of child pornography and a lot of other stuff. No one wants to defend pornography. There is too much of it around, too much of it on the newsstands and on television. But we have a defense. We don't have to buy it or watch it. We have the same defense in regard to the Internet. We can heed the increasingly frequent warnings and just not download. And as the U.S. Supreme Court noted in 2002 when it struck down two provisions of the Child Pornography Prevention Act, Shakespeare's *Romeo and Juliet* would have been considered pornography under this act. The First Amendment's freedom of speech provision was intended to protect us from arbitrary definitions of what is OK and not OK for us to see.

As someone who has spent a lifetime in the broadcasting business, it has never been clear to me why the government thinks that it owns the airwaves. I have never seen the bill of sale or the certificate of title. Yet, while newspapers and other printed means of communication are protected from regulation by the First Amendment, electronic media have always been subject to arbitrary and capricious acts of Congress.

There was good reason for the federal government allocating frequencies so that broadcasters didn't interfere with one another. It is quite another thing to decide that broadcasting media must be owned by U.S. citizens, carry public service programming, and adhere to the Federal Communications Commission's idea of fairness. Then, just when most of these regulations were repealed, Congress decided to control what you send over your personal computer. This is directly equivalent to opening your mail.

Of course this seems small potatoes compared to the Patriot Act and the data mining done by the George W. Bush administration under the guise of fighting terrorism. It's not just Congress that wants to lean over our shoulder at the computer and listen in on our telephone conversations.

Our various wars on drugs, state, and federal, have been expensive failures. In August 2006 a *New York Times* report concluded that the six-year $4.7 billion effort to eradicate Colombia's coca fields made no difference in the price, quality, or availability of cocaine on the streets of America. In fact, according to this report that policy, along with the effort to eradicate the opium poppies in Afghanistan, has fueled organized crime, contributed to the resurgence of the Taliban, and made the United States even more unpopular in those parts of the world. What if the Afghans tore up grain fields in Tennessee because Muslims are not supposed to drink bourbon?

But the war on drugs has accomplished some things! About half a million Americans are arrested annually for possession of marijuana. And doctors can lose their licenses for prescribing marijuana to relieve pain and nausea in terminal cancer victims.

Getting tough on crime means getting tough on taxpayers. When the *Ruiz* case was in trial in 1979, the state had eighteen prisons for 25,000 inmates. In the late 1980s and early 1990s, the state built eighty-nine more prisons that could house 140,000 more inmates.

Between 1987 and 1995, Texas built 110,000 prison beds. We borrowed $2 billion from present and future taxpayers to do it. Tony Fabelo, director of the Texas Criminal Justice Policy Council, noted that no other state locked up as many of its citizens (636 of every 100,000).

Fabelo, who was much applauded but rarely heeded when he was head of the Criminal Justice Policy Council, found that reduced crime most strongly correlated with reduced numbers of people between the crime-prone ages of thirteen and twenty-four. Most criminologists agree. In the United States this population started declining in 1983 and with it the crime rates.

Another factor is the economy. When more people have jobs, property crime decreases.

Sometimes even our steady supply of inmates faltered and we imported some from other states. In 1995, eight new state jails were nearly empty and costing taxpayers nearly $1.5 million a month in debt service.

We rented space out to other states. But by 2006 we apparently needed 11,000 more beds.

At that time, Sen. John Whitmire, chair of the Senate Criminal Justice Committee, pointed out that some five thousand beds were occupied by low-risk inmates serving time for property and drug crime—good candidates for parole. They were also good candidates for drug and alcohol treatment programs. The late great Governor Richards instituted a program of rehabilitation for prison inmates identified as good prospects.

Richards was aware of a 1988 study that showed that 80 percent of Texas inmates had done drugs and 54 percent needed treatment for severe addictions. She proposed operating 14,000 drug treatment beds at a cost of about $160 million a year. But Bush won the election for governor in 1994, and he didn't believe in rehabilitation. "Incarceration is rehabilitation," he said when he was campaigning.

Bush cut the number of drug treatment beds to 5,300. He also signed into law tougher penalties on drug offenders—one bill to increase penalties on possession of less than a gram of cocaine and one bill stiffening penalties for selling drugs near a school bus. But the Texas Criminal Justice Policy Council in 1999 released a study showing that the inmates who got into drug treatment were less likely to be back in prison in a year—63 percent less. Those out for three years were 20 percent better than those who had no treatment. In 2003 another Republican governor, Rick Perry, pretty much totally eliminated drug treatment for inmates.

But a good idea won't die, and in 2007, largely because of Senator Whitmire, the state started building 6,000 treatment and rehabilitation beds. The new rehab program included expanded drug and alcohol treatment and counseling and transition centers to help inmates succeed when they left prison.

The result—"Just what we expected," Whitmire said. By 2009 the prison population had actually stopped growing. Corrections officials agreed that the program was having a dramatic impact. "It's been proven before that these types of programs have an impact on recidivism so these new numbers are no surprise," said Michelle Lyons, a spokeswoman for the Texas Department of Criminal Justice.

22

The Poor We Always Have With Us

I N 1970 Lt. Gov. Ben Barnes named me chair of the Senate Interim Committee on Welfare Reform. It wasn't exactly a high honor—welfare in Texas has pretty much always been associated in the public mind with lazy, shiftless folks who won't work—"welfare queens" who supposedly live high on the hog on welfare payments, which would be difficult considering that Texas's welfare payments have always been among the lowest in the nation.

The state's philosophy has been pretty much summed up in Clayton Williams's statement: "If you don't have an oil well, get one." Claytie Williams is a West Texas oilman who ran for governor unsuccessfully against Ann Richards. The most memorable point of his campaign was when he compared bad weather to rape, saying "if it's inevitable, just relax and enjoy it."

Back to our work on the Senate committee. In the introduction to our report, titled "Breaking the Poverty Cycle," our committee reported that the state's welfare system up to then had treated the blind, the disabled, and the poor in essentially the same way, "as persons to be maintained only on a level at or below that of decency."

The irony is that Texas is not a wealthy state. Despite the oil tycoon mythology, Texas was and is a state with below-average median income and with some of the poorest counties in the nation. The Texas median income for a family of four was $54,554 in 2007, compared to the national median of $65,093. And Texas shares the challenges of many large states in educating and assimilating a large immigrant population.

A 2006 study showed that Texas ranks sixth in the nation in terms of needs (such as the need for public education as measured by the number of school-age children) and thirty-seventh in revenue effort. In fact, Texas ranks forty-seventh among the fifty states in expenditures to meet human needs, according to the same study.

As is usually the case, the interest in welfare reform stemmed not from concern for the least among us as much as it did from the fact that the cost of payments to the needy and to people with disabilities was going off the charts.

The committee's welfare reform report was a good one. We hired consultants to analyze parts of the complex Medicaid system and we asked Ross Perot's company, Electronic Data Systems, to make a pervasive study of the operations, systems and data processing of the Department of Public Welfare. (Perot, of course, would sell that company, start another, lead a highly successful effort to upgrade Texas public education, then run for president and unintentionally help elect Bill Clinton.)

We made sweeping recommendations, some of which were actually adopted, such as removing the constitutional ceiling on state appropriations for welfare, the replacement of food commodities with food stamps, and the garnishment of wages for child support, though some of those reforms took a long time. Some of our recommendations went nowhere, such as providing for a statewide system of day care. Some were less controversial then than they would be now, such as an expansion of family planning services. All in all, it was a good piece of work, and my participation left me with a better understanding of the arcane and impossibly complex laws surrounding the provision of health and human services.

It also introduced me to the dedication and brain power of the people who commit themselves to pushing this particular rock uphill. A little-known state senator who was about to be elected to Congress was on the committee. Her name was Barbara Jordan.

June Hyer, a University of Houston at Clear Lake administrator, directed the staff and was my parliamentarian after I was elected lieutenant governor. She also served as executive director of a Special Committee on Delivery of Human Services that I created in 1980.

The chair of that committee was Helen Farabee of Wichita Falls, a visionary who became my advisor on all matters relating to health and human services. Helen was the first director of what is now the Center for Public Policy Priorities. Helen produced a report called "The Potential in the Patchwork" that is still cited today. Not only did Helen's committee identify the issues (lack of comprehensive planning, different funding streams, a confusing patchwork of agencies and services) it endeavored to chart a path to a less costly, more efficient system. One of the committee's members was a Travis County commissioner named Ann Richards. One of the things that Helen articulated better than most advocates was the extreme costliness of our neglect. She said we could pay now or pay later — and later will cost more.

Most of the progress in Texas's health and human services system was born of crisis, and in the early 1980s a crisis was brewing. President Reagan called it the New Federalism, but the gist of it was that states were to get more responsibility, more flexibility, and less money.

Texas's state constitution makes counties responsible for indigents, paupers, and lunatics. Then as now, Texas made it difficult for people to become eligible for Medicaid, the federal-state health care assistance program. Then, as now, Texas ranked among the highest in the nation in children and adults without health insurance. In 2007 the Texas Health Institute confirmed that Texas had the highest rate of uninsured in the nation. At that time, 25 percent of Texans, about 5.6 million people, were without health insurance. About 72 percent of them lived in households where at least one family member worked full time.

Urban counties with public hospitals were overrun not only with their own indigent patients, but also with patients from counties that chose not to provide a public health care option—in other words, most of them.

There were spectacular cases of patient dumping. This occurs when the very ill patient arrives at the hospital, receives a wallet biopsy, and is sent on his or her way, often with catastrophic results. An East Texas man with a knife in his back died after being turned away from several hospitals. A South Texas child with diarrhea died after being refused care.

So in 1983 I asked Helen to tackle the problem of indigent health care, and the Governor's Task Force on Indigent Health Care was assembled. Bryan Sperry, later on my staff and director of the Texas Association of Children's Hospitals, directed the task force staff. Sperry is one of the state's best thinkers about health care policy.

When Helen died in 1988 at the age of fifty-three, her husband, Ray, had recently left the Senate to become general counsel for the University of Texas System. Her death was memorialized in the Senate chamber. Rebecca Canning of Waco was one of the speakers. Becky described Helen as a problem-solver and compared her to Ariadne of Greek mythology, who gave Theseus the golden thread that enabled him to find his way out of the labyrinth after he had slain the minotaur.

DeAnn Friedholm, then Gov. Mark White's staff expert on health and human services, was an important contributor to the committee's work. DeAnn became Texas's Medicaid director and later advised the government of South Africa on human service programs.

That task force conducted thirteen hearings and site visits and pulled in some important allies. One of them was Ernie Cortes, a MacArthur Fellow who headed the innovative Texas Industrial Areas Foundation, a well-organized network of community groups that lobbied for better services for their low-income members.

The task force recommended a package of five bills introduced in the 1985 legislative session. They included:

- The county responsibility bill—the guts of the package. This defined a county's responsibility for indigent care and set up a mechanism for state payments when the county exceeded its budgeted limit.
- The Maternal and Infant Health Improvement Act. This act allowed Texas to participate in the federal program, later covered by Medicaid, which greatly expanded prenatal and postnatal care for low-income women and children.
- The Primary Care Act. This act laid the foundation for primary care clinics, which are still recognized as the keystone for preventative care.
- The Patient Dumping Act. Still a national model, this act required a hospital to stabilize a person whose life is in danger before transferring him or her to a tax-supported public hospital.
- A data collection bill.

Financing is always a problem with improvements in health and human services. In this case, the modest $70 million needed to provide an incentive to counties to participate in the indigent care program was dubbed the "sick tax" by the Texas Hospital Association. That pretty much killed that plan. With the clock ticking and DeAnn Friedholm and Bob McPherson searching desperately for funds, we cobbled together a package that Comptroller Bob Bullock could certify.

In those days, the end of the session was pandemonium. Any mistake could spell doom for a proposed bill. The conference committee redrafted the indigent care bill and sent it back to the floors of the Senate and House with only a few hours to go. The Senate adopted the conference committee report. But in the House someone raised a point of order that the conference committee report had not been distributed to members' boxes.

Maybe the failure was malicious. Maybe it was a mistake. But it was critical. Under House rules, the bill could not again come to the House floor until three minutes to midnight. Members who favored it were yelling, "Vote! Vote! Vote!", but Bill Cerverha, a Republican from Richardson, easily talked it to death.

House members were screaming. Ernie Cortes had thousands of his community activists in the galleries specifically to support indigent health care. They blocked the doors to the governor's office. We spent the next hour trying to persuade Governor White to call an immediate special session. At 1:30 a.m. he agreed and called the session for nine the next morning.

The Senate took approximately five minutes to approve the bill and send it to the House, but the drama wasn't over. Republicans now saw a chance to embarrass Mark White. Then U.S. Sen. Phil Gramm called Republicans asking them to vote against the bill. Sen. John Leedom, a Dallas Republican, was on the House floor lobbying the Republicans to vote for a crippling substitute amendment.

Rep. Jesse Oliver, a Dallas Democrat, fielded questions brilliantly at the front mike. The vote came up 73 to 71. House members voted by pushing a button on their desks, and it was easy for members to push buttons for absentees. A verification of the vote was called for. The verified vote was a tie, 71 to 71. At that point, Speaker Gib Lewis took a stand. He said, "Show the chair voting Aye." The bill passed.

These changes were modest, but important. The bills set up the system of disproportionate share, which Texas used very successfully to capture more Medicaid dollars. Disproportionate share (DSH) is a source of federal funds for hospitals that treat sizable numbers of uninsured and low-income patients. The legislation began some important Medicaid expansions that greatly improved care for pregnant women and children. It created the first state legislation on patient dumping.

In the next few years many other states studied indigent health care and took various steps. Most states stepped up to their responsibility in a limited way. But Texas's struggle illustrates the difficulty states face in dealing with the ongoing challenge of health care.

The 1985 session was notable not just for the indigent health care bills but for a bill requiring mandatory insurance coverage of alcoholism treatment and bills providing unemployment and workers' compensation coverage for farm workers. I was pleased when Comptroller Bob Bullock stated "This session did more for the indigent, the afflicted, the forgotten than any session I remember and the person I think is totally responsible is Bill Hobby."

We made another good try at a comprehensive health and human services package in 1989. With the help of spin doctor Glenn Smith, then my press secretary, we named it the Hobby Anti-Crime Package of 1989. We reasoned that since crime-fighting was hugely popular and prison construction was breaking the budget, we could fashion a program that would be more effective and less expensive than putting thousands of Texans in prison.

Our package included expansions in the Medicaid health care program, alcohol and drug prevention programs, and pilot pre-kindergarten programs for low-income children. The artistry of it was that much of it was financed by leveraging federal funds with a modest amount of state money. An impressive group of organizations, including law enforcement, lined up to support the package.

Our bill was compromised, of course, as it worked its way through the legislature. But most of it survived. We successfully patched a few holes in Texas's skimpy health and human services safety net. Patience is important when working for progress in Texas. Great leaps forward are rare, perhaps non-existent, and those who selflessly dedicate themselves to achieving progress in this sometimes thankless sector deserve a position high in the panoply of saints.

Among these saints are the staff of the Center of Public Policy Priorities in Austin. Founded as the Benedictine Resource Center in 1985 by Benedictine nuns, the center has grown into a respected nonpartisan, nonprofit think tank that provides the strong foundations for constructing policy initiatives. Helen Farabee, DeAnn Friedholm, Dianne Stewart, and Scott McCown have been executive directors of this great resource. I have been honored to serve on its board.

As I have been writing these memoirs, the stage is once again set for a national health care program. DeAnn is once again in Washington, as she was during the Clinton administration's effort to create a better health care system. This time she heads the Consumers Union health care initiative. It seems a shame that in all these years we haven't made more progress.

We spend far too much on health care for what we get. In 1985, health care spending was 6 percent of GDP; in 1991, it was 12 percent. Today it is closer to 15.2 percent, according to the World Heath Organization. The percentage is still rising. Only the Marshall Islands spends a greater percentage of its wealth on health care than the United States.

About 15 percent of the population is uninsured—45.7 million people. I have mentioned previously that Texas leads the nation in this sector, with about one in four persons uninsured. About 8 million children are uninsured. The rate of uninsured children in Texas, one in five, is also the highest in the nation.

We have a much better model just north of us. Canada has had publicly funded universal coverage for medically necessary health care for more than forty years. Health care is based on need, not a patient's ability to pay. Canada even calls it "medicare."

Our northern neighbor spends less on health care than the United States—$3,678 per capita compared to $6,714 in the United States, according to a 2006 comparison by the Organization for Economic Cooperation and Development. This is about 10 percent of Canada's GDP compared to our 15.3 percent.

Our country's high per capita health care costs could be overlooked if our health outcomes vastly outpaced the rest of the world. But we don't live longer than our Canadian and European counterparts—average life expectancy in Canada is 79.9 years, while in the United States, it's 77.5 years. The United States has higher infant mortality rates than Canada— 6.9 deaths per 1,000 births in the United States compared to 5.4 per 1,000 in Canada.

Americans are not particularly happy with our system. A CNN poll in March 2009 was just one of many to show high dissatisfaction with the present situation—about 72 percent favored government programs to improve our health care system. It wasn't the number one concern—considering the wretched state of the economy at that time, but it ranked number three. If Canadians are unhappy with their health care, it's not ranking among their top concerns.

It is true that our health care system is a technological marvel that often makes people well in ways that would have seemed miraculous just a few years ago. But it also impoverishes many of our citizens and neglects millions of others.

Federal programs, except Medicaid, basically tie health care to employment. That doesn't work because there are millions of people whose employers can't afford the insurance and millions more who have no employer at all.

The price of health care goes up faster than other things because price competition does not work well. Doctors and hospitals are paid largely by insurance companies and governments. We all ultimately pay those costs, but we don't realize it in the same way we do when we pay a lawyer for legal services.

There is no great mystery about how to cut the cost of any particular medical service. It can be done in two ways: 1) cut what doctors, hospitals, and drug manufacturers are paid, and 2) cut administrative costs—including malpractice payouts.

But cutting the total bill is another matter. Any number of studies show that people who have health care coverage see the doctor more than people who do not. Those who do not are more apt to seek expensive emergency room care or wait until more expensive care is required.

A reasonable national goal would be to have a system efficient enough to provide regular coverage for those who do not have it—at no increase in total cost. Surely we are smart enough to figure out how to do with 15 percent of our national effort what the Canadians do with 10 percent of theirs?

Canada has a single-payer system—the government pays the bills directly. Citizens choose their own doctor, just as we do. Canadians have to wait longer for some kinds of care than do our citizens who have health care coverage. Some Canadians come to the United States to get quicker treatment with expensive machines (CAT scanners, magnetic resonance imagers), which are not as widely available in Canada. On the other hand, Canadian costs are lowered by the more efficient use of hospitals, which are always full. And we still have a number of citizens crossing the northern border to buy prescription medication at lower prices.

President Barack Obama made a health care plan a top priority, and he succeeded in passing an insurance reform bill in 2010. His determination reflected the hopes of the American people and the simple need for a system that does more and costs less. I hope it is successful.

23

The Legislative Redistricting Board

In Texas, since 1962, the constitution has said that if the legislature fails to redistrict itself in the first regular session after a federal census, the job will be done by the Legislative Redistricting Board (LRB). In fact almost all legislative redistricting has been done by the LRB ever since it was created. That has happened not because the legislature has been unwilling or unable to redistrict itself on time, but usually because of circumstances beyond the legislature's control. Those circumstances have included a veto by the governor and state and federal court decisions.

The LRB is made up of the lieutenant governor, the Speaker of the House, the attorney general, the comptroller, and the land commissioner. The two members of that board who have the greatest interest in the result are, obviously, the lieutenant governor and the Speaker. They are the ones who have to live with the results on a personal, day-to-day basis.

Typically each house redistricts itself, and the other house passes the bill without amendment or even much discussion. But there have been times when paranoia has interfered with that logical and orderly process. At least once in the past the mutual suspicion was so great that the doors of the two chambers were opened so that the two presiding officers could see one another across the rotunda and coordinate final passage of the two bills. Both wanted their gavels to fall at the same moment.

If the task does end up with the LRB, that same comity and respect for the other presiding officer's position usually prevails. That means that each presiding officer redistricts his own house and supports the other officer's plan. That leaves each presider with the job of getting one more vote from among the other three on the LRB. That doesn't sound like too hard a job, but in 1981 it was difficult. That year, the LRB redistricted the Senate because Governor Clements had vetoed the Senate bill. It redistricted the House after a state court threw out the House bill because the court thought the House's bill cut too many county lines.

Speaker Billy Clayton and I each had been advised by our predecessors on the basis of their experience in the 1970s not to vote on the plan for either house until the board was ready to vote on both houses. So Clayton and I produced plans for our respective houses, published the plans, took testimony, consulted with other board members, and made the indicated changes. We were still one vote short.

The constitution gives the LRB ninety days to do its work. On the morning of the last day the board could meet, the matter was still unresolved. The board met in the morning, determined that the votes weren't there for either plan and recessed for an hour or so. And recessed. And recessed. Finally, early in the evening, the board met for the severalth time in the Senate chamber. I told Billy that I had just gotten then-Attorney General Mark White's commitment. Since both of us thought that commitment was good for about ten minutes, the board went ahead and voted out the Senate plan, even though the votes were not there for the House plan. Billy's House plan was voted out later in the evening.

Texas's judicial districts haven't been redrawn in over a century. They bear no relationship to population or caseloads. Several lawsuits have attacked judicial elections on the grounds of discrimination against minorities. Federal Judge Lucius Bunton in Midland even went so far as to order a hasty and ill-advised redistricting based on outdated figures. He was reversed by the Fifth Circuit.

In 1985 the legislature added a fail-safe to the constitution on judicial districts, creating a Judicial Districts Board that would redraw those districts should the legislature fail. The state's senior judges and a lawyer appointed by the governor and confirmed by the Senate make up this board. This redistricting has been working pretty well, improving the administration of justice in Texas.

24

TEN YEARS IN ACADEMIA

FROM 1991, WHEN I LEFT THE OFFICE OF LIEUTENANT GOVERNOR, until 2001, more or less, I worked in higher education. From 1991 to 1997 I was the Sid Richardson Professor of Public Affairs at the Lyndon B. Johnson School of Public Affairs at the University of Texas at Austin. From 1995 to 1997 I was chancellor of the University of Houston System. Since 1993 I have been the Radoslav Tsanoff Professor at Rice University. Each of these was a very valuable experience. In each I got to try my hand at teaching and administering at one of Texas's finest, although very different, institutions of higher education.

I also have been a regent of the University of Houston (1965–1969), trustee of Rice University (1989–1993), trustee of St. Edwards University in Austin (1990–1995), and a member of the board of visitors of the Kennedy School of Government at Harvard (1995–2001). The LBJ School is housed in part of the long, graceful building next to the Lyndon B. Johnson Library and Museum. It was founded to produce skilled and knowledgeable practitioners of government who would work in the agencies that make our country work—local, state, and federal governments.

With that philosophy, the LBJ School has produced some remarkable alumni: Billy Hamilton, who, as chief deputy comptroller for the state, guided tax policy for more than twenty years; Bill Owens, former governor of Colorado; Rodney Ellis, Texas state senator; DeAnn Friedholm, a former state Medicaid director who spent three years advising the treasury department of the Republic of South Africa on health and social services safety net programs; and Susan Rieff, former deputy chief of staff for the U.S. Department of the Interior.

Working with idealistic and strong-minded students was a great pleasure. They cared about government and still do. Their plan was to make it work by bringing their intelligence and skills to bear, and, for the most part, that is what they did. Most of them sacrificed much higher earnings in the private sector to do what they loved—making public policy.

Another great pleasure from my time at the LBJ School was getting to know the other faculty members. I co-taught a number of budget classes

From left, Chet Brooks, Grant Jones, Ray Farabee, Bill Hobby, and Max Sherman, November 17, 2000. *Courtesy of the Hobby family.*

with Tom Keel, whose practical experience included directing the State Legislative Budget Board staff and serving as chief fiscal officer for the University of Texas System. After Tom retired, his grateful students established a scholarship in his name that is awarded each year.

Another great friend was Dean Max Sherman, a former state senator from Amarillo, who was one of the state's better public servants. An unfailingly smart, courteous, and witty gentleman, Sherman led the LBJ School to national prominence. After he left the deanship, he continued to teach a course in ethics.

The most famous faculty member at the LBJ School was Barbara Jordan, who died in 1996. The first African American woman to serve in the Texas Senate and as a congresswoman from the South, her eloquence galvanized the nation during the Watergate hearings. Barbara left a legacy of integrity and courage that no one has challenged to this day.

One time, the Rev. Jesse Jackson was in Austin to speak to the Black Caucus of the Texas Legislature. I was the only white person in the meeting, having been invited by Sen. Eddie Bernice Johnson. Jackson gave a terrible talk, all about showing those white m—therf—ers a thing or two. He asked Barbara Jordan if he could come to the LBJ School to see her that afternoon. Barbara told him she would be teaching then, but he could visit her class.

Barbara told her class that Jackson would probably drop by. She predicted that Jackson would come in, call her "Sister Barbara," and kiss her on the forehead. Barbara was a person of enormous personal dignity and reserve, and nobody who knew her very well would do either of those things. But Jackson did both. Barbara had set Jackson up to play the fool, and he did.

One of my favorite projects at the LBJ School was producing the Texas Budget Simulator. At the LBJ School, students take a two-semester course during which they produce a product for a paying client. Our client for this project was the Legislative Budget Board. The purpose was to help people understand the elements of budget decision-making—the constitutional and statutory parameters and the federal restrictions. This class produced a DOS program that allowed users to construct a state budget electronically, make policy decisions, and see their impact on the budget.

The LBJ School's niche has been state and local government, but it has since added more national and international experts to the faculty and has increased the enrollment of doctoral candidates. However, it has not lost sight of its goal. The curriculum remains sound, with a healthy dose of courses in budget preparation, economics, and statistics.

If the LBJ School's mission needed validation, it came loud and clear with the cavalier attitude of the second Bush administration toward the business of government. The idea that friends, cronies, and political hacks can run massive and critical government agencies has been demonstrated as lunacy.

Texas Senator Lloyd Bentsen (1921–2006) did not attend the LBJ School, but as congressman, senator, and secretary of the treasury, he personified all of its ideals, as well as setting the gold standard for government service. As President Clinton said at Bentsen's eulogy, he "excelled at every single thing he set his mind to." Bentsen approached national issues as a problem solver, not as an ideologue, and his legacy of important health and human service legislation and sound fiscal policy will live on. Bentsen learned, he was open to ideas, and he sought expert advice. I am proud that Lloyd Bentsen was my friend.

While I was still teaching at the LBJ School, I was asked by the Board of Regents at the University of Houston to be chancellor of the UH System on an interim basis. At that time, 1995, I wondered why I might want the job. UH had its share of problems. The turnover among administrators was high. Chancellors, campus presidents, provosts, deans, and vice presidents had come and gone at a great rate. The old joke about "When the

Hobby with Ann Richards and Lloyd Bentsen, May 2000. *Courtesy of the Hobby family.*

boss calls, find out who he is" could have been written about the University of Houston.

But I felt that the dust kicked up by the comings and goings obscured the greatness and vitality of the institution. UH's greatest asset and virtue is that it is located in Houston, a dynamic, growing city that I have called home all my life. Houston is the world center of the energy industry, a great international port, and a city with a powerful sense of entrepreneurship. Its economy is as diverse as its citizenry. It has been blessed with extraordinary political leadership—at that time the mayor was Bob Lanier and his wife, Elyse, was a UH regent.

Few institutions of higher education boasted the same level of community support that UH had. Houstonians may not have wanted to see the Cougars play football, but they were willing to speak with their pocketbooks. In 1994, UH ranked second in the nation, behind Harvard University, in private foundation support. In 1995, UH was thirty-first, outranking all Texas institutions except the University of Texas Southwestern Medical School.

The main University of Houston campus is a nationally recognized research institution with world-class programs in creative writing, drama, law, physical sciences, and hotel management. The main campus is the home of the superconductivity lab run by Dr. Paul Chu. It has a renowned creative writing program where students, many of whom go on to win national prizes, sit at the feet of the masters such as Chitra Banerjee Divakaruni, Seamus Heaney, Grace Paley, Ann Beattie, and E. Annie Proulx, all of whom and many others have been on the permanent and visiting faculty. Its School of Theatre, where Dennis and Randy Quaid learned their trade, has Pulitzer Prize-winner Edward Albee and Tony award-winner Stuart Ostrow both in residence. UH has an Honors College of selected students who explore western civilization and a Scholars' Community that deepens the university experience for commuting students.

Then as now, UH believed in going to the customer. UH faculty members teach all over the greater Houston area—in the Texas Medical Center, the Woodlands, West Houston, and at Compaq Computer. In 1995 there were three institutions beside UH. UH Downtown is an open-admission university. It offers classes at night, on weekends, and electronically, and was then entirely undergraduate. UH Downtown still takes students where they are, whether they are high school students with little hope of attending college or young urban professionals looking for another degree, and moves them where they want to go.

UH Clear Lake is a model for upper-level institutions, catering to adult professional students who want education in business, science, education, or the humanities. Unlike upper-level institutions elsewhere in Texas, it has stayed true to its role as a senior institution and never sought to become a four-year university. It seems to thrive, even without a football team.

UH Victoria (UHV) expands the system's reach to serve South Central Texas. UHV had pioneered a program called Move It Math, which teaches elementary and junior high school teachers how to teach math. UHV not only teaches this skill in South Texas, but also in Dallas, where they really need it.

Higher education is responsible for Texas's economic shift from a Third World state dependent on minerals and vegetables that come out of the ground to a technological power dependent on what comes out of people's heads.

The world has changed. No longer do we go to school, train for a career, find a job, and work until we retire. Not many of our children will follow that traditional pattern. The opportunity in the new economy is for the knowledge worker—the person who can acquire complex new skills quickly as the needs of the economy change. The knowledge worker may have three or more careers. The knowledge worker goes to school all his life and rarely has the luxury of taking several years off from earning a living.

Hobby with Bill White, October 1995. *Courtesy of the Hobby family.*

That is why I thought it was so insightful that UH student Dominic Corva described UH as "exactly what this city needs: a continuing opportunity rather than a one-time shot." UH adapted to the needs of the students, who needed to be able to acquire education at times and places convenient to them. It was open to telecommunications technology as a teaching tool. What we worked on, as this perceptive student pointed out in the *Daily Cougar* (the UH student newspaper), is not a UCLA or a University of Chicago but a higher education system that met Houston's needs. It still specializes in part-time students. It specializes in diversity. It combines excellence with access.

In 1995, however, the university was in turmoil. The faculty at the largest campus was in active revolt—they contended that the UH System administration was wastefully consuming resources that should be used at the main university. Enrollment was declining, and the football team was losing. My job at the UH System was basically to calm things down enough so that a well-qualified individual would be interested in the job of running the system. It was to my advantage in taking on this job that Houston was my hometown and that people thought well of my advocacy for higher education while I was lieutenant governor.

The main argument was whether the University of Houston, with its four institutions, should have a system form of governance, which it had had since 1977. Faculty at the UH main campus, by far the largest of the system's institutions (with its 34,000 students), believed the system was draining resources from the university and thwarting its mission as a major research institution.

I appointed task forces to study the functions of the system and the campus organizations and to identify overlaps and inefficiencies. The outcome was a somewhat reduced system office and the decision that the system chancellor would also serve as University of Houston president. System offices were moved to the UH campus from their separate downtown location.

I hope I did the job well, but my successors have done it even better. My immediate successor was a superbly qualified administrator, Dr. Arthur K. Smith, former president of the University of Utah. Dr. Jay Gogue, former president of the University of New Mexico, succeeded him, and Renu Khator, former provost at the University of South Florida, now very ably leads UH.

I was more interested in goals other than governance. I wanted to ensure that the university served its many students in the fastest-growing sector of the Houston metropolitan area—Fort Bend County. As noted, urban university students tend to be part-time and take longer to complete a degree. They tend to be older, and many of them are retooling for a new career in a society where yesterday's skills have no application. An urban university also has more minority students. Furthermore, Houston sprawls all over the Gulf Coast. The nation's fourth-largest city, it is the second largest in geographic area. A student living in Fort Bend County, for example, may be thirty miles from the main campus and has only very sketchy public transportation options.

But creating a new university in Texas isn't easy. The Texas Higher Education Coordinating Board must determine it is necessary and cost effective. The legislature must fund it—and the legislature in the 1990s wasn't much in a mood to finance the construction of new institutions. We took the recommended route—combining offerings from a number of universities to create a multi-institution teaching center. Students at what is now the University of Houston System at Sugar Land can take courses from any of three UH universities. The partnership with Wharton and Houston community colleges ensures a smooth transition for students who start their academic careers there.

Another challenge was location. Turns out that the Texas Department of Transportation (TXDOT) owned 256 acres of prime property in Fort Bend County and had no immediate plans to use it. Herb Appel, CEO of the Greater Fort Bend County Economic Development Council, was an enormous help here. He understood the value of higher education to his community. He identified the land and recommended the location for the higher education center.

I would have to say that my meeting with TXDOT officials didn't meet with enthusiastic endorsement, but they didn't push back too hard, and I decided to take the matter to the legislature. When you are trying to pass a bill, there are an impressive number of obstacles that can doom it. One early on was that our bill needed a neutral bill number. The week it came before committee, a bill numbered 666 was killed because the number apparently had satanic significance.

We weathered the storms and passed the bill. Afterward, Bob Lanier, then mayor of Houston and previously chair of the Texas Transportation Commission, asked me: "Isn't that the land you forced me and the department to buy from the prison system because you needed the money to balance the budget, and now you want them to give it away?"

The University of Houston System at Sugar Land opened its first building in 2002 and has another underway.

I was also concerned with state funding for higher education, which had been trending steadily downward. In 1995 all of the chancellors of Texas public institutions (including community colleges) started working together to build the case for more funding. The reason seemed self-evident—education is our future. We will succeed or fail based on the ideas and innovations that come out of the well-educated brains of our people.

What is evident to me is not always evident to everyone else. The state demographer, Steve Murdock (soon to be director of the U.S. Census Bureau) painted a dramatic picture that is still true today:

- Texas's population is growing fastest among groups (African Americans and Hispanics) in which educational attainment has been relatively low.
- Texas lags behind the nation in the production of college and university graduates.
- Texas per capita income is below the national average.
- If current trends continue, the average household income in Texas will decline by 2030.
- State support for public higher education has declined since 1985.

The united higher education coalition produced a case statement called "Back to Basics" that made the argument for an increase of $926 million in state funding. We got a substantial portion of what we asked. In

1997 the legislature increased funding by $593 million, in no small part due to Sen. Bill Ratliff's interest in a more effective, efficient higher education system. The product of the funding increase was a 22 percent increase in higher education degrees by the end of the phased-in program.

I wish I could say this started a favorable trend, but neither increased total funding nor a per capita increase in higher education degrees has been achieved. You get what you pay for. In this case, what we fail to pay for may cost Texas its future.

Another hope of mine as chancellor of the UH System was to chart a direction for institutions that seemed in need of a goal that everyone could agree on. My solution was a Vision Commission. The commission's job was to see what UH should look like in 2020. Get it?

Kenneth L. Lay, chair of the board of Enron Corporation, chaired the commission (it seemed like a good idea at the time). He had chaired the UH Board of Regents. He spent many hours as commission chair and did a good job. Better than he did at Enron.

This commission, with its nineteen members and its widely diverse points of view, generated fascinating debate. Participants were loosely divided between two camps. One envisioned the University of Houston as a highly innovative, open, and accessible institution that celebrated diversity, its urban location, and its role in assimilating a new immigrant culture and in re-educating the city's residents who needed new skills for new careers. The other faction envisioned "Harvard on the Bayou," a more traditional major research institution modeled after such education powerhouses as the University of Michigan. I can't say that UH achieved its vision—to become the pre-eminent metropolitan university system of the twenty-first century—but it is a worthwhile goal, and the debate was valuable.

When I left UH the *Houston Chronicle* said "UH has made steady progress and now seems poised to claim the long-sought mantle of a major urban research campus that offers excellent undergraduate education. . . . Much of the credit for that development and promise goes to a single man, former Lt. Gov. Bill Hobby." Dr. Bill Fitzgibbon, a mathematics professor who helped organize the faculty group that pressured for reform, told the *Dallas Morning News* in 1996 that he didn't "know anybody else who could have done it."

Rice University, where I taught political science, was a different experience. I was teaching undergraduates and never had the uninterrupted time to teach more than one course a semester. I am proud that Rice is my alma mater—I had been editor of the *Rice Thresher* and a history major when I graduated in 1953. I had intended to be a math major until my math professor told me I would be a much better history major.

One of my great pleasures at Rice was teaching with and getting to know Bob Stein, then dean of social sciences. Stein is a fine academician, but he is also a political junkie who conducts political polls, sometimes with his friend Dick Murray, a political scientist at the University of Houston. Stein and I enjoyed our co-teaching experiences, but even more than that we enjoyed our political discussions.

Sometime in the early 1990s, I discovered the statistics summer camp at the Inter-University Center for Political and Social Research at the University of Michigan. Since then, I have spent part of every summer in Ann Arbor learning to work with data sets and software. I worked my way up to become a teaching assistant when I was seventy-six, proving that it's never too late to find a new job.

25

The Commission on a Representative Student Body

I N 1992 CHERYL HOPWOOD and three other Anglo students filed suit against the University of Texas at Austin for denying them admission to the School of Law. In 1996 the Fifth Circuit ruled that the Fourteenth Amendment prohibits universities from considering race when admitting students. The same year, the U.S. Supreme Court let the circuit decision stand.

For higher education in Texas, that created a painful dilemma. At the time I was chancellor of the University of Houston. The chancellors of Texas public universities had asked state demographer Steve Murdock to project the state's future demographics based on Texas's present population. His study showed that the minority population was increasing but that its educational achievement was not. It does not take a demographer to know that the outlook for the future is grim if we cannot educate all our citizens to the level necessary to make a living in a post-industrial society.

Almost immediately after the Supreme Court's ruling, Texas Attorney General Dan Morales, a Democrat, issued "guidelines" to universities that advised universities to stop considering race in everything from admissions to financial aid. His ill-considered action turned a rather narrow ruling, based largely on the admittedly flawed admission policies of one law school, into a sweeping mandate covering hiring, procurement, and financial aid policies of higher education in Texas.

I asked him for an attorney general's opinion. When reporters asked why, I said, "The attorney general has held a press conference and written a letter but that does not have the effect of law." There was another important reason. Those of us serving as officers or regents of universities could be held personally liable for our actions if they thwarted a legal ruling. I thought the people of the state deserved something more than a political "have it both ways" statement on this critical issue.

The Hopwood decision was pretty strange. One of the two judges who decided the case had never read the opinion. Cheryl Hopwood and other plaintiffs claimed they were not admitted to the University of Texas Law School because they were white. Federal District Judge Sam

Sparks found that they were not admitted because they were not qualified.

The plaintiffs appealed to the Fifth Circuit. A three-judge panel sent the case back to Judge Sparks, who found they were not any better qualified than they had been a few months earlier. The Fifth Circuit panel did more than that, however. They passed a new law, 2–1, banning the use of race in determining admissions and invited enforcement by personal liability lawsuits.

A few weeks after the Fifth Circuit decision I ran into Hal DeMoss, one of the two judges who had passed the new law.

"Bill, what did you think of the Hopwood decision?" Hal asked.

"Well, Hal, I'm not a lawyer or a federal judge but I was surprised that you encouraged people to file personal liability lawsuits. I didn't think you Republicans liked that sort of thing." I replied.

"Bill, there wasn't anything in there about personal lawsuits," said Hal. Obviously he hadn't read it.

One columnist, Susan Richardson, who then wrote for the *Austin American-Statesman*, was kind enough to say that "Hobby's challenge of Morales' guidelines shouldn't be surprising for at least three reasons: Almost half the students at the University of Houston system are minorities; Hobby is a multimillionaire and beholden to no one; and most important, he has a spine."

It would have been nice to think that my letter to Morales resulted in a legally proper, narrow interpretation of the Hopwood decision, but that was not the case. Morales took a bad opinion and made it worse. His opinion essentially required that all programs at Texas public universities be race neutral. The chancellors of the state's public universities had created the Texas Higher Education Coalition to advocate more money for higher education. We now determined that there was another important task—how to attract, retain, and graduate students of all races and ethnicities in a post-Hopwood world.

The result was the Texas Commission on a Representative Student Body, created in 1997 and charged with assessing current efforts to recruit and retain minority students and to make short- and long-term recommendations for improving that record. I was asked to chair that group, which included a very experienced and talented group of academicians and citizens.

Not surprisingly, one of our main findings in 1998 was that money is a major barrier for minority students who want to go to college. At that time, a student from a family with an income above $75,000 a year had an 86 percent chance of entering college before age twenty-four while a student from a family earning less than $10,000 a year had a 38 percent chance. One of the commission's key recommendation was the creation of a fund of $500 million to provide scholarships based on need and high school grades to students who applied to a technical college, a community college, or a public or private university. The formula for the aid program was based on the premise that each student could receive a maximum of $5,000 a year to pay for higher education, with the amount received to be based on the family's ability to contribute. We asked the legislature to create a fund of approximately $60 million to be used for recruiting minority students. We also asked that work-study programs be expanded and that universities be given more funds to provide retention programs for at-risk students.

Another tactic for increasing the number of students, particularly minorities, was to develop a marketing communications plan that would appeal to prospective students. Roy Spence, one of the founders of the prestigious Austin advertising firm GSD&M, worked with us in developing a plan that included market research, production, and air time. The estimated cost was $18 million for an adequate five-year plan.

Did we get what we wanted? Yes and no. In October 2000 the Texas Higher Education Coordinating Board adopted an ambitious plan called "Texas Higher Education: Closing the Gaps," which incorporated many of the goals identified by the Commission on a Representative Student Body. Specifically, the plan set a goal of increasing overall college participation by 500,000 students by 2015. The number of African Americans enrolled was to increase by 19,300 by that time and the number of Hispanics by 120,000. These goals were based on 1999 enrollment data showing that only 4.6 percent of African Americans and 3.7 percent of Hispanics attended college, compared to 5 percent of whites.

"Closing the Gaps" also recommended increases in the grants and loans available to lower-income students as well as a sustained campaign to raise public awareness of the value of a college education, the preparation required, and the availability of financial aid.

In 2005, the goal was revised to enroll 630,000 students in higher education by 2015, 5.6 percent instead of 5 percent of the eligible population. The percentage of African Americans was to increase by 5.6 percent and the number of Hispanics by 4.8 percent. How are they doing?

Overall enrollment increased by 5.2 percent between 2000 and 2005, meeting the 2005 goal two years early, and in 2008 enrollment was on-target to reach the 5.6 percent goal. Likewise, the number of African Americans increased faster than the target rate. By fall 2005, 30,000 more African Americans were enrolled, and in 2008 it looked likely that the 5 percent goal would be met. In 2008, African Americans lagged behind whites only .001 percent in college enrollment in Texas. But Hispanic enrollment lagged, and in 2008 only 3.9 percent of eligible Hispanics were attending colleges and universities. Nor are they succeeding as well as could be hoped. In 2008, the number of associate and bachelor's degrees granted to African American and Hispanic students was approximately 1,500 short of the goal.

In 1999, Sen. Bill Ratliff and Sen. Rodney Ellis created the TEXAS (Towards Excellence, Access and Success) grant program for students with financial need. Students who complete the more rigorous Recommended High School Program or Distinguished Achievement Program in an accredited Texas high school and who meet certain eligibility requirements are automatically considered for grants of up to $4,392 per year if they enroll in a Texas public university within sixteen months of graduating from high school.

According to Ellis, in just five years, more than 115,000 young Texans received 235,000 TEXAS Grants totaling more than $648 million to help them pay for college. Forty-six percent of TEXAS Grants have gone to Hispanic students, while 13 percent have gone to African American students. Since the program began 6,758 young Texans have received $56,510,529 in TEXAS Grant funding to attend UT Austin. The UT System overall has received $187,859,907 to help 25,000 students go to college.

But funding for TEXAS grants was threatened in a matter of years. In 2003, budget cuts and rising tuition rates resulted in 22,000 students losing their grants. The program continued, however, and in 2007-2008, 53,467 students received grants, according to the Coordinating Board.

The marketing campaign Roy Spence recommended was implemented, with a Web site and television commercials boasting about the $4 billion available in financial aid to Texas students. But funding for this effort was cut in 2003, well before the campaign had achieved any significant penetration of the market.

Affirmative action, to my thinking, worked pretty well. People who think we live in a meritocracy usually have just gotten a promotion that they actually think they deserve, and they think they got it because of their unique talents. It rarely occurs to them to credit the immeasurable advantage of being a white person in a country where white people are not only the majority, but have wealth and power. Historical disadvantage, language issues, and a whole host of other factors mean that many African American, Hispanic, and Asian people don't enter school at the same level as middle-class white children, so it didn't seem controversial to give them a little extra help in getting a college education, since it's to all our benefit that they do. I was wrong.

26

The Census

VIRTUALLY ALL GOVERNMENTS TAKE CENSUSES for one purpose or another. The U.S. Census is unique in that it is an essential part of our political process. The census is required by the Constitution, Article 1, Section 2. The writers provided for a process by which seats in the U.S. House of Representatives could be apportioned among the states according to the size of their population.

Throughout history censuses have frequently been controversial and occasionally fatal. The most famous fatal census was the most storied event in history. It happened in Israel in Y-Zero-K. (Even then the census was taken in decennial years.) Joseph and the pregnant Mary traveled from Nazareth to Bethlehem to be counted and to pay taxes. They had to stay in a stable. (And today people complain about having to fill out the long form.) Herod, mindful of a prophecy that a rival king would be born at about that time and in that place, ordered the slaughter of male infants so born—the Holy Innocents. But Mary and Joseph escaped with their infant to Egypt. So Herod failed to kill the infant that, sure enough, became known as Jesus of Nazareth, King of the Jews.

In 1937 a census was taken of the Soviet Union. Premier Joseph Stalin thought the numbers were too low and shot the members of the census board for "diminishing the population of the Soviet Union." You won't be surprised that the 1939 census takers found millions more Russians.

The U.S. Census, like the historic Judean count, has been used for purposes other than demographic. In 1942, 1940 census data was used to round up and intern U.S. citizens on the West Coast who happened to be of Japanese descent. How ironic, then, that Secretary of Commerce Norman Y. Mineta, the boss of the Census Bureau from 2001 through 2005, was one of those internees. Mineta, when he was a California congressman, successfully sponsored legislation to pay $20,000 to each surviving internee.

During the Civil War, Gen. William Tecumseh Sherman used census office maps to chart his march through Georgia to the sea. The maps showed the number of whites, free blacks, and slaves in each county. They also showed how much his army could forage: the amount of improved land, the number of horses and mules, and the amount of wheat, corn, oats, and other crops in each county. "No military expedition was ever based on sounder or surer data," Sherman wrote to his daughter Ellen. The census data enabled Sherman's army to live off the land without supply lines and to move faster than traditional armies.

American history is full of pre- and post-census politics. That is the subject of a textbook *The American Census* by Margo Anderson. Margo is a historian. I am a politician, so my interest in the census is how it has affected electoral politics at various times in our history, mainly through reapportionment and redistricting. Reapportionment is about arithmetic. Redistricting is about geography.

Congress reapportions 385 seats in the House of Representatives and, therefore, in the Electoral College. The first 150 seats in the U.S. Congress are apportioned by the Constitution, which requires that each state, regardless of size, have two Senate seats and one House seat. The states redistrict the congressional seats apportioned to them and redistrict their own legislatures. Local governments redistrict county commissioners' precincts, city council districts, school board districts, etc. In a way, Congress redistricts, too—when it admits a new state.

First, here are some interesting historical episodes relating to the census.

The first census, taken in 1790, was conducted by Secretary of State Thomas Jefferson. The first bill vetoed by our first president, George Washington, was a reapportionment bill. Congress had prescribed a reapportionment method involving the fractions that result from dividing the apportionment base by the number of seats in the House of Representatives. The apportionment base is not the same as the census count. The apportionment base is the people counted by the census who are included in the state population figure that is used for the apportionment of House seats. At first all slaves were counted, but only 60 percent were included in the apportionment base. Overseas government personnel, while counted, have not always been included in the apportionment base.

The Constitution says that seats shall be apportioned among the states "according to their respective numbers." Jefferson successfully urged President Washington to veto the bill because the Constitution does not mention fractions and because the bill would have allocated more seats to Connecticut than permitted by the constitutional maximum of 1 to 30,000.

The end of the Civil War left an extraordinarily vicious Republican majority in Congress with two unexpected problems: a southern president and the prospect that the readmitted Confederate states might gain seats in Congress because freed slaves would be recognized for apportionment purposes.

The Republicans tried to deal with the first problem by passing a law saying that President Andrew Johnson from Tennessee couldn't fire his own cabinet members. They then impeached him for doing so. The impeachment of Johnson by the House and his trial by the Senate was a sorry chapter in U.S. history with which the 1999 Bill Clinton impeachment fiasco has made us all too familiar.

The U.S. Constitution excluded 40 percent of the slaves from the apportionment base. When slavery was abolished by the Thirteenth Amendment all former slaves were to be included. It was one thing to free the slaves. But putting more Democrats in Congress was quite another! Some Republicans feared that the inclusion of all freed slaves in the population count of the former Confederate states would gain them an additional sixteen seats. Sixteen new Southern electoral votes and additional Democratic seats in Congress certainly were not what the Republicans had in mind. After all, the North won the war, right?

The Republicans need not have worried. The former Confederate states did not, in fact, increase their share of seats in the House of Representatives. The 1870 census showed that the apportionment base of the former Confederate states increased by only 14 percent, less than the national increase of about 25 percent. Also, later figures showed that the South had probably been undercounted by 1.26 million (about 3 percent). The actual undercount was probably greater. Until 1880, U.S. marshals did the counting. The western states of California, Iowa, Michigan, Minnesota, Missouri, and Oregon had grown more than 50 percent, thanks to the passage of the Homestead Act in 1862. Eastern states lost population but not seats in Congress, partly because the size of the House of Representatives was increased from 243 to 292.

The 1920 census showed that the U.S. population had grown by 14 million during the decade. The Republicans' problem was that the rural population had dropped by 5 million. Therefore, the urban population increased by 19 million. Many of the new city dwellers were European immigrants. Nativist Republicans feared that Irish and German immigrants would vote for Democrats. As a consequence, the 1920 House simply ignored the Constitution and did not reapportion seats in the House of Representatives.

Here is how reapportionment works: Think of population as a variable with several different values, with the values descending rather than ascending.

The first and largest value (POP_0) is the actual (and unknown) population of the United States at 12:01 a.m. April 1, 2000.

The Census Bureau's adjusted figure (POP_1) may be used to distribute about $150 billion a year in federal aid under many different programs, the largest being Medicaid.

The traditional Census Bureau unadjusted figure for the nation and the individual states (POP_2) is the sum of the POP_2s of each state. The undercount, many of whom are children and minorities, is determined by subtracting POP_2 from POP_0.

The apportionment base (POP_3) changes from time to time. Originally the Constitution excluded two-fifths of the slaves and "Indians not taxed by this Constitution." The Thirteenth Amendment eliminated the partial slave exclusion. The untaxed Indians remained excluded until 1940. The Fourteenth Amendment was a rather weird (and ignored) attempt to reduce the apportionment bases by excluding males over twenty-one who were denied the right to vote due to their involvement in crime or rebellion. The 1990 apportionment base was 249,022,783. U.S. Government employees overseas have been in and out of this group. They were in in 1971, 1991, and 2001, out in other years. Their inclusion in 1991 switched a House seat from Massachusetts, home of the former Speaker Tip O'Neill, to Washington, home of the then-Speaker Tom Foley. Odd coincidence.

The population eligible to vote (POP_4) is currently POP_2 minus minors, aliens, and felons. POP_4 was changed in 1865 by the Fifteenth Amendment to include former slaves, in 1920 by the Nineteenth Amendment to include women, in 1971 to include those between eighteen and twenty-one years old.

Lest you think felons are unimportant in reapportionment just because they can't vote, ask Rep. Eddie Bernice Johnson from Dallas. As a state senator in 1991 she drew her own congressional district. She was asked if she had drawn the district to include every African American in south Dallas County, Texas. She said no, she had excluded felons.

Speaking of felons, let's go back to the apportionment base for a moment, using Wisconsin as an example. Wisconsin farms out many of its felons to Texas and other states. Should Wisconsin's farmed-out felons be in Wisconsin's POP_3 or Texas's? Wisconsin is on the cusp of losing a congressional seat. The census counts prisoners where they are incarcerated, not where they lived before imprisonment. In 2008 a Wisconsin representative introduced a state constitutional amendment that would not count incarcerated prisoners at all—an attempt to deal with the skewed counts for Wisconsin counties, mostly rural, that have large prisons. A Wisconsin congressman introduced a bill directing the Census Bureau to count Wisconsin felons as if they were in Wisconsin, wherever they may be. Governor Thompson was afraid he may have exported a congressman among the felons, but he won't say which one. On Wisconsin.

Registered voters are POP$_5$. The Census Bureau does not register voters. POP$_5$ is changed from time to time as people tinker with registration rules. Poll taxes, property ownership, and literacy tests have been eliminated as voting requirements. Voter registration rules change. One recent effort has been the "motor voter" law passed in 1993, under which a citizen is given the opportunity to register to vote whenever he or she has contact with almost any state agency. Changes to POP$_5$ are mostly a waste of time. People who have to be begged to register aren't likely to vote.

Since 1911 the size of the House of Representatives has basically been 435, but it has not always been so and could be changed by Congress at any time. I say "basically" because it blipped to 437 when Alaska and Hawaii were admitted, then reverted to 435. Margo Anderson has argued for increasing the size of the House as population increases, as was done in the eighteenth and nineteenth centuries. Generally, the size of lower houses in large democracies is approximately the cube root of the population. For example, the Census Bureau count for 2000 was 281,421,906, which according to that guideline would mean a House numbering more than 650 members.

Redistricting is a morass of confusing federal law and court opinions. The Voting Rights Act commands legislators not to pack districts with minority voters and not to dilute them, but also commands the legislators to create "majority-minority" districts.

States under Section 5 of the Voting Rights Act must get pre-clearance for redistricting plans from the Justice Department, so their plans must conform to DOJ guidelines. But in a recent case involving Georgia congressional districts, the Fifth Circuit in New Orleans said, in effect, we make the law around here, not the Department of Justice.

In other words, the law of redistricting is confused, confusing, and ever changing. It was even more confusing in 2001 when two sets of census figures–adjusted and unadjusted–were available to each jurisdiction. Redistricting used to be a mysterious process conducted in the semi-secrecy of legislative offices. Now anybody with a computer can play. Redistricting software is readily available. Here is a recipe for litigation that will go on for the entire decade. Then the process will start all over again.

27

THE NATIONAL RIFLE ASSOCIATION

I WAS NEVER A GREAT FRIEND of the National Rifle Association. When I was lieutenant governor, I used to get letters inspired by the NRA wondering why I wasn't a better gun advocate. I'm a hunter, but sometimes my lack of support was because I found it hard to keep the NRA's position clear. For example, what is the National Rifle Association's (NRA's) position on criminal background checks and waiting periods?

The NRA has waffled a lot on the issues of background checks and waiting periods for the last several decades. In the mid-1970s the NRA published a firearms control pamphlet in which it said "a waiting period could help in reducing crimes of passion and preventing people with criminal records or dangerous mental histories from acquiring guns."

The NRA is hardly alone in waffling on gun control. When Lloyd Bentsen beat George Bush for the United States Senate in 1970, Bentsen made a campaign issue of a pro-gun-control vote by then-congressman Bush. In 1988 presidential candidate George Bush made an issue of Massachusetts Governor Dukakis's support of gun control. Bentsen, of course, was Dukakis's running mate. What goes around comes around.

By the early 1980s the NRA took a strong stand against criminal background checks, charging that they were an invasion of privacy and divert police from real crime to paperwork.

Congress passed the Brady Bill in 1983. The Brady Bill is named for James Brady, former press secretary to President Ronald Reagan. Brady was crippled for life by a pistol-wielding would-be assassin targeting Reagan. The Brady Bill required a seven-day waiting period to buy a pistol. When the U.S. House of Representatives was considering the bill in 1988, the NRA opposed a waiting period. In an effort to kill the bill, the NRA abandoned its earlier opposition to "gun control" laws and supported instant background checks at the point of sale. Such checks would require an expensive and (at that time) non-existent federal computerized system of criminal records to be created and made accessible to gun dealers. Talk about invasion of privacy!

Of course, the NRA's real objective was to pass a measure that would be impossible to implement. It took ten years and hundreds of millions of dollars to develop and install such a system. This National Instant Criminal Background Check System came online in 1998 and trumped the seven-day waiting period.

Later the NRA supported legislation extending Oregon's five-day waiting period to fifteen days. And here in Texas, NRA supporters pushed state Sen. Gene Green's concealed weapons bill to allow citizens to carry guns around with them after undergoing a background check. Is the NRA schizophrenic? Why it is OK to conduct background checks under the Green bill—for concealed permits—but not for handgun sales?

In 1991 the NRA opposed a Brady Bill renewal because it *only* requires a waiting period but not a background check. In an effort to compromise, Senate Majority Leader George Mitchell attached an amendment to the bill requiring a background check and providing federal money for states to update their criminal records databases. Yet the NRA remains opposed to the revised gun control bill. The Brady Bill didn't make the streets safe overnight, but it was a step in the right direction.

The NRA's flip-flopping has been going on for decades. The NRA used to be a fairly benign group interested in teaching people about gun safety, target shooting, and hunting techniques. (I won some NRA marksmanship medals when I was a boy.) But somewhere along the line the association leaders went crazy. In the early 1980s, for example, they opposed the nation's law enforcement officers who were working to outlaw the armor-piercing ammunition that police call "cop-killer" bullets. By 1986, they opposed a ban on plastic pistols, which don't set off metal detectors in airports and government buildings. And even after several mass murders with assault rifles triggered the introduction of bills in congress to ban the sale of assault weapons, the NRA remains opposed to this legislation. What do legitimate gun owners need with weapons that kill cops and aid terrorists?

The NRA has dug itself into a hole by taking positions that include supporting waiting periods and background checks, but in reality were only designed to delay and weaken bills when their passage seemed inevitable. In fact, the association's positions revolve faster than the chamber on a Saturday night special.

On one issue the NRA is consistent. Whenever there is an issue between armed robbers and policemen, the NRA favors the criminals. Moreover, the NRA, generally thought of as a right-wing group, likes to rewrite history just as much as the left-wing "politically correct" forces on some university campuses.

The NRA said I was incorrect in my belief that the NRA opposed the bill banning armor-piercing ammunition (known as coiller bullets to police).

The NRA, through its spokesman Weldon Smith, says the NRA not only supported the ban, but drafted the legislation and helped pass it. Not quite.

Cop-killer bullets were originally designed for the police. But police stopped using the bullets because they ricochet, endangering both police and bystanders. By 1982, when legislation was first introduced to ban the bullets, the only people using them were criminals who wanted to kill policemen wearing bulletproof vests.

Nevertheless, the NRA opposed the ban on coiller bullets, charging that the issue was a "media-made hoax." Police officers whose lives were threatened by the bullets did not agree. Many police chiefs testified on behalf of the bill. In 1984 the Reagan administration proposed a compromise bill that would outlaw the manufacture and importation of cop-killer bullets. Finding itself backed into a corner, the NRA gave in and said it wouldn't oppose the administration's bill, but it would continue to oppose any bill that banned the *sale* of cop-killer bullets. But the bill Congress passed did ban the sale of armor-piercing, or cop-killer, bullets.

The NRA denied, in letters to me, that it opposed legislation banning pistols made from polymer or ceramic that have a few small metallic parts. So small, in fact, that they don't set off the metal detectors in airports and government buildings. These guns are potentially dangerous weapons in the hands of terrorists.

In 1987 the U.S. Senate considered a bill to ban such guns. When asked to take a stand on the issue, the NRA said they could not support a ban on these guns because no such guns existed, hence they were not a realistic threat. They also said the bill was a back-door effort to ban thousands of guns that already existed, even though the bill specifically exempted all legally owned guns.

More than half a dozen people testified before the Senate that prototypes of this gun existed and that the technology was available to produce them in vast numbers. Senators also heard from police officers, the U.S. Secret Service, and airline representatives who testified that the proliferation of these guns would create dangerous security problems. Faced with this expert testimony, the NRA decided that plastic guns did exist but that they had legitimate hunting purposes and shouldn't be banned.

Unlike some issues before Congress, this time senators on both sides of the aisle were bound and determined to prevent a problem before it became one. The only way to ensure that these weapons would never get into the hands of terrorists and assassins was to ban them before they hit the market. And that's what Congress did. Thanks to the wisdom of the U.S. Congress—and no thanks to the NRA—plastic guns cannot legally be made or sold in the United States.

28

The Hobby-Eberly Telescope

WHEN I LEFT OFFICE, after serving longer than any other lieutenant governor of Texas, there were few monuments to Bill Hobby. A state prison and a state office building in Austin acquired at the depths of the 1980s bust bore my name. The deficit of desirable namesakes has been remedied. My favorite monument is the Hobby-Eberly Telescope (HET).

This very large telescope—the fourth-largest optical telescope in the world—scans the dark skies of West Texas from Mount Fowlkes at McDonald Observatory. It started out as a pipe dream. It was a dream first for two Penn State astronomers, Dan Weedman, an extra-galactic scientist, and Larry Ramsey, who studied stars in the Milky Way, our home galaxy. In 1983 Weedman was wrestling with the problem of making large telescopes with the light-collecting ability necessary to reach into deep space. Eight-meter telescopes were so expensive as to be beyond reach for Penn State, and time on the existing large telescopes was so limited that access for those wishing to study faint, distant objects was difficult.

Weedman had an idea that an optical telescope could borrow from the concept of the giant radio telescope. That is, it could be pointed at one part of the sky with the revolution of the earth to add scope. Such a telescope would be built for spectroscopy, the science of discovering the evolution of stars from their chemical compositions. Weedman wondered if it could be formed from several mirrors, which would be much cheaper to construct than the prohibitively single large mirror. He talked to his colleague Larry Ramsey, an expert in the construction of spectrographs.

In 1984 they took their idea, now developed into the Penn State Spectroscopic Survey Telescope, to a conference near Munich, Germany, that was exploring new concepts for telescope construction. Another presenter was Harlan Smith, the director of the University of Texas's McDonald Observatory. Smith was a Texas visionary who had conceived a plan for a telescope that used a very thin mirror that could be shaped by computer-assisted drivers.

Harlan Smith had big dreams. His dream was called the Eye of Texas, a 7.7-meter telescope with a price tag of $50 million. The University of Texas at Austin was committed to the project and had already raised $2 million for it by 1984. But Texas was then descending into one of its periodic oil busts, which doomed the project. Meanwhile, Weedman had connected with UT radio astronomer Frank Bash and had arranged a meeting with Smith. An optimist, Smith embraced Weedman's idea, which had the advantage of being $44 million cheaper. With a cost estimated at $6 million, Smith got then-UT Chancellor William Cunningham to sign on. Cunningham committed $1.5 million, so more than half of the price was already in hand.

In 1989, Bill Cunningham and George Christian asked me to help with the fundraising. What was to become the Hobby-Eberly Telescope was a new idea. Building a working telescope producing good science took more time and money than anyone realized.

When Harlan visited me about the telescope, I didn't yet know him (although his wife, Joan, remembers them cheering for me at a parade in Midland, and my wife, Diana, and Joan were schoolmates at Radcliffe). Later, when I eulogized Harlan at his funeral in 1991, I said that he was "gentle and joyful in all that he did—a patient and lucid expositor in a way that only someone of great wisdom, as well as knowledge, can be."

I liked Harlan and his idea of the telescope. I liked visiting West Texas. He invited me to visit McDonald Observatory in 1987 and learn more about his proposal to build a very large telescope with segmented mirrors for less money than a traditional telescope with a single large mirror.

Raising money for a telescope, even an inexpensive telescope, is a more difficult proposition than raising money for, say, a football stadium. And the oil bust had extended to agriculture and real estate and was proving very persistent. But my friends and colleagues brought enthusiasm and persistence to their task.

Houston banker Ben Love became the chief fundraiser. A luncheon presentation at the Houston Club netted $300,000 and pledges of even more. Meanwhile, Penn State was raising money on its own, finding a patron in Robert Eberly, a chemist and businessman who had been generous to the Eberly College of Science at Penn State. The telescope would be jointly named.

Money rolled in fast enough that the astronomy departments of the two universities were able to proceed with detailed plans and an outside technical review. The 1991 review made it clear that the $6 million estimate was low. The new benchmark was $10 million. One of my frustrations with the project was that the projections increased in astronomical fashion. But the astronomers were never discouraged. They decided they needed new partners to put up the cash. Georg-August University in Goettingen, Ludwig-Maximilians University in Munich, and Stanford University all bought in.

By now Harlan's health was failing, and Frank Bash had succeeded him as director of McDonald Observatory. Bash is a radio astronomer with an interest in large-scale star formation processes in spiral galaxies. He had been awarded several teaching honors and is a first-class communicator, as well as a warm and genial person. He is as adept as Smith at making others see the vision of a very large telescope. He created the multi-university team that would fund and benefit from the HET.

In 1992 the project got underway. Tom Sebring, an optics engineer who has since managed construction at the Southern Astrophysical Research Telescope and the Lowell Observatory Discovery Channel Telescope, was hired to manage construction. Sebring's first task was a top-to-bottom review. He concluded that some of the plans would not work. As a result, the idea of building a truss, the Pyrex mirrors, and even the original location of the telescope on Mount Locke were all scrapped.

Sebring's philosophy, based partly on his budget constraints, was "the better is the enemy of the good enough." He set out to design and build the project in a "direct, lean, mean and innovative way." HET's structure had to withstand winds of more than one hundred miles per hour, the high level of dust common to desert environments, and the daily temperature shifts that would play havoc with the mirrors and delicate instrumentation.

I joined Robert Eberly and officers from the five universities in breaking ground for the telescope in 1994. First light came on December 12, 1996. I was there again for the telescope's dedication in October 1997, after many trips with Frank Bash to see the progress in erecting this monument to innovation. During the dedication Frank said the project had been on budget and on schedule. When it was my turn, I asked him, "Which budget and which schedule?"

Most telescopes go round and round and up and down. One reason the HET cost only about a fifth of what comparable telescopes cost is that it just goes round and round. It is permanently pointed fifty-five degrees above the horizon. That means the astronomer has to wait for his part of the sky to come by. The telescope floats on air bearings, which allows it to turn to track objects across the sky.

When a telescope is traversing from one part of the sky to another it is not observing and doing science. A computer schedules observations to maximize observing time and readjusts the schedule when cloudy skies

Bill Hobby and the Otto Struve 82" Telescope, Fort Davis, c. 1997. *Courtesy of the Hobby family.*

make observation impossible. The uncertainty of observation times makes it pretty hard for an astronomer from Goettingen to know when to show up in West Texas. He doesn't have to. The results show up on his computer.

Nobel Prize-winning astrophysicist Steven Weinberg gave the dedication address. "The Hobby-Eberly Telescope will take the students and the faculty members who use it on quite a voyage," Weinberg said. "They will be traveling out thousands of lightyears, to visit stars and clusters of stars within our own galaxy, and millions of lightyears farther on to visit other galaxies, and billions of lightyears beyond that to see the most distant objects that can be seen, objects that were formed when the universe was about one-tenth its present age."

At first the HET didn't work well. It was a prototype baby, and, like many difficult children, it had issues. In 2000, with the HET operating far below its intended capacity, Frank Bash made a plea to the University of Texas at Austin for increased funding to make changes that would make the HET far more functional.

The HET was a challenge to engineering and an experiment in economics, as Stanford University astronomer Roger Romani noted. With its complex moving parts and first-of-its kind configuration it was remarkable that it worked at all.

As is always the case at a major research university, the competition for dollars was fierce. There were other priorities, other urgent needs, even some grumbling that the HET was turning into a West Texas white elephant that would never function correctly. But McDonald Observatory receives part of its funding from the state legislature as a special item—a specific appropriation earmarked for its use. I wasn't lieutenant governor any longer, but I still had some friends in high places. Working with other friends of the University of Texas, we secured the funding, and while we were at it, we added in a little warning to the university. A rider on the 2001 appropriations bill stated that universities that fail to follow the wishes of donors on projects funded with private contributions would find those contributions subject to refund. I know you can't do that in a rider, but it sent a good message.

The 2001 repairs brought the HET close to fulfilling its promise. All the problems are not solved. Among the ongoing challenges the telescope faces are

- the "adobe effect," mud buildup on mirrors resulting from West Texas dust and humidity
- difficulties with the tracker, a complex instrument that adjusts the scope to find new targets
- a limited field of view
- poor image quality
- long setup time.

Nevertheless, by 2005, after five years of observing, HET data had appeared in eighty peer-reviewed journals. Discoveries included detection of the most distant objects in the universe, one of the smallest known planets orbiting a nearby star, and the identification of the nature of many of the faintest known X-ray sources. Technical innovations were continuously being applied to the telescope, in particular to the challenging task of aligning the ninety-one segments of the primary mirror. By 2007 the fraction of time required to maintain the shape of the mirror had been reduced from over a third to less than 10 percent.

In recent years the HET has concentrated on programs that emphasize its combination of special capabilities: large light-gathering power and use of queue scheduling. These traits have allowed the HET to become a key player in the exciting fields of discovery and characterization of planets outside of our solar system and observations of titanic cosmic explosions (supernovae and gamma ray bursts) that reveal the fundamental structure of the universe.

UT astronomer Karl Gebhardt said the HET competes very well with other eight-meter telescopes. Long exposures on single objects do work, he said.

In addition to producing good science, the HET enabled the University of Texas at Austin to gain a new observing point in the southern hemisphere and provided an opportunity for South Africa to build its own large telescope. The South African Large Telescope (SALT) design was based on the HET, and the telescope's designers used the experience at HET to make innovations and improvements. HET is a 10 percent partner in SALT, the South African Astronomical Observatory having traded observing time at SALT for the HET plans and design advice from the HET team.

SALT is located in the high, dry region called the Karoo in the Northern Cape, a four-hour bus ride from Cape Town. Those of us who attended SALT's inauguration rode a bus through lush vineyards and imposing mountains—a long tunnel was one feature of the trip. The little town of Sutherland, above which the SALT stands, has a welcome sign that says "Sutherland: Twin Town to Fort Davis, Texas." In fact, the landscape, with its scrub brush and scorpions, looks a lot like West Texas. SALT is the largest telescope in the southern hemisphere.

The $36 million eleven-meter SALT is the result of an ambitious plan by the South African government to keep its country on the global astronomical charts. "Maybe it sounds fantastic for South Africa to want to play in the big leagues of astronomy," said Dr. Khotso Mokhele, president of South Africa's National Research Foundation. "Does it not have more pressing needs, more pressing problems that it should tackle now and maybe contemplate astronomy sometime else? Yes, but unless we start to make the sort of investments that SALT is, then we never come out of poverty."

South Africa's President Thabo Mbeke spoke at the inauguration of the telescope. "Even those of us who know nothing about astronomy have awaited this day with great anticipation, feeling, perhaps instinctively, that this giant eye in the Karoo would tell us as yet unknown and exciting things about ourselves," he said.

To the UT astronomers who struggled with the Hobby-Eberly's birth, SALT "is a beautiful vindication of the effort we put into HET, that the South Africans chose to build a copy of it," said David Lambert, director of McDonald Observatory.

And much is ahead for the HET itself. One of the most ambitious proposals for the HET is the HETDEX (Hobby Eberly Telescope Dark Energy Experiment) a survey intended to solve one of the great mysteries of the universe. Understanding dark energy—what it is and how it works—is considered the number one problem in astrophysics. If HETDEX is successful, the HET will be the first telescope in the world to characterize dark energy.

"What is dark energy? We have no idea," Karl Gebhardt, associate professor of astronomy at the University of Texas at Austin, told the McDonald Observatory Board of Visitors in July 2005. Gebhardt estimated that 73 percent of the universe is dark energy, 23 percent is cold dark matter, and only 4 percent is atoms. In other words, Gebhardt said, "we are completely insignificant in terms of the universe."

But it appears that dark energy is responsible for the acceleration in the rate of universe expansion. After the Big Bang, galaxies moved apart, but as time passed, gravitational expansion slowed the rate of the expansion of the galaxies. Astronomers speculate that dark energy grows while the rate of expansion slows and then pushes bodies apart at a faster rate. The HETDEX plan is to map with very high precision the positions of 2 million galaxies in order to construct a three-dimensional map of the universe.

The HETDEX survey will consume most of the dark time (when the moon is not in the sky) spring viewing nights for several years and produce huge amounts of data. To implement it, the research team is using a $3 million federal grant to expand the field of view for the survey observations. Construction is underway for VIRUS, a combination of perhaps 145 spectroscopes that can rapidly replicate the data coming in from deep sky probes by the telescope. The cost of the dark energy project is about $34 million and the hope is the Department of Energy and private donations will pay for it. Like other science projects, the cost keeps going up, but like the telescope that will be used, HETDEX is cheap compared to other dark energy proposals.

In 2007, UT astronomers were still full of dreams. The astronomy department, with university commitment, was moving full steam ahead on the $90 million Giant Magellan Telescope (GMT), with seven 8.4-meter mirrors, which would be located in Chile. The Magellan will be fully steerable and have five times the light-gathering ability of the HET. UT is partnering with the Carnegie Institution of Washington, Harvard University, Massachusetts Institute of Technology, the Smithsonian Astrophysical Observatory, Texas A&M University, the University of Arizona, and the University of Michigan. "It's a high-stakes game and not for the faint of heart," said UT Provost Sheldon Eckland-Olson at the Board of Visitors meeting in July 2005. So what else is new?

29

Hobby for President

I DECIDED IN 2000 that I should run for president, and it would have been a whole lot better for everyone if I had followed through with it. Too bad I didn't make up my mind until the primaries were nearly over. Even then, I thought I still had a chance. Certainly Gov. George W. Bush would have tried to keep me off the ballot, but he wasn't very good at keeping Ross Perot off the ballot. I'm not nearly as crazy as Ross Perot, and he was on the ballot in every state!

The platform I adopted had two parts. First were the things I said I would NOT do.

- I will never raise your taxes. Or lower them either. Presidents can't do either one. Only Congress can pass a tax bill or an appropriations bill. Any candidate who says differently hasn't read the Constitution. Nor will I insult your intelligence by telling you that I will eliminate the deficit but spend more on defense and education or by telling you we have a "surplus" when we owe $2.5 trillion. (The national deficit now is $10.6 trillion.)
- I will not go to war in a country unless I've heard of it.
- I will not be your spiritual leader. I will not tell you what church I go to, if any. It's against the law—or at least the spirit of the law. Congress won't let an employer ask an employee about religion, and I want to be your employee. Also, it's bad manners to flaunt your religion, plus it's none of your business.
- I will not be your nanny. I will not tell you to stop smoking by putting a warning label on the pack you have already bought. I won't tell you to fasten your seat belt. If you are smart enough to vote for me, you can figure those things out. I will not put pills in bottles nobody can open. I will stop putting airbags that may kill you in your car. I will not let the government search you every time you get on an airplane.
- I will not tell states what flag to fly over their capitols. If the folks in South Carolina are so boorish as to fly a Confederate flag to deliber-

ately infuriate African Americans, that is not the concern of the president or Congress.

- Speaking of civil war, I will not tell Russians how to handle their civil war in Chechnya, even though we handled our own civil war so well.
- I will not tell other countries whom to elect as their president. That's their business. For that matter, I won't even tell you whom to vote for any other office. If you're smart enough to vote for me, you're smart enough to make up your own mind.
- I will not take contributions from greedy special interests. Greedy special interests contribute to my opponents.
- I will not let people call you at dinner to sell you something over the phone nor let companies play music when they put you on hold. Press no. 8, and they will be fined $5,000.

In the interest of full disclosure, there were things I wanted to tell voters that I would not have been able to tell them once my campaign started. I am a minority candidate. I am an aging white male. If you vote for anybody younger, I will sue you for age discrimination. But enough of negative things. Here's what I WILL do.

- I will declare victory in the war on drugs. We have put more of our citizens in prison than such democracies as Russia and South Africa, so we must have won. After all, Prohibition worked. Right?
- I will make anybody who sues you unsuccessfully pay you whatever amount he was trying to extort from you. That will clear up the backlog in the courts so I won't have to appoint any more judges. Since I won't appoint any more judges, the U.S. Senate won't be able to embarrass itself further by listening to idiots like Strom Thurmond and Jesse Helms.
- Most important of all, I WILL do a superb job of running the executive branch of the federal government. After all, that's what the U.S. Constitution says the president is supposed to do.

Of course, I decided not to run, but think about it . . . would we have been better or worse off if I had?

30

Just Vote No

J UST BEFORE EACH BIENNIAL SESSION of the Texas Legislature, I feel compelled to offer legislators some advice.

Dear Legislator:

Congratulations on your recent election! The easy part is over!

Between now and the end of May you will set the state's priorities for the next two years. You will consider thousands and pass hundreds of bills. The bill that really counts is the general appropriations bill. In that one bill you will decide how well Texans will be educated, regulated, imprisoned, and medicated for the next two years.

Spend every nickel you can on education. Every nickel you don't spend now will cost dollars in the future for welfare and prisons.

Then go home. Please don't pass any more laws.

Specifically, anybody who wants to "amend the Penal Code by adding a new section to read as follows . . ." probably thinks they are "getting tough on crime" by creating another law. What they are really doing is getting tough on taxpayers. It's cheaper to send a person to college for a year than to lock that person up for a year. People have been passing laws for about 5,000 years now—ever since the Code of Hammurabi. If we could eliminate, or even reduce, crime by passing laws, we wouldn't have built new prisons in years. New laws in the Penal Code create new crimes and new criminals. We have enough criminals already, so Just Vote No.

Don't try to tell people what it is you don't want them to put into their minds or bodies. (See above.) People won't appreciate your advice, or even pay attention, so Just Vote No.

Whenever somebody wants to "reform" something, hold on to your purse or wallet tightly. What they really want to do is transfer money or power from some other group to their own group. Maybe that's all right. In fact, that's why legislatures meet every year or so—to change power and money relationships to fit the political realities of the day. But when somebody tells you he or she wants to "reform" something, they are saying

"Trust me." Just don't think the world is going to be a better place after it's "reformed"—or be disappointed when it isn't, so Just Vote No.

Somebody will probably want to "reform public schools" by "amending the Education Code by adding a new section to read as follows . . ." Nothing in the Education Code makes any difference in the classroom anyway, so give it a rest and Just Vote No.

Don't react to a tragedy by passing a law. Don't vote (as Congress did) to give the cops more power because a right-wing nut blew up the federal building in Oklahoma City. Don't vote to create "hate crimes," however heinous the deed. Such crimes are already first-degree offenses (murder, etc.) and carry the heaviest penalties available, so Just Vote No.

Don't be silly. Don't decide how much water will flush a toilet, as Congress did a few years ago. Don't decide that the circumference of a circle is three times the diameter, as a legislature in the last century did. Don't decide that the earth is only four thousand years old, as legislatures have when they made monkeys of themselves by passing evolution laws. In short, don't make a fool of yourself—Just Vote No.

And, speaking of people making fools of themselves, please repeal the law against libeling cows. The Panhandle ranchers must have caught mad cow disease just before they sued Oprah Winfrey, and legislators who passed the law certainly need a check-up.

Resolutions: Vote against the little stuff, too. Seemingly harmless resolutions can be as bad as bills.

Nobody can sue the state of Texas in state court unless you vote to let them by passing a "resolution to sue the State." Anybody who does business with the state knows that. These resolutions cost the state millions of dollars a year in needless legal costs and judgments. When you pass these resolutions, you are giving away the state's money. Would you waive your own immunity, the statute of limitations, for example, to let somebody sue you personally? You wouldn't give your own money away that way, so Just Vote No.

Legislators are forever introducing "memorial resolutions." These are not in honor of departed constituents but are resolutions "memorializing" Congress to do something or other. Nobody in Congress ever reads these things, nor is there any reason why they should. Somebody is trying to make you vote on some issue that is not before the legislature. You should vote "Present not voting" or Just Vote No.

Legislative rules are set by resolution early in the session. The rules authorize the lieutenant governor and the Speaker to appoint legislators to committee chairmanships and other important positions on the basis of the legislator's effectiveness and experience, not on the basis of partisanship. Neither party has a patent on statesmanship or leadership. If somebody tries to amend the rules resolution to make the legislature more partisan, to make the legislature look more like Congress, Just Vote No.

I know that it just plain feels good to get tough on crime, reform all sorts of things, mess around with the schools yet again, fight the war on drugs, and so on. Especially if you borrow the money and don't have to pay for it. Maybe the best rule is: If it feels good, Just Vote No.

But don't vote "No" on everything! Here are a few ideas that will reduce the size of state government and might save some money, too.

You have lightened the attorney general's workload by not letting people sue the state. Why not save even more money by privatizing the office? There are able lawyers in the attorney general's office, but the turnover rate is high. A lot of time is wasted because of the lack of continuity. Many agencies, particularly those outside Austin, will be better served by private counsel. Appropriate money to each state agency for its legal expenses and let the agency decide whether to use the attorney general's office or a private law firm. Reduce the attorney general's appropriation accordingly. (How would you feel if you couldn't select your own lawyer for your own business?)

Make the loser pay all court costs and attorney fees, plus an insult charge to a successful defendant. Reduce judicial appropriations accordingly. Why should you and I foot the bill every time somebody goes to court to whine that it was somebody else's fault?

Remove the requirement that the Texas Higher Education Coordinating Board approve every course offered by every state university and community college. Universities get paid by the number of students that take a course, so they don't teach courses that nobody wants. Hundreds of people, both at the coordinating board and the schools, now do this busywork that the law requires. And you are for local control, aren't you?

Abolish the State Securities Board. The federal government (Securities and Exchange Commission) regulates the securities business. We don't need two nannies.

SINCERELY,
BILL HOBBY

31

Parting Thoughts

I hope that reading these memoirs has been as instructive and enjoyable for you as writing them has been for me. My life has centered around public affairs, first as a journalist and then as a public official. It was the same for my parents, who were my role models.

My lasting friendships began about the time I became lieutenant governor: Saralee Tiede, Max Sherman, Betty King, George Christian, to name a few. Most of my newspaper friends passed away long ago.

The greatest satisfaction of my life has come from my wife, Diana, a scholar and editor. Diana is also that rarest of people—someone who enjoyed being married to a public official. Our four children, Laura, Paul, Andrew, and Kate, and their spouses are all wonderful people who have produced nine grandchildren who are fine, productive citizens.

What more could one ask of life?

Writing this book has, of course, brought back many memories that would have been lost forever but for the process of setting them down.

The most important lesson of my life, that I hope I have imparted in this book, is that public officials should think of their oath of office as a Hippocratic oath:

First, do no harm. For example, don't lock up people whose lifestyle you don't like. Don't try to tell people who they can sleep with or what drugs they can take. They won't appreciate your messing in their business or even pay any attention to you.

Don't pass any more laws. We have quite enough already. Don't create more crimes. We have enough criminals already. Free the people now serving time because of the foolish laws described above. Get them back to work and off the taxpayers' back.

Second, don't make a fool of yourself by trying to inflict your views on other people. Galileo was a better astronomer than the pope. Darwin was a better biologist than the creationists. Don't try to secede from the union, either. That didn't work so well the last time we tried it.

Bill and Diana Hobby with Ann Richards, 1994. *Courtesy of the Hobby family.*

Family portrait, c. 2004. *Courtesy of the Hobby family.*

Don't try to save the world. The world will not appreciate your efforts. It has steadfastly resisted salvation for millions of years. The most important service government can provide is education.

To help people, government has to work. Dedicate yourself to the process of governing. Make the system work.

BILL HOBBY

THE THREADS OF HISTORY

HANK YOU, MAX SHERMAN, FOR THAT INTRODUCTION—understated as it was. And thank you, Molly Sherman, for organizing this dinner.

Thank you, Dolph, Rodney, and Betty for those kind words.

And thank you, Governor Richards, for being here tonight. And welcome to the Bob Bullock Museum. We all know how glad Governor Bullock is that you are here.

Ann had agreed to tape the interview in one of the heavenly courtyards, but St. Peter thought the TV crew was from Fox News and wouldn't open the pearly gates. After he checked with the boss he told them to go to hell.

Ann was eager to come. Seems that the angels spend their days and nights singing and praying—not exactly Ann's idea of a good time. And it's not a long trip. Austin isn't far from heaven—just a short trip on Southwest Airlines. No farther than Houston.

One hundred and seventy-three years ago today Texas declared independence from Mexico. We would not be celebrating that anniversary but for Sam Houston's victory at San Jacinto, so the San Jacinto rule is in effect.

The San Jacinto rule forbids speakers from talking about the Texas Revolution longer than the eighteen minutes it took Sam Houston to win it at San Jacinto. It won't take me even that long to put you to sleep!

But let's take a few of those minutes to explore some of the threads that run through Texas history and tie it together in unexpected ways.

There's no better place to start than Sam Houston, a legendary figure in American history. In fact, he spans it. At the suggestion of his mentor Andrew Jackson, Houston, on his way to Washington for his first session as a Tennessee congressman in 1823, stopped at Monticello to meet Thomas Jefferson.

In other words, a veteran of the War of 1812 and an acquaintance of the third President of the United States, of the Marquis de Lafayette and

Alexander de Tocqueville, was the father of a United States Senator from Texas who served within my lifetime.

Sen. Andrew Jackson Houston held the same seat his father held.

The Houston seat was later held by Lyndon Baines Johnson, whose grandfather Brother George Washington Baines helped baptize Sam Houston. Told that immersion in Rocky Creek would wash away all his sins, Houston said "I hope so, but if they were all washed away, the Lord help the fish down below." How's that for a thread of history?

Houston's great-granddaughter Jean Houston Daniel was married to Price Daniel, attorney general of Texas, U.S. senator, and governor of Texas. Houston's great-great-grandson, Price Daniel III, was Speaker of the Texas House while I was lieutenant governor.

Picking up another thread, Thomas J. Rusk was elected to the U.S. Senate at the same time as Sam Houston. Senator Rusk's law partner's great-great-granddaughter, Sen. Kay Bailey Hutchison, is with us tonight.

Enough of the threads of history. Let's get back to my favorite subject—Sam Houston.

In April 1832, Houston, then a citizen of the Cherokee Nation, went to Washington to get some stimulus for the Cherokees from the Great White Father (Andrew Jackson).

Congressman William Stanberry of Ohio insulted Houston (and Jackson) in a speech on the floor of the House and ignored Houston's challenges. Not a good career move.

After a convivial dinner with some of his congressional buddies (including the Speaker of the House) on April 13, Houston encountered Stanberry on Connecticut Avenue. Armed with his signature hickory stick, Houston beat Stanberry to the ground.

Stanberry tried to shoot Houston, but the gun didn't go off. For some reason, that made Houston mad, so he raised Stanberry's legs and beat him severely about his nether regions.

The House charged Houston with violating the Constitution, which says that a congressman "shall not be questioned in any other place" for a speech made on the floor of Congress. Out of deference to the ladies in the audience at the trial, nobody specified that "other place."

Houston was a violent man. Had his dinner companions not intervened, the governor of Ohio would have had to call a special election.

The House ordered Houston arrested and tried. While awaiting trial Houston, clad in his Indian garb, had dinner with Andrew Jackson at the White House. Jackson told Houston to get a proper suit for the trial before the House. Houston said he couldn't afford a suit, so Jackson bought him one.

Houston was convicted. The Speaker pronounced judgment, saying "I reprimand you," then went on to other business.

The prominent Baltimore lawyer Houston had hired couldn't get him acquitted but at least got him off with a brief sentence. Three words is a pretty brief sentence. The lawyer is better known to history as the songwriter Francis Scott Key. How's that for a thread of history?

When Houston returned to Texas he wrote President Jackson thanking him for his support and hospitality. In that letter Houston prophesied his own role in Texas's independence from Mexico and its subsequent admission to the Union by writing "I shall lay before you a new Estremadura."

When Texas was admitted to the Union on December 29, 1845, Houston's promise was redeemed, his prophecy fulfilled—for a while.

The controversy over Texas's admission echoes in the current session of the legislature. All states before Texas had been admitted by treaty requiring a two-thirds vote of the U.S. Senate. More than one-third of the U.S. Senate didn't want Texas in the union, so Texas had to be admitted by a resolution requiring only a simple majority.

The current Texas Senate has been divided over a practice of requiring a two-thirds vote to pass a bill. The controversies are similar. More than a third of the Republican-dominated U.S. Senate didn't want Texans to vote there. More than a third of the Republican-dominated Texas Senate doesn't want Democrats to vote here.

A group of legislators called on Governor Houston on March 16, 1861, and told him he had to swear a loyalty oath to the Confederacy. They met in Houston's office—the first room on the left as you enter the Governor's Mansion.

Houston refused in these words:

"Fellow-Citizens, in the name of your rights and liberties, which I believe have been trampled upon, I refuse to take this oath. In the name of the nationality of Texas, which has been betrayed by the Convention, I refuse to take this oath. In the name of the Constitution of Texas, I refuse to take this oath. In the name of my own conscience and manhood, which this Convention would degrade by dragging me before it, to pander to the malice of my enemies . . . I refuse to take this oath."

Maybe Governor Houston had a problem with taking the disloyalty oath because he had already sworn, as required by the Texas Constitution, to "preserve, protect, and defend the Constitution and laws of the United States and of this State, so help me God."

When all else fails, read the directions.

A lot of Texans had just died in a long and bloody war to secede from Mexico and be admitted to the United States. Then the Texas Legislature decided that a lot more Texans should die to secede from the United States.

Not good thinking! Sam Houston knew better.

Houston's personal life was at least as colorful as his political life. While serving under Andrew Jackson at Horseshoe Bend in 1814 Houston was wounded in the groin by an arrow. The wound never healed and may have caused the breakup of his eleven-week marriage to Eliza Allen when he was governor of Tennessee in 1827.

Houston just wasn't Texan enough for the Texas Legislature, so they kicked him out of office twice for supporting the union—first from the U.S. Senate for opposing the Kansas-Nebraska Act, then from the governor's office.

Sam Houston even anticipated Abraham Lincoln with the words "A nation divided against itself cannot stand."

Now let's pick up another thread of history. Here's one you never heard of unless you have read Patsy Spaw's history of the Texas Senate. Benjamin Franklin, a founder of the United States, had a grandson who tried to keep Texas from becoming one of them.

Franklin's grandson, Richard Bache, followed his grandfather into the family business as postmaster in Philadelphia. Bache first appears in Texas history when Houston assigned him to guard the captive Santa Anna after San Jacinto.

He next appears as a state senator from Galveston and the only member of the 1845 Texas annexation convention to vote against joining the union.

Why did Bache vote against joining the union?

Maybe he was drunk. When he ran for the Senate from Galveston an opponent said he was drunk and he fell off the platform. Bache won anyway and became one of Babe Schwartz's predecessors. Babe is with us tonight.

Maybe he wanted to avoid extradition. As postmaster he went missing from Philadelphia in a big hurry because $50,000 had gone missing from the post office.

Maybe he wanted to save his brother-in-law George Mifflin Dallas, vice president of the United States, the bother of presiding over a couple of Texas senators. I can identify with that.

You remember Vice President Dallas. They named some little town up near Fort Worth for him.

How's that for a thread of history?

We Texans are still wrestling with history. As William Faulkner wrote in *Requiem for a Nun*, "The past is never dead. It's not even past."

Abraham Lincoln and Charles Darwin were born on the same day two hundred years ago last month. We Texans have pretty well accepted Sam Houston's view of Lincoln, but some of us are still not sure about Darwin.

We Texans have struggled for millions of years to become human beings—and we have made it! We walk erect and have opposable thumbs! We have evolved from Neanderthals into homo sapiens!

But now come members of the State Board of Education with an "intelligent design" to say we haven't evolved at all! And they are partially right! They themselves have not evolved! I have never actually met any of them, but I suppose they walk erect—but with Neanderthal brains.

Not good thinking!

Any University of Texas regents here tonight will be pleased to know that astronomers at the McDonald Observatory, under the leadership of Dean Mary Ann Rankin, who is with us tonight, have confirmed what we see on the red-and-blue political map of the nation.

For years McDonald astronomers have measured the distance to the moon and found that the moon gets farther away from Texas all the time! Then the astronomers look through the big telescope and see billions of galaxies fleeing Texas so fast they turn red! And they are turning redder all the time!

Scientific proof that Texas is the most red-shifted state in the entire universe!

Good thinking! Let's give those astronomers astronomical bonuses!

Three weavers of our threads—historians of these events—are with us tonight.

- Patsy Spaw is the historian of the Texas Senate and its secretary.
- James Haley is the definitive biographer of Sam Houston.
- H. W. Brands wrote *Lone Star Nation*, the story of the Texas Revolution, and a biography of Senator Bache's grandfather Benjamin Franklin.

Ted Fehrenbach is the dean of Texas historians. Ted could not be here tonight to answer the charges, but he and Bill Brands have vandalized Texas history. They have taken away our cherished myths! How can you have a Texas Revolution without the line in the sand and the yellow rose?

Patsy, James, Bill, Babe, Mary Ann—would you please rise.

Well, I don't hear any more musket fire. The Twin Sisters from Ohio are silent. But I hear terrified shouts of "Me no Alamo!" and "Me no Goliad!"

The San Jacinto rule has kicked in. The battle is over. Texas is free—and so are you.

Good night!

BILL HOBBY
Texas State History Museum Foundation Dinner
Bob Bullock Texas State History Museum
Austin, Texas
March 2, 2009

Index

Page numbers in *italic* refer to illustrations.